METAPHORS IN MIND

Also by James Lawley and Penny Tompkins

A Strange and Strong Sensation (DVD)

METAPHORS IN MIND

Transformation through Symbolic Modelling

James Lawley
and
Penny Tompkins

The Developing Company Press

Published by The Developing Company Press, 2000
www.cleanlanguage.co.uk

Reprinted 2001, 2002, 2003, 2005

Distributed by Anglo American Book Company Ltd.
www.anglo-american.co.uk

A catalogue record for this book
is available from the British Library

ISBN 0-9538751-0-5

and the Library of Congress, No.2002491763

Metaphors in Mind has been translated into Italian.
Mente e Metafore (ISBN 8-8815001-2-4) is available from:
Gruppo Editoriale Infomedia
www.infomedia.it

This book is dedicated to
DAVID GROVE
who has paid due diligence to his craft.

CONTENTS

Foreword

An eighteenth century botanist planted a willow sapling in a barrel after first weighing both the sapling and the soil. After the sapling had grown for five years, he weighed the tree and discovered that it had increased in mass by 195 pounds. Upon weighing the soil he was surprised to find that it had decreased in weight by only 13 ounces. The question is, where did a 195 pound tree come from if not from the soil? The only answer is, out of thin air!

And it is by delving into thin air itself that we discover an explanation for this mystery. During the light of day a tree absorbs carbon dioxide through its leaves. Then at night, during the dark phase of photosynthesis, the carbon dioxide molecule is separated into one carbon atom and two oxygen atoms. The tree releases the oxygen atoms back into the air and forms the carbon atoms into a six carbon simple sugar ring which is a building block for cellulose. The hidden beauty in this system is the deconstruction, release and recombination of basic elements from one structure to another. The mass and structure of the tree is the result of this mysterious process.

Just like building blocks of a carbon atom that have been re-combined to form more complex compounds, Penny Tompkins and James Lawley have synthesized elements from a variety of sources such as Neuro-Linguistic Programming, Clean Language and systems thinking—and added both mass and structure. Although my original work was in a therapeutic context, their synthesis has made it available to others who have taken it into the fields of business, education, health and social services. I have tremendous admiration for the innovative work they have developed.

My first encounter with Penny and James appeared to materialize out of thin air. Penny's tenacious 'won't take no for an answer' style and James' inquiring, penetrating questions formed my initial introduction to them. My life continues to be enriched by our ongoing interactions. 'Developing' is a word that I strongly associate with both of them. Not only is it the name of their company, but it also describes what I have come to recognize as a constant theme which they apply to themselves as well as the clients with whom they work.

I congratulate Penny and James on completing this valuable book. The immense degree of dedication and devotion that they steadfastly maintained during the course of this project has resulted in a richly stimulating text that gently escorts the reader on a captivating journey. Be prepared for this book to launch you on a personal journey of change and development. The parade of thought provoking concepts, stories and challenges contained within will provide a reliable travelling companion to accompany you along the way.

David J. Grove

4 July, 2000

Acknowledgments

Our thanks to Lynne Preston for pinning us down to start writing at 7:00am on 1st August, 1997 and her continued faith ever since.

Our early drafts benefited from the supportive comments of: Tom Allport, Clive Bach, Gilly Barton, Dee Berridge, Roger Butler, Judi Buttner, Bob Janes, Gina Sanders, Graham Smith, Hugh Smith, Sheila Stacey, Wendy Sullivan, Caitlin Walker and Thomas Zelenz.

Thanks also to Ann Kritzinger for steadying our nerves about the publishing process, Ruth 'the proof' Shadwell, Judy Strafford for her artistic talent and Chris Tidy for graphic design advice.

Particular mention is due to Richard Stacey who reviewed the entire manuscript with his characteristic clarity and precision.

An extra special thanks to Philip Harland who read every word, twice, and whose skilful feedback contributed to us learning the art and craft of writing. His gentle challenges prompted us to reconsider and refine our descriptions and his encouragement kept us going when it seemed like the project would never end.

Norman Vaughton, a great teacher and raconteur, helped fill the gaps in our knowledge of David Grove's early work. And conversations with Steve Briggs stimulated our ideas and broadened our view of David's approach. We are also grateful to Brian van der Horst for introducing us to the ideas of Ken Wilber at just the right time.

We also appreciate Charles Faulkner, whose own work in metaphor has significantly influenced our thinking, not least during our long chats in various Hampstead and Highgate cafes. As Charles says, "We're walking down different sides of the same street." And what an exciting street it is.

Acknowledgement also to Cei Davies who has made such a valuable contribution in supporting David Grove and helping make his work available to the public.

We continue to learn from our students and from members of the London Clean Language Practice and Research Groups. We thank them for helping us sharpen our skills and test our ideas.

And lastly, we are grateful to our clients whose courage has inspired every page, and who continually remind us to expect the unexpected and to trust the wisdom in the system.

Introduction

"James, I know you'll ask a hundred questions about this workshop, and I don't think I'll be able to answer a single one. But I do know this guy David Grove is doing something special. I've just had one of the most profound experiences of my life. Why don't you postpone your holiday and come and see him? Maybe together we can figure out what he's doing."

Unbeknown to Penny, this telephone conversation was to decide the direction of our lives for the next five years.

David J. Grove, M.S.

David Grove is a New Zealander whose unique psychotherapeutic approach, experience and style make him one of today's most skilful and innovative therapists.

In the 1980s he developed clinical methods for resolving clients' traumatic memories, especially those related to child abuse, rape and incest. He realised many clients naturally described their symptoms in metaphor, and found that when he enquired about these using their *exact* words, their perception of the trauma began to change. This led him to create Clean Language, a way of asking questions of clients' metaphors which neither contaminate nor distort them.

Initially David Grove specialised in 'healing the wounded child within'. These days his interests have widened to include nonverbal behaviour, perceptual space and inter-generational healing. He is constantly developing new ideas and creative methods which continue to fascinate and inspire us.

Our contribution

To "figure out" what David Grove was doing we used a process called modelling. This involved observing him work with clients (including ourselves) and spending hour after hour poring over recordings and transcripts. We looked for patterns in the relationship between what he was doing and the way clients responded that contributed to the changes they experienced. We combined these patterns into a generalised model which was tested and fine tuned—cycling through observation, pattern detection, model construction, testing and revising many times.

While our model is based on David Grove's work and incorporates many of his ideas, he has a different way of describing his approach. Our model was derived more from our observation of him in action than from his explanation of what he does. It was also shaped by our desire for others to learn the process easily and for it to apply to a range of contexts in addition to psychotherapy.

As well as employing many of David Grove's ideas, we have also drawn upon cognitive linguistics, self-organising systems theory and Neuro-Linguistic Programming (NLP). The result is a process called Symbolic Modelling.

Symbolic Modelling in a nutshell

Symbolic Modelling is a method for facilitating individuals to become familiar with the symbolic domain of their experience so that they discover new ways of perceiving themselves and their world. It uses Clean Language to facilitate them to attend to their metaphoric expressions so that *they* create a model of their symbolic mindbody perceptions. This model exists as a living, breathing, four-dimensional world within and around them.

When clients explore this world and its inherent logic, their metaphors and way of being are honoured. During the therapeutic process their metaphors begin to evolve. As this happens their everyday thinking, feeling and behaviour correspondingly change as well.

Some clients benefit just from having their metaphors developed with a few clean questions. For some the process leads to a reorganisation of their existing symbolic perceptions, while for others nothing short of a transformation of their entire landscape of metaphors will suffice. As a result clients report that they are more self-aware, more at peace with themselves, have a more defined sense of their place in the world and are more able to enrich the lives of others.

What you will learn from this book

What do you do as a therapist, teacher, doctor or manager when your client, student, patient or colleague says "It's like I'm hitting my head against a brick wall" or "I'm so wound up I can't see straight" or "Things keep getting on top of me"?

Do you ignore the metaphorical nature of their communication? Do you unwittingly introduce your own metaphors ("Why do you continue *punishing* yourself?" "I can tell you're *stressed*." "How does that *make* you feel?")? Or do you take their metaphors as an accurate description of their way of being in the world and ask questions within the logic of the information—without introducing any metaphors of your own ("And is there anything else about that brick wall?" "And what kind of wound up is that?" "And whereabouts on top of you?").

This book describes how to do the latter.

When using Symbolic Modelling you give your clients, students, patients or colleagues an opportunity to discover how their symbolic perceptions are organised, what needs to happen for these to change, and how they can develop as a result. In order to do this proficiently, you need to be able to:

- Attend to client-generated verbal and nonverbal metaphors
- Communicate via Clean Language
- Facilitate clients to self-model
- Be guided by the logic inherent in their symbolic expressions.

Our primary focus in this book is psychotherapy. And while we describe a complete process that can be used in its own right, many therapists and counsellors have found ways to combine Symbolic Modelling with their preferred approach. In addition, in Chapter 10 we describe how Symbolic Modelling is being used in education, health and business.

Structure of the book

We have arranged the book in five parts. Part I provides theoretical and background knowledge about metaphor, modelling and self-organising systems. Part II introduces the basic questions, philosophy and methodology of Clean Language. Part III contains a stage-by-stage description of the Five-Stage Therapeutic Process, with extensive client transcripts to illustrate and explain how the process unfolds. In Part IV we describe a number of applications of Symbolic Modelling outside the field of individual psychotherapy. Finally, Part V contains annotated transcripts of our work with three clients.

How to use this book

We have designed the book to be used iteratively. This means that you will benefit from revisiting each chapter with the accumulated knowledge gained from reading later chapters, and from having put into practice what you have learned. In this way the book is like a travel guide. It gives useful information about the places you are about to visit, what to look out for, and if you reread it after you return, it will mean so much more.

You do not have to begin this book at the beginning. Depending on your preferred learning style there are various entry points. You can start with Part I if you like general concepts and theory first. If you prefer to learn by doing, the information in Part II will enable you to start practising immediately. If you want to find out how you can apply the model in a variety of contexts, go to Part IV. And if you learn best by first seeing an example of the entire process, start with Part V.

And finally

Like learning to play the piano, no amount of theory or observation can substitute for the actual experience of your fingers moving over the keyboard. Our main purpose in writing this book is to encourage you to *use* Symbolic Modelling because only then will you discover how much your clients can benefit from this approach.

And it is not only your clients who will benefit. As a result of using Symbolic Modelling we have developed acute listening and observation skills, an improved ability to retain and recall information and an increased capacity to think systemically and at multiple levels.

Also, being facilitated to model *our* metaphors and patterns has been an indispensable part of learning to facilitate others to model theirs — not to mention the gift of our own personal development.

Yet perhaps the most unexpected benefit of regularly facilitating Symbolic Modelling has been learning to become comfortable with 'not knowing', to be in the moment with whatever is happening, and to trust the wisdom in the system.

I

BACKGROUND KNOWLEDGE

1

Metaphors We Live By

*Metaphor is perhaps one of man's most fruitful potentialities.
Its efficacy verges on magic, and it seems a tool for creation
which God left inside His creatures when He made them.*
Jose Ortega y Gasset

Imagine you are standing behind Michelangelo. He is standing in front of a large block of marble, hammer and chisel in hand. He knows there is a sculpture in the stone, yet has no idea what the final creation will look like. How do you support Michelangelo to transform the marble into a work of art and in the process transform himself?

On the surface this book is about a new approach to psychotherapy called Symbolic Modelling. But really it is about a new way of thinking about the process of change—of artfully facilitating the Michelangelo's who are your clients to transform themselves.

In Symbolic Modelling a client's metaphors are the raw material, the marble, out of which their creation emerges. Your role is to facilitate them to use their metaphors and symbols for self-discovery and self-development. Before learning the skills required to do this, some background information will be useful. Therefore this chapter covers:

> The Symbolic Domain of Experience
> Metaphor and Symbol Defined
> How the Symbolic Domain is Expressed
> Metaphor and Cognition

The Symbolic Domain of Experience

Assume the following statements refer to the same experience. Take a moment to say them out loud, and notice your internal response.

1. When she looks me in the eye, and speaks in that high-pitched tone of voice, my whole head starts to throb.
2. I'm angry because of her attitude.
3. It's like I'm the dynamite and she's got the detonator.

The first statement describes an experience using language related to the senses, to what is seen, heard and felt. The second uses abstract concepts to label the experience. The third is metaphoric and symbolic.

Most people report a subtly different response when saying and considering each one. This is because each represents a different type of language with its own vocabulary and internal logic, and each involves different ways of understanding, thinking, reasoning, and perceiving. We refer to these three domains of experience as *sensory,* *conceptual* and *symbolic.*

SENSORY

People know about the environment, the material world, and the behaviour of others and themselves through seeing, hearing, touching, smelling, tasting, and by their emotions and inner-body feelings of orientation, movement, balance and position. People also see pictures, hear sounds and feel feelings in their imagination when they remember a past event or imagine a future event.

CONCEPTUAL

All categories, comparisons, beliefs and judgments are constructs of the human mind. They only exist as abstract concepts. While everyone has experienced being part of a group of related people, no one has ever touched the concept 'family'. Concepts are a different order of reality from the sensory-material world. Concepts are *labels* for complex gestalts of experience.[1]

SYMBOLIC

A number of philosophers, linguists and cognitive scientists claim that much, if not most, everyday language and thinking is neither sensory nor conceptual, but is actually metaphoric.[2] Metaphors allow people to express and give a form to complex feelings, behaviours, situations and abstract concepts. Most metaphors make use of the sensory-material world to describe, comprehend and reason about the conceptual and abstract. For us 'symbolic' means more than the dictionary definition of 'relating to a symbol', it also involves *connecting with a pattern that has personal significance.*

Distinguishing between domains

To further clarify the distinctions between these three domains we describe a well-known object, the American Flag, with sensory, conceptual and symbolic language:

Describing something in *sensory* terms requires a specific example and words that directly relate to what we see, hear or feel. In this case it is made of red, white and blue pieces of cloth, which together are displayed as a rectangle four feet long by two feet high. The upper left-hand corner has 50 white five-pointed star-shaped pieces sewn onto a dark blue background. The rest of the rectangle comprises six red and seven white alternating stripes sewn horizontally. The left-hand side is connected to a wire on top of a pole where it moves in response to variations in direction and intensity of the wind.

The *conceptual* label is, simply 'the American flag', called The Star Spangled Banner.

The *symbolic* description of 'Old Glory' will vary from person to person. One American may pledge allegiance to it and say it symbolises "the land of the free and the home of the brave." To another it might symbolise "the police force of the world." If we were to pursue the matter further each person would likely tell stories and give examples from their personal history in an attempt to capture the significance of the symbol for them, and in the telling would probably discover a deep personal connection to this cultural icon.

These three types of description—sensory, conceptual and symbolic—represent distinct yet interrelated ways of perceiving the world.

The world of solid objects and sensory input is fundamentally different from the world of ideas and abstract notions, which in turn is different from the world of symbol and metaphor. Each domain has its own vocabulary, its own logic and brings forth its own perceptions. Nevertheless, people effortlessly switch back and forth between them and sometimes enjoy all three simultaneously.

To access and work within each domain, a process tailored to the characteristics of that domain is needed. Most research into how people perceive the world, and most approaches for helping them create new and more enriching perceptions, have been sensory and conceptually based. Symbolic Modelling is a process for working with symbolic and metaphoric perceptions directly.

Metaphor and Symbol Defined

In this section we define metaphor and symbol, and discuss the concept of isomorphism before considering why metaphors have such magical properties.

We have entitled this chapter *Metaphors We Live By* as a tribute to George Lakoff and Mark Johnson's innovative and mind-expanding book. They say:

> The essence of metaphor is understanding and experiencing one kind of thing in terms of another.[3]

We like this definition for a number of reasons. First, it recognises that metaphor is about capturing the essential nature of an experience. For instance when a client of ours described his situation as, "It's like I'm a goldfish in a deoxygenated pond having to come up for air," his sense of futility and impending doom was instantly apparent. Second, the definition acknowledges that metaphor is an active process which is at the very heart of understanding ourselves, others and the world around us. Third, it allows metaphor to be more than verbal expression. Metaphors are also expressed nonverbally, by objects and as imaginative representations. Thus whatever a person says, sees, hears, feels, does or imagines has the potential to be an *autogenic*, self-generated metaphor.

Metaphors themselves are comprised of a number of interrelating components which we call *symbols*.[4] So a metaphor is a whole and a symbol is a part of that whole. For instance, "I feel like my back is being pinned against a wall" refers to three symbols (I, my back, and a wall), with a fourth (whatever or whoever is doing the pinning) being implied.

Carl Jung noted that there is always something more to a symbol than meets the eye, and no matter how much a symbol (or metaphor) is described, its full meaning remains elusive:

> What we call a symbol is a term, a name, or even a picture that may be familiar in daily life, yet that possesses specific connotations in addition to its conventional and obvious meaning. It implies something vague, unknown or hidden from us.[5]

Although we may not be able to fully explain a symbol's "unknown or hidden" meaning, we can still *know* it is significant for us. And the more its symbolism is explored, the more its significance emerges.

While symbols such as a national flag or religious icons have a shared cultural meaning, they may also contain a unique *personal* significance. It is this personal connection which brings the cultural meaning to life.

In Symbolic Modelling we are *only* interested in the personal nature of symbols and metaphors. This idiosyncratic symbolism connects a person to their history, their spiritual nature, their sense of destiny and to the "unknown or hidden" aspects of their life. Metaphors and symbols have the potency to carry information from the mundane to the extraordinary, and for some, to the sacred.[6]

Isomorphism

Metaphors correspond in a special way to the original experience they are describing—through isomorphism. In other words, the form of a metaphor is *different* from the original experience, but it has a *similar* organisation. This means that the attributes of its symbols, the relationships between symbols and the logic of the whole matches the organisation of what is being described. While there will be some correspondence of tangible components, the key role of metaphor is to capture the essence, the intangible, the relationships and the patterns. Isomorphism is the "pattern which connects" two different kinds of things.[7] When a person comprehends a metaphor, it is their intrinsic ability to recognise and utilise isomorphism that allows them to infer the organisation of the original experience from the metaphor.

The following examples are based on George Lakoff's detailed analysis of metaphors used for anger. They demonstrate the isomorphic correspondence between anger and:

SOURCE:	METAPHOR:
Hot fluid	I've reached boiling point. He blew his top.
Fire	Those are inflammatory remarks. He's been smouldering for days.
Insanity	He went crazy with anger. Stop or I'll go berserk.
An opponent	She fought back her anger. I was seized by anger.
A dangerous animal	He had a ferocious temper. She unleashed her anger.
Trespassing	You're beginning to get to me. You've stepped over the line.
A burden	Get it off your chest. Losing my temper was a relief.

Although these metaphors refer to the same class of experience conceptually labelled 'anger', each addresses a subtly different quality of this highly complex emotion. George Lakoff has found about three hundred phrases related to anger which display a remarkable degree of experiential coherence. Thus:

> We can see why someone who is doing a slow burn hasn't hit the ceiling yet, why someone whose anger is bottled up is not breathing fire, why someone who is consumed by anger probably can't see straight, and why adding fuel to the fire might just cause the person you're talking to to have kittens.[8]

While concepts can be used to *define* anger (a feeling of great annoyance or antagonism), they cannot capture the particulars of a person's experience. Sensory terms can *describe* anger, but for all their accuracy and detail, much of the *quality* of the experience will be lost.

The magic of metaphor

Having facilitated hundreds of clients to explore their metaphors, we know that metaphor can heal, transform and enrich lives. Why is this? Why does metaphor's efficacy verge on magic? Why is metaphor such a universal tool for description, comprehension and explanation? How is it that metaphor produces such novel perspectives?

Andrew Ortony points out three remarkable properties of metaphors: *inexpressibility, vividness and compactness.*[9] Put simply, because metaphors embody that "something vague, unknown or hidden," they give form to the inexpressible. Because they make use of everyday concrete things to illustrate intangible, complex and relational aspects of life, they are vivid and memorable. And because of isomorphism, only the essence of an experience needs to be captured; the rest can be reconstructed from inferential knowledge. In short, metaphors carry a great deal of information in a compact and memorable package.

There is a fourth vital property of metaphor and it is the one which most impacts people's lives. A metaphor describes one experience in terms of another, and in so doing it *specifies and constrains* ways of thinking about the original experience. This influences the meaning and importance of the experience, the way it fits with other experiences, and actions taken as a result. Lakoff and Johnson state:

> In all aspects of life … we define our reality in terms of metaphors and then proceed to act on the basis of the metaphors. We draw inferences, set goals, make commitments, and execute plans, all on the basis of how we in part structure our experience, consciously and unconsciously, by means of metaphor.[10]

Metaphors embody and define the intangible and abstract, but this process limits and constrains perceptions and actions to those which make sense within the logic of the metaphor. Metaphors are therefore both descriptive and prescriptive. In this way they can be a tool for creativity or a self-imposed prison.[11] Symbolic Modelling is designed to unlock creativity and open prison doors. It does so by working directly with the symbolic domain.

How the Symbolic Domain is Expressed

Consider the types of metaphor expressed in the following:

> It's like dancing with a tiger [arms raised, torso swaying]. [Picks up pillow and holds it as if it is a partner.] I can see it all now, the room, the chandelier, hear the music, feel my heart pounding as we swirl between other couples on the dance floor—I'm on the edge of life and death.

This example and Figure 1.1 show how metaphors can be classified into four groups: Verbal, Nonverbal, Material and Imaginative. This section describes each category, how information can be translated between categories, and how the totality of a client's metaphors and symbolic expressions combine to form a Metaphor Landscape.

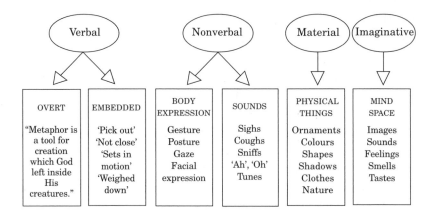

FIGURE 1.1 Ways to express the symbolic domain

Verbal metaphor

We refer to words and phrases which are obviously or conventionally metaphoric as *overt* verbal metaphors. This distinguishes them from the less obvious verbal metaphors *embedded* in everyday speech. There is nothing absolute about this distinction; it entirely depends on the speaker or listener's awareness of the metaphorical nature of language. Although embedded metaphors are not usually recognised as metaphorical, they are an essential and universal feature of language.

OVERT VERBAL METAPHOR

Conventionally, metaphors are those everyday sayings and phrases used to spice up language. Here is a selection from our clients:

> I've got my head in the clouds.
> I'm carrying the whole world on my shoulders.
> I've got a knot in my stomach.
> I'm banging my head against a brick wall.

These expressions are obviously metaphoric. Our clients know there is not an actual cloud surrounding them, that they have not turned into Atlas, and that there is no real knot or brick wall. Instead an inbuilt mechanism registers the figurative nature of these expressions and accepts them as symbolising an experience rather than being the experience itself. They know that everyday things and behaviours—clouds, carrying, shoulders, knots, banging and walls—are being used to represent *other* experiences: absent-mindedness, excessive responsibility, an unwanted feeling, and a lack of progress.

Overt metaphors evoke rich images and a felt sense of what is being described. They can vividly express a single idea or a lifetime of experience. Although some linguists dismiss them as 'merely figurative', we accept them as a highly accurate description of experience. Because of their graphic and embodied nature, overt metaphors convey the essence of what is being said better than dozens of sensory or conceptual words ever could.

EMBEDDED VERBAL METAPHOR

When everyday language is examined in detail, it is apparent that metaphor is far more common than first realised. In fact it is 'hard' to 'put together' an 'everyday' sentence which does not 'contain' a 'hidden' or 'embedded' metaphor:

My mind has just gone blank.
There's a gap in my knowledge.
I'm feeling down today.
I'm going round in circles.

These sentences are not obviously metaphoric until 'blank', 'gap', 'down' and 'going round in circles' are examined more closely. We call these and similar expressions *embedded* metaphors since their metaphoric nature is disguised in ordinariness and familiarity. Once you recognise embedded metaphors you will notice them everywhere:

METAPHOR:	PRESUPPOSED SOURCE:
I got out of my relationship.	A relationship is a container.
I see what you mean.	Understanding is like vision.
The deadline is approaching.	Time is a moving object.
We've sorted out our ideas.	Reasoning is manipulating objects.
She made me change my mind.	Others can exert a force on our mind.

The things, events and behaviours presupposed in these sentences have no physical reality and are entirely metaphoric. Nevertheless we accept them as if they are true and tend to forget they are describing what the experience is *like*.

Embedded metaphors are especially important because they often indicate how the speaker is 'mentally doing' the abstract experience they are describing. For example, changing the embedded metaphor in the following sentences has a noticeable effect on the type of experience we assume the speaker is describing:

I'm thinking *about* what you said.
I'm thinking *over* what you said.
I'm thinking *around* what you said.
I'm thinking *beyond* what you said.
I'm thinking *past* what you said.
I'm thinking *outside of* what you said.
I'm thinking *through* what you said.
I'm thinking *on* what you said.[12]

Mark Johnson's *The Body in the Mind* gives a wealth of evidence for the *embodied* nature of embedded metaphors.[13] He shows that the majority of embedded metaphors are based on that which is most familiar: the human body, the environment it inhabits and how the two interact. Steven Pinker in *How the Mind Works* notes that:

> Location in space is one of the two fundamental metaphors in language, used for thousands of meanings. The other is force, agency, and causation. ... Many cognitive scientists (including me) have concluded from their research on language that a handful of concepts about places, paths, motions, agency, and causation underlie the literal or figurative meanings of tens of thousands of words and constructions, not only in English but in every other language that has been studied.[14]

He goes on to say "Space and force don't act like figures of speech intended to convey new insights; they seem closer to the medium of thought itself."

During Symbolic Modelling you need to pay particularly close attention to your client's metaphors because these specify *how* they are mentally doing and embodying what they are describing. And more important, as the client becomes aware of their own embedded metaphors, they can recognise how these limit or empower them.

Nonverbal metaphor

While metaphor is generally thought of as a linguistic device, non-verbal behaviour—*body expressions* (postures and movements of the body and eyes) and *nonverbal sounds* (grunts, coughs, hems and haws)—can also be metaphoric. They are metaphoric in that they can be used to understand and experience one kind of thing in terms of another.

BODY EXPRESSIONS

David Grove noticed that many of his clients' gestures, looks, facial expressions, postures and body movements were encoded with, and were containers for, idiosyncratic symbolic information. These non-verbal metaphors ranged from the subtlest glance, twitch of a finger or change in breathing to enacting an entire symbolic event.

When clients pay attention to their body expressions, a just-outside-of-awareness symbolic world is revealed. For example, one client discovered that their hands-out-in-front-grabbing movement symbolised "holding on when I really need to let go"; another with hunched posture found this expressed "feeling like the whole world is on my shoulders"; while the client who sat motionless, leaning forward and staring down was surprised to find that the angle of their gaze represented "looking over the edge into a bottomless pit."

NONVERBAL SOUNDS

David Grove also noticed that nonverbal sounds such as throat clears, sighs, clicks, blows, giggles, 'Ah', 'Oh', 'Mmm', 'Umm' or humming tunes, may be encoded with symbolic meaning. For example a client who regularly cleared their throat before speaking found it symbolised "being unable to speak my truth"; another's nervous giggle whenever they were complimented "prevented the pride that comes before a fall."

In Symbolic Modelling when working with body expression and non-verbal sounds your aim is twofold: for the client to recognise and preserve the idiosyncratic, symbolic significance of their nonverbal behaviour; and, if appropriate, for the client, and *only* the client, to encapsulate the experience in an equivalent verbal metaphor.

Material metaphors

The mind has a remarkable capacity for seeing, hearing and feeling symbolism in a material object or the environment. As Aniela Jaffe´ notes, *any* object can be imbued with personal symbolism:

> The history of symbolism shows that everything can assume symbolic significance: natural objects (like stones, plants, animals, men, mountains and valleys, sun and moon, wind, water and fire), or man-made things (like houses, boats, or cars), or even abstract forms (like numbers or the triangle, the square, and the circle). In fact, the whole cosmos is a potential symbol.[15]

In our consulting room, shadows, wallpaper and carpet patterns, curtains, ornaments, pictures, book titles, mirrors, furniture and door handles have caught a client's attention and activated a symbolic response. We have lost count of the number of times a client has remarked that the shape, size, colour or layout of something in our consulting room, or their clothes and jewellery, 'coincidentally' matches a symbol in their imagination.

Given the choice, clients attempt to position themselves so that there is maximum alignment between the configuration of their inner symbolic world and the layout of the physical environment. This may mean sitting where they can see out of a window, being near a door or having us on their left or their right. For this reason we follow David Grove's practice of asking clients to choose where they would like to sit and then to position us. Their preferences invariably turn out to have symbolic significance.

Imaginative symbolic representations

In addition to material, nonverbal and verbal symbolic expression there is another, *imaginative,* which occurs in the private world of thoughts and feelings. The 'seeing' of objects and events in the mind's eye, the 'hearing' of sounds and internal dialogue, and the 'feeling' of emotions and other sensations, together create a personalised virtual reality.

John Grinder and Richard Bandler were among the first to apply the correlations between language, behaviour and imaginative representations to psychotherapy.[16] David Grove extended this to *symbolic* representations such as: *seeing* an image of 'a pot of gold at the end of a rainbow' or 'shadows on the wall of a cave' or 'my life's path in front of me'; and *hearing* the 'perfect pitch of a bell at the bottom of the sea' or 'a silent scream' or a witch saying 'if I say black's white, it's white'; and *feeling* the sensation of 'a knot in my stomach' or 'hands around my throat' or 'the warmth of an everlasting sun on my back'.

To have a conscious imaginative representation requires an imagined 'object of perception' to be located somewhere in a "mind-space" that Julian Jaynes says is the "first and most primitive aspect of consciousness."[17] For instance, think of a cat:

> *Where* do you 'see' it? In front of you? To one side or the other? Above or below eye-level? What is your emotional response to this cat? *Where* are you experiencing the sensation of that feeling? If you have an inner dialogue about the value of owning a cat, *where* do the words appear to come from? Does each side of the dialogue originate from the same or a different place? Do they seem to be spoken from inside or outside your head?

According to Daniel Dennett, there is no physiological seat of consciousness, no theatre in the brain where the cat lives—although it sure seems that way.[18] Because of this, when clients notice what is in their imaginative mind-space they have very real responses. In fact, changes to imaginative representations have been correlated with changes in heart rate, galvanic skin response, blood pressure, and a host of other chemical and neurophysiological effects.[19]

During Symbolic Modelling we regard a client's imaginative realm as existing in a *perceptual space* that is as real as any physical environment. This space can exist inside and outside their body or in an entirely imaginary environment happening somewhere and somewhen else. By recognising and honouring their experience exactly as they describe it, clients can be facilitated to discover the metaphors they live by.

Translating metaphors

Because the four categories of symbolic expression are interrelated it is possible to translate a metaphor from one form to another. In Symbolic Modelling there are two common forms of translation: *verbalising* and *physicalising* (see Figure 1.2).

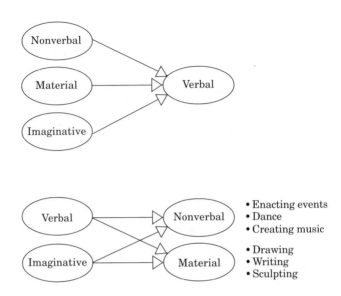

FIGURE 1.2 Two common ways of translating metaphors

VERBALISING

Much of the Symbolic Modelling process involves facilitating the client to *verbalise* the symbolism they ascribe to their imaginative representations, their nonverbal behaviour and to the material objects that draw their attention.

PHYSICALISING

The other common type of translation involves the client *physicalising* their spoken and imaginative metaphors, that is, intentionally creating a physical symbolic representation. This could be drawing, painting, sculpting, poetry, prose and making music. Or they could use their body to mime, act or dance their metaphor. Physicalising a metaphor often enables clients to depict things they cannot say, and to encapsulate and convey the overall wholeness of an experience in a single material representation.

Carl Jung discovered that externalising his inner-symbolic world produced life-long learnings:

Gradually, through my scientific work, I was able to put my fantasies and the contents of the unconscious on a solid footing. Words and paper, however, did not seem real enough to me; something more was needed. I had to achieve a kind of representation in stone of my innermost thoughts and of the knowledge I had acquired. Or, to put it another way, I had to make a confession of faith in stone. That was the beginning of the "Tower," the house which I built for myself at Bollingen.

From the beginning I felt the Tower as in some way a place of maturation— a maternal womb or a maternal figure in which I could become what I was, what I am and will be. It gave me a feeling as if I were being reborn in stone. It is thus a concretisation of the individuation process, ... during the building work, of course, I never considered these matters. I built the house in sections, always following the concrete needs of the moment. It might also be said that I built it in a kind of dream. Only afterwards did I see how all of the parts fitted together and that a meaningful form had resulted: a symbol of psychic wholeness.[20]

Once he had this realisation, for the next 35 years Jung continued to modify and add to his Tower as a way of reflecting and physicalising the development of his inner experience.

Metaphor Landscapes

Verbal, nonverbal, material and imaginative metaphors coexist, interrelate and maintain each other. While sometimes they contradict or conflict, they do so in ways that are consistent and meaningful within a larger context. This larger context—the sum total of a client's embodied symbolic perceptions—is their *Metaphor Landscape.*

Once a client pays attention to their symbolic expressions, the content of their Metaphor Landscape begins to enter their awareness. When they describe a symbol they implicitly acknowledge its existence and form. When they look at, gesture to, or orientate their body towards a symbol, they explicitly reference its location. From the client's perspective, the space around and within them becomes inhabited by their symbols. It is in this space that symbolic events take place. The client finds they are inhabiting a living, breathing symbolic world, and the more they attend to it, the more real and significant it becomes.

As symbols form and their relationships to each other become clear, the whole Landscape becomes psychoactive: that is, the client has thoughts and feelings in response to the symbols and events, which in turn generate further activity in the Landscape. After a time the Landscape becomes a four-dimensional, multilayered, systemic, symbolic world which with uncanny accuracy represents and reflects how the client experiences, behaves and responds in 'real life'.

For example, a client who described his problem as like "looking over the edge into a bottomless pit" discovered "I'm standing on barren soil with my toes extending just over the edge of a black hole" and "the more I look into it, the more I have to hold myself back from a strange gravity-like attraction toward the blackness." These concurrent images and feelings of attraction and holding back were a replica of "a long-standing conflict in my life." While describing this metaphor the client was looking down, face ashen, body swaying back and forth, embodying the conflict, in the moment, in the room.

The more the client explores the attributes of their symbols, the relationships within their metaphors and the patterns of their whole Metaphor Landscape, the more they realise there is a consistent and coherent logic operating. The symbolic logic of, "I've been adrift in an open boat for years but I'm still anchored to my family," does not necessarily conform to the laws of science nor to the logic of philosophy, but it will make perfect sense to the client. The self-reflection, self-understanding and self-awareness made possible by interacting with their Metaphor Landscape resonates with a deeper, more fundamental cognition.

Metaphor and Cognition

In this section we consider why metaphorical expressions are not arbitrary and why they are not independent of each other. Instead they have a coherent and consistent organisation *because* there is a coherent and consistent organisation to cognition.[21] Many cognitive scientists now conclude that people not only talk in metaphor, but also think and reason in metaphor, they make sense of their world through metaphor, and they act in ways that are consistent with their metaphors. For George Lakoff and Mark Johnson:

> Metaphor is not just a matter of language, that is, of mere words. ... On
> the contrary, human *thought processes* are largely metaphorical. This is

what we mean when we say that the human conceptual system is metaphorically structured and defined. Metaphors as linguistic expressions are possible precisely because they are metaphors in a person's conceptual system.[22]

Thus the *organisation* of a client's language and behaviour will be isomorphic with the *organisation* of their cognitive processes, and both will be grounded in the embodied nature of experience. This is why changes in a Metaphor Landscape reflect changes in cognition which in turn generate new thoughts, feelings and behaviour.

Isomorphism is central to Symbolic Modelling because it makes it possible for the client to construct a model of the organisation of their cognition from their metaphoric expressions. As neuroscientist Karl Pribram writes:

> Analogical reasoning sets in motion a self-reflective process by which, metaphorically speaking, brains come to understand themselves.[23]

Summary

The key points about metaphor and symbolism made in this chapter are:

- Metaphor is pervasive in English and probably every other language.

- Metaphor works by representing one experience (usually more abstract, vague or intangible) in terms of another experience (usually more concrete, explicit or commonplace) which has a corresponding (isomorphic) organisation.

- Metaphor enables people to understand, reason about and explain abstract concepts. The primary sources for these metaphors are the human body, the physical environment and their interaction.

- Metaphor helps people organise complex sets of thoughts, feelings, behaviours and events into a coherent whole.

- Most metaphors are so pervasive, so familiar and so embedded in thought and body that their metaphorical nature is usually overlooked.

- Symbols are the identifiable components of a metaphor.

- The sum total of a person's verbal, nonverbal, material and imaginative metaphors comprise a self-consistent and coherent Metaphor Landscape.

- A Metaphor Landscape is part of a more inclusive process, that of cognition, which itself is fundamentally metaphorical in nature. As a result, metaphors can limit and constrain or be a source of creativity and development.

Concluding Remarks

The patterns of our metaphoric language, symbolic behaviour and imaginative representations express the way we make sense of the world. Metaphor and symbolism enable us to give form to those aspects of life which are the most mystifying; namely, our relationships, our problems and their solutions, our fears and desires, our illness and health, our poverty and wealth, and the love we give and the love we receive. Furthermore, metaphors allow us to reflect on and describe our own cognition in a manner that is isomorphic with that which is being reflected upon. It is through this iterative, systemic and wheels-within-wheels process that metaphors for who we are, why we are here, how we are a unique part of a larger whole, and other questions of knowing and being, become amenable to exploration.

2

Models We Create By

If you want to understand mental processes,
look at biological evolution.
Gregory Bateson

From birth we create mental models of how the world works. These inform our decisions, guide our behaviour and enable us to learn and change. Later, in an attempt to understand and explain the processes by which we give meaning to the world, we also construct models of our models. This gives us a degree of freedom, a semblance of choice, because it allows us to recognise that our models are just that—*our maps*, and not *the territory*—and are therefore subject to revision, modification and improvement.[1] With this awareness it becomes possible to change the way we construct our models, thereby opening up new ways of perceiving the world and our place in it.

How people create their models of the world can be revealed by a process called modelling. Although there are a number of ways to model in the sensory and conceptual domains, this book is about Symbolic Modelling—a new methodology for working in the symbolic domain. Metaphor, modelling and Clean Language are the bases of Symbolic Modelling. Metaphor was the subject of Chapter 1. Clean Language will be described in Chapters 3 and 4. And modelling, interwoven with a number of ideas from self-organising systems theory, is the subject of this chapter.

This chapter includes a description of:

Modelling
Symbolic Modelling
The Organisation of Metaphor Landscapes
How Metaphor Landscapes Change and Evolve
The Five-Stage Therapeutic Process
Principles of Symbolic Modelling

Together these represent a new way of thinking about human cognition, how people change, and how they do not.

Modelling

Modelling is a process whereby an observer, the modeller, gathers information about the activity of a system with the aim of constructing a generalised description (a model) of how that system works. The model can then be used by the modeller and others to inform decisions and actions. The purpose of modelling is to identify 'what is' and how 'what is' works—without influencing what is being modelled. The modeller begins with an open mind, a blank sheet, and an outcome to discover the way a system functions—without attempting to change it.[2]

Steven Pinker uses an analogy from the world of business to define psychology, but he could just as easily be describing the modelling process:

> Psychology is engineering in reverse. In forward-engineering, one designs a machine to do something; in reverse-engineering, one figures out what a machine was designed to do. Reverse-engineering is what the boffins at Sony do when a new product is announced by Panasonic, or vice versa. They buy one, bring it back to the lab, take a screwdriver to it, and try to figure out what all the parts are for and how they combine to make the device work.[3]

Pinker is not saying that people are machines; he is saying the *process* of making a model of human language, behaviour and perception can be likened to the *process* of reverse-engineering.

When 'the system' being observed is a person, what usually gets modelled is behaviour that can be seen or heard (sensory modelling), or thinking processes described through language (conceptual modelling).[4] Figuring out how great tennis players serve is an example of the former, while identifying their beliefs and strategies for winning is an example of the latter.

We used sensory and conceptual modelling to study David Grove at work, and as a result discovered a new way of modelling never previously documented—Symbolic Modelling.

While this book focuses on psychotherapy, Symbolic Modelling can also be applied to the more general endeavour of modelling human cognition and learning (see Chapter 10).

Symbolic Modelling

We define Symbolic Modelling as a process which uses Clean Language to facilitate people's discovery of how their metaphors express their way of being in the world—including how that way of being evolves. It differs from traditional modelling in three ways:

- What is modelled—the organisation of a Metaphor Landscape
- Who is modelling—*both* the client and the facilitator
- How self-modelling is facilitated—by using Clean Language.

What is modelled

Metaphor is a fundamental means of making sense of life. When a client identifies and examines the metaphors they live by they can use the information to construct a model which corresponds to the way they perceive themselves, others and the larger scheme of things. In other words their metaphors give a form to what it is *like* to be them. The result is a symbolic model-of-self, a Metaphor Landscape of the way they "bring forth a world."[5]

The metaphors used to describe thoughts, feelings, relationships, complex behaviours and abstract concepts are primarily derived from the workings of the physical world; that is, a world where things with a characteristic form exist at a location and which, as a result of internal and external events, change over time. In addition, everyday language and thought rely on (the metaphor of) an observer separate from what is observed; that is, a separate subject and object. This use of objects, places, events and observers as a source for metaphor is apparently universal. We therefore presume that metaphors of *form, space, time and perceiver* constitute the raw material of symbolic perception from which Metaphor Landscapes are constructed.[6]

In Symbolic Modelling the client is facilitated to develop a Metaphor Landscape as a means to model the *organisation* of their metaphors. But what is 'an organisation'? According to Fritjof Capra:

> The organization of a living system, [Maturana and Varela] explain, is the set of relations between its components that characterizes the system as belonging to a particular class ... The description of that organization is an abstract description of relationships and does not identify the components ... Maturana and Varela emphasize that the system's organization is independent of the properties of its components, so that a given organization can be embodied in many different manners by many different kinds of components.[7]

A system's organisation cannot be modelled directly; it has to be inferred from modelling the pattern of relationships between components. In Symbolic Modelling, components are the symbols contained in a client's metaphoric expressions—verbal, nonverbal, material and imaginative. Together these describe the client's in-the-moment embodied symbolic perception, and the sum total of these perceptions make up their Metaphor Landscape.

Pinker's reverse-engineering analogy can illustrate the Symbolic Modelling process if we split the role of a boffin into two: a client who figures out the design of *their own* device (the Metaphor Landscape), and a facilitator who assists the client by asking Clean Language questions. The facilitator facilitates the client to recognise the components of the device (the symbols) which comprise the internal mechanism (the metaphors) and the logic of the design (how the symbols and metaphors are arranged into patterns). This enables them to infer the manufacturing process (the organisation of their Metaphor Landscape).

Who is modelling

During Symbolic Modelling, instead of a dialogue there is a 'trialogue' where "a triangulation occurs between the therapist, the client and the [metaphoric] information."[8] The client models the organisation of their Metaphor Landscape while the therapist uses the client's metaphoric expressions to construct an equivalent model (Figure 2.1). In other words, *your* model will be your description of your perception of your experience of their description of their perception of their experience.

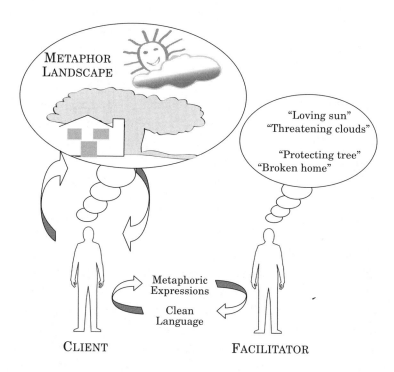

FIGURE 2.1 A trialogue

Both the client and the facilitator model the client's *in-the-moment* experience. Central to Symbolic Modelling is the perspective that every memory, behaviour, description, symptom, explanation, problem, solution or 'ah-ha' is an expression of the way the client brings forth their world, which in turn is isomorphic with the way their cognition is currently organised. Whether the client is remembering the past or imagining the future, they are experiencing it in the here and now. From this viewpoint, all experiences that relive the past or prelive the future are metaphors.

THE CLIENT
As a client describes their experience in metaphor, a symbolic perception manifests in front, around and within them so that they see, hear, feel and otherwise sense their symbols. At the same time their body

responds, mostly out of awareness, by gesturing, enacting or marking out aspects of the symbolic perception being described. For example, if the client says "I feel pulled in two directions" they can become aware of where they feel the two pulls, what kind of pulls they are, and in what directions they are being pulled. Maybe they also see who or what is doing the pulling and hear their conflicting demands. After a while, the client realises that they are actually embodying what they are describing. These sensations are not emotions; they are feelings, images and sounds which are experienced in a physical and real way. Of course the client may have emotional responses *about* feeling pulled in two directions, and these can be symbolised and incorporated into their Metaphor Landscape too. In short, it is the *embodiment* of their metaphors, their symbolic mindbody-knowing, that the client self-models.[9]

As self-modelling continues an amazing phenomenon occurs—the client begins to generate new experience. Describing this in metaphor triggers further experience and awareness, and so on, in a recursive, developmental spiral. When the client has an outcome to change and enough new experiences, or an experience of sufficient significance occurs, their Metaphor Landscape evolves. This results in a corresponding change to their day to day feelings, thoughts and behaviours. In Symbolic Modelling, therefore, change is a *by-product* of the modelling process. Over time the client not only learns how their system functions and how it changes but, because they have learned how to self-model, they can monitor their own evolution.

THE FACILITATOR

To facilitate a client to model the organisation of their Metaphor Landscape you will need to create your own model of their symbolic world. First you take their metaphors and nonverbal behaviours literally and assume that, within the privacy of their perceptual space, they are doing exactly what they are describing. If they say "My future is shrouded in mist" while gesturing in front and to their right, you assume they are pointing out the location of their future and that it is, indeed, shrouded in mist. Second, you verbally and nonverbally acknowledge the reality of the client's perceptual space and in so doing you "bless its characteristics."[10] Third, you invite them to attend to their Landscape so that they notice 'what is', and thereby learn about themselves.

Because facilitating is a dynamic process you must allow each client response to update the model of their Metaphor Landscape you are constructing. This updated model informs your choice of which question to ask next, and the process repeats. Therefore the formation of your model is a *by-product* of the client specifying their Metaphor Landscape. The relationship between what the client self-models and what the facilitator models is shown in Figure 2.2.

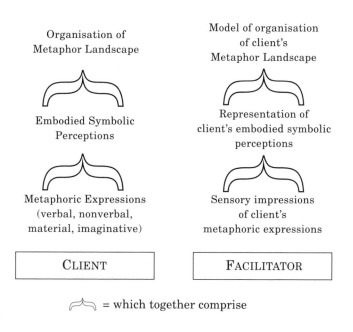

FIGURE 2.2 Who is modelling what

Your purpose is not to analyse or interpret the client's experience. It is not even to understand it. Rather it is to offer *them* the opportunity to become aware of their symbolic perceptions with minimal 'contamination' by your metaphors.

How self-modelling is facilitated

Given all languge influences, how do you play an active part without contaminating the client's perceptions? By asking questions that conform to the logic of their metaphors and which invite *them* to discover and understand the workings of their symbolic perceptions. To do this you need to pay exquisite attention to the metaphoric nature of what is being said and done, and then to incorporate this information into your Clean Language.

It is the 'cleanness' of your questions that minimises the imposition of your 'map' (metaphors, assumptions and perceptions) upon the client's Metaphor Landscape. In fact, the introduction of your metaphors will likely distract the client from their symbolic perceptions. It will require them to engage in extra, unnecessary processing in order to convert or translate your metaphors into a meaningful form. Not only does this interfere with the self-modelling process, it may also replicate hundreds of past impositions experienced by the client.

Clean Language is an honouring, affirming and facilitatory language. It acknowledges whatever the client is describing in a way that allows space and time for their symbolic perceptions to emerge and take form. This is why Clean Language is ideally suited for modelling autogenic metaphors (both verbal and nonverbal) and why it is central to the Symbolic Modelling process.

Creative States

The states which clients access during Symbolic Modelling seem to have many characteristics in common with those involving heightened creativity. For example, Arthur Koestler found that:

> The creative act, insofar as it depends on unconscious resources, presupposes a relaxing of controls and a regression to modes of ideation which are indifferent to the rules of verbal logic, unperturbed by contradiction, untouched by the dogmas and taboos of so called common sense. At the decisive stage of discovery the codes of disciplined reasoning are suspended—as they are in a dream, the reverie, the manic flight of thought, when the stream of ideation is free to drift, by its own emotional gravity, as it were, in an apparent 'lawless' fashion.[11]

This statement appears to be describing a journey into landscapes similar to those pioneered by David Grove. Koestler accurately reflects what happens when a client is fully involved self-modelling their symbolic perceptions. Clients often report a moment when they realise they have a choice to relax the controls, or as one client described it, "take the handbrake off." Another client spoke for many by saying:

> There was a point when I realised I couldn't make all the connections
> back to my real life and focus on what was happening in my head. I
> thought 'what the hell?' and just went with it.

Ernest Rossi, in his extensive investigation of *The Psychobiology of Mind-Body Healing,* describes such moments as creative breaks:

> What we usually experience as our ordinary everyday state of aware-
> ness or consciousness is actually habitual patterns of state-dependent
> memories, associations, and behaviours. I have conceptualized "crea-
> tive moments" in dreams, artistic and scientific creativity, and everyday
> life as breaks in these habitual patterns. The new experience that
> occurs during creative moments is regarded as *"the basic unit of origi-
> nal thought and insight as well as personality change."* [12]

Symbolic Modelling seems to induce creative breaks in our habitual patterns which result in the creation of novel ways of thinking, perceiving and being in the world.[13]

Three frameworks—The Organisation of Metaphor Landscapes, How Metaphor Landscapes Change and Evolve, and The Five-Stage Therapeutic Process—provide a theoretical basis for the practice of Symbolic Modelling and these are discussed next.

The Organisation of Metaphor Landscapes

People can be regarded as self-organising systems—and so can their Metaphor Landscapes:

> The organisation common to all living systems is a network of production
> processes, in which the function of each component is to participate in
> the production or transformation of other components in the network.
> In this way, the entire network continually 'makes itself'. It is produced
> by its components and in turn produces those components. 'In a living
> system,' [Maturana and Varela] explain, 'the product of its operation is
> its own organisation'.[14]

While each self-organising system is unique, collectively they exhibit common features. We borrow from Ken Wilber's description of these features and show how they apply to Metaphor Landscapes.[15]

- Self-organising systems are organised into *levels*. These determine what the system can and cannot do, its capacity to conserve and to transform itself, and its evolutionary direction. We distinguish four levels of organisation that comprise Metaphor Landscapes: *symbols; relationships* between symbols; *patterns* across those relationships; and a *pattern of organisation* of the entire configuration of patterns, relationships and symbols (Figure 2.3).[16]

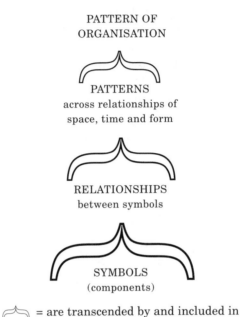

PATTERN OF
ORGANISATION

PATTERNS
across relationships of
space, time and form

RELATIONSHIPS
between symbols

SYMBOLS
(components)

⁀ = are transcended by and included in

FIGURE 2.3 Organisational levels of a Metaphor Landscape

- Each level of organisation is simultaneously a whole/part—a holon, to use Arthur Koestler's term.[17] Whether a symbol, a relationship or a pattern is perceived as part of a whole, or as a whole comprising parts, is simply a different way of punctuating experience.

- A self-organising system simultaneously *self-preserves* and *self-adapts*. At the same time as it seeks to preserve its own recognisable pattern, wholeness and identity, it adapts to maintain relationships with other systems, the environment, and to express its 'partness' of something larger. Metaphor Landscapes reflect this balance. Each symbol seeks to maintain *both* itself as an individual agency *and* its communion with other symbols, relationships and patterns.

- Each level exhibits its own *emergent properties*. These are not properties of any individual component and they do not exist at other levels. For example, 'salty' is not a property of either sodium or chlorine, both of which are poisonous. Neither is it a property of the compound sodium chloride. 'Salty' only emerges from the relationships between salt, taste buds and the nervous system—a higher level of organisation than its components. The same is true for the symbols, relationships and patterns of a Metaphor Landscape.

- Each lower level is nested within a hierarchy of higher levels and each higher level "transcends and includes" all lower levels.[18] In a Metaphor Landscape a relationship is more than the sum of its component symbols—it transcends them. But without those symbols the relationship does not exist—so it must include them. Symbols are necessarily included in a relationship but they do not define it because a relationship is a different class of information, a different organisational level from symbols.

Recognising levels of organisation

Becoming familiar with the characteristics of organisational levels of Metaphor Landscapes means you will be able to distinguish between them, to shift your attention from one to another and to recognise how each level influences the Landscape as a whole. This in turn will enhance your ability to cleanly invite clients to switch their attention within and between the four levels (symbols, relationships, patterns and pattern of organisation).

A description of these levels is followed by an example of how they manifested in a client's Metaphor Landscape.

Symbols

Symbols are the tangible components of a metaphor. They form the content of symbolic perception—that which can be seen, heard, felt or otherwise sensed directly (whether physically or imaginatively). A symbol is a 'something' that exists 'somewhere' and 'somewhen'.

A symbol's *attributes* (its characteristics and properties) give it a particular form, and its *location* specifies its position or place within the Metaphor Landscape. Together these distinguish it from other symbols and describe its unique identity. If a client says a symbol is

"A huge castle door that's very thick, very old, very heavy" you can be sure that every one of the door's attributes—its hugeness, thickness, oldness and heaviness, and that it is located in a castle—hold significance.

The minimum configuration of a symbolic perception is one perceived symbol and one perceiver of that symbol. If the client says "It's like I'm behind a castle door," the symbol 'castle door' is perceived by a perceiver called 'I' whose *point of perception* is located 'behind' a castle door (and presumably on the inside). The perceiver can be regarded as a special kind of symbol—one that has attributes which enable it to perceive other symbols in a particular way and from a particular location. In general, Metaphor Landscapes comprise multiple symbols and most involve several perceivers, each with their own point of perception.[19]

RELATIONSHIPS

While symbols have a form and a location which can be seen, heard, felt or in some way perceived directly, relationships do not. When two symbols connect, co-operate, balance, fight, avoid or scare each other, they are part of a functional or logical relationship. A relationship is an interaction, connection or correlation 'between', 'across' or 'over' *two* symbols (or one symbol over two spaces or times).

At a minimum, there will always be a relationship between each symbol and the perceiver of that symbol. In the above example the perceiver 'I' is "trying to open" the castle door. "Trying to open" specifies the relationship between the two symbols and also provides a wealth of presupposed relational information: the door is closed, 'I' has been trying for some time, 'I' is still trying, and although 'I' wants to open the door, 'I' is unable to at the moment.

PATTERNS

Symbols and their relationships to each other do not exist in isolation. They are part of wider contexts and larger systems consisting of higher level patterns. According to Fritjof Capra, patterns:

> Cannot be measured or weighed; they must be mapped. To understand a pattern, we must map a configuration of relationships. The study of pattern is crucial to the understanding of living systems because systemic properties ... arise from a configuration of ordered relationships. Systemic properties are properties of a pattern.[20]

Patterns emerge from a network of relationships. They connect components across multiple spaces, times and forms. They exist as stable configurations, repeating sequences and recurring motifs.

Once a pattern has been identified the client can embody it in a metaphor or symbolic representation and thus directly attend to this higher, more inclusive and more significant level of organisation.[21]

By recognising the patterns which emerge from their metaphors, clients often become aware that their presenting problem is symbolic of a whole class of problems. For instance, a client came to us with "a dilemma. I have to decide whether to stay with my partner or leave her." Through modelling his symbolic perceptions he recognised that his dilemma was not just about this particular partner, but about commitment in general. To his surprise he further realised that the metaphorical structure of the dilemma was the same as for every important decision he had ever made. With this heightened awareness his perception of the unwanted thoughts, feelings and behaviours previously associated with the dilemma began to change. Then it was easier for him to decide what to do—to stay with his partner and work through their difficulties. As often happens, he later discovered that his pattern contained the ingredients for its own evolution, and rather than getting rid of it, he found he could make use of it when "choosing the direction I want my life to take."[22]

PATTERN OF ORGANISATION

A Metaphor Landscape is more than its symbols, more than the relationships between those symbols and more than the patterns of those relationships. It exists as a unit, an entity, an identity, a whole unified system, a pattern of patterns that specifies and describes the unique nature of the system—a pattern of organisation. For Fritjof Capra, "The *pattern of organisation* of any system, living or nonliving, is the configuration of relationships among the system's components that determines the system's essential characteristics."[23]

A client's pattern of organisation will be so pervasive and so habitual, it is as if without it they would not be themselves. When a client uses metaphor to express a pattern of organisation, they give form to who they are.

Consider a person with 'an addiction' or 'a compulsion' or any other abstract concept which labels a set of repetitive behaviours about which they have little or no choice. The addiction is not the addictive substance, it is not even the particular sensations, perceptions, behaviours and beliefs experienced by the addict. It is the organisation of the relationships between these experiences that ensures the pattern repeats over and over. While the components specify the form the addiction takes, it is the pattern of organisation which specifies the near-certain probability that the addictive behaviour will continue. This is why stopping the addictive behaviour is only a part, albeit a fundamental part, of changing the addiction. Later, when a fully recovered addict says "I'm not the person I used to be" they are describing an organisational truth.

An example of levels

The Jubilee Clip transcript in Part V neatly illustrates the four levels of organisation. The client felt vulnerable and was waiting to be exposed. He symbolised these feelings as like a screwdriver tightening a jubilee clip around a hose:

SYMBOL	The metaphor consists of three symbols: a screwdriver, a jubilee clip and a hose.
RELATIONSHIP	The relationships between the symbols are: the screwdriver is *tightening* the jubilee clip, and the jubilee clip in turn is *tightening around* the hose.
PATTERN	The pattern which emerges later in the transcript can be summarised as: an ongoing conflict between wanting to undo the clip and the fear of an unknown risk if the clip is undone. This results in a continuation of the tightening and therefore a greater desire to undo the clip, which increases the fear, which tightens the clip, and so on. The end result is helplessness.
PATTERN OF ORGANISATION	After identifying other relevant metaphors, the client realised he had been repeating the same pattern of behaviour for more than 30 years. He symbolised this as: "I have to keep on climbing a mountain that gets higher the more I climb."

As the organisation of his Metaphor Landscape transformed, so did his perception of himself, his situation and his role in life.

It is because self-organising systems are organised into levels that they can be regarded as a whole or a part, that they can balance self-preservation with adapting to others, that emergent properties can exist, and that limitations and contradictions can be transcended and included.

We have distinguished symbols, relationships, patterns and patterns of organisation to illustrate how Metaphor Landscapes are organised into levels. Although for simplicity we have chosen to highlight four levels, symbols are themselves made up of components, and patterns of organisation are nested in larger contexts (as they, like everything else, are simultaneously whole/parts). More important than the precise number of levels is the way upward, downward and sideways influence is crucial to how self-organising systems change and evolve.

How Metaphor Landscapes Change and Evolve

Our second framework relates to the way self-organising systems evolve. We describe six characteristics of systemic change and map these onto the way Metaphor Landscapes, and thus clients, change and evolve.

CHANGE MANIFESTS AS A DIFFERENCE OF FORM OVER TIME

Gregory Bateson makes clear that "Difference which occurs across time is what we call 'change'."[24] What is different is detectable in the *form* of the system. Even changes to higher-level patterns will be embodied in changes to lower levels of form—but not necessarily vice versa. When a person moves, all their cells move with them, but when a cell changes, it rarely changes the person.

This means for a change in a Metaphor Landscape to be noticed, one or more attributes of a symbol, or group of symbols, has to be seen, heard, felt or in some other way sensed by the client as different compared to how they were before. Even changes to organising patterns will be embodied in differences to the attributes and location of symbols.

CHANGE IS SPECIFIED BY THE EXISTING ORGANISATION

Although an external stimulus can trigger an internal reconfiguration, it is the system's existing organisation that specifies the nature of any change that takes place. Because each new organisation emerges from the fundamental features of its predecessor, the system maintains a continuity of identity—despite changing over time. Therefore the current organisation is a product of its entire history of changes.[25]

Change requires a context, a Metaphor Landscape, from which to emerge. And as Landscapes can only change in ways that are congruent with their current form and organisation (doors may open and birds may fly, but generally not vice versa) it is not the past that keeps clients from changing, but the way their perceptions are *presently* organised. Equally, the current organisation will be the source of, and set the direction for, the client's next creative development.

LIVING SYSTEMS ALWAYS CHANGE—EVEN IF JUST TO STAY THE SAME
In response to a universe in constant flux, living systems are forever adapting, learning and evolving—that is, changing in an effort to preserve and maintain their coherence and identity. Homeostatic, self-perpetuating processes make changes at one level in order to maintain stability at other levels. The result is a constantly changing state of dynamic stability—ably demonstrated by a tightrope walker.[26]

The same processes that keep a system from disintegrating and from escalating out of safe bounds, can also act to inhibit, trap, stick, prevent, constrain, hinder, block or somehow bind development and transformation. We use *bind* as a generic term for any self-preserving pattern which the client finds inappropriate or unhelpful, and which they have been unable to change.[27]

Often binds are conceptually labelled as a conflict, dilemma, impasse or paradox. When a binding pattern is represented symbolically its ethereal nature is made tangible and the logic inherent in the pattern that perpetuates the bind can be attended to directly. Then clients discover that the organisation of their Metaphor Landscape prevents the very changes they seek. Or they realise that, within the existing organisation, their problem is simply unresolvable. Or they become aware that what they are trying so hard to achieve is actually causing the problem.

In the Jubilee Clip example above, the client is in a binding pattern because he *has to* climb the mountain, but the more he climbs the higher the mountain gets. By trying to get to the top he is actually getting further away from his goal, which means he *has to* renew his efforts to climb, and so on. The result is a stalemate, a game without end. However, recognising the binding nature of the pattern creates conditions for change.

CHANGE OCCURS WHEN SUITABLE CONDITIONS ARISE

Homeostatic processes tend to prevent significant change, except under threshold conditions. Then the slightest perturbation can trigger a change—like the straw that breaks the camel's back, or the speck of dust that activates a supersaturated solution to transform into a crystal. The primary way the conditions for change arise is through the client learning how their system is organised, how it maintains the status quo, and how it currently changes. These conditions arise:

- When symbols, relationships and patterns are separated and distinguished enough that they become available for a new synthesis.

- When the Landscape gets complex enough that a simpler, more inclusive pattern emerges.

- When certain structures, processes or motifs are recognised as inherent, then a new responsiveness and flexibility becomes possible.

- When symbols and patterns are perceived within larger contexts and outcomes, then perception itself becomes ready to change.

THERE ARE TWO WAYS SYSTEMS EVOLVE

Systems evolve by *translation*—their form changes but not in a way that significantly affects higher-level patterns, or by *transformation*— a new pattern of organisation emerges and the whole system changes into a fundamentally new form.

There is an important difference between quantitative translation and qualitative transformation. Translations ripple 'horizontally' within the same level of organisation without transforming the nature of the system itself. In contrast, transformations percolate or cascade 'vertically' through the levels such that the system's essential nature evolves. In a desert, no matter how much the size, shape, composition and number of sand dunes translate, the desert remains a desert. The formation of a range of mountains, however, will transform the desert into a variety of ecosystems. In short, "Translation shuffles parts; transformation produces wholes."[28]

As a client learns about the organisation of their Metaphor Landscape, usually they either accept their existing organisation as is, or a
translatory change satisfies them. Changes of this nature account for
most of what people wish to achieve through psychotherapy. In some
cases however, neither the status quo nor a translatory change is
acceptable. Then the system needs to find a new way of being. As Ken
Wilber elegantly explains:

> With translation, the self is simply given a new way to think or feel
> about reality. The self is given a new belief—perhaps holistic instead of
> atomistic, perhaps forgiveness instead of blame, perhaps relational
> instead of analytic. The self then learns to translate its world and its
> being in the terms of this new belief or new language or new paradigm,
> and this new and enchanting translation acts, at least temporarily, to
> alleviate or diminish the terror inherent in the heart of the separate
> self. But with transformation, the very process of translation itself is
> challenged, witnessed, undermined, and eventually dismantled ...
>
> And as much as we, as you and I, might wish to transcend mere
> translation and find authentic transformation, nonetheless translation
> itself is an absolutely necessary and crucial function for the greater
> part of our lives. Those who cannot translate adequately, with a fair
> amount of integrity and accuracy, fall quickly into severe neurosis or
> even psychosis: the world ceases to make sense—the boundaries
> between the self and the world are not transcended but instead begin to
> crumble. This is not breakthrough but breakdown; not transcendence
> but disaster.
>
> But at some point in our maturation process, translation itself, no
> matter how adequate or confident, simply ceases to console. No new
> beliefs, no new paradigm, no new myths, no new ideas, will staunch the
> encroaching anguish. Not a new belief for the self, but the transcend-
> ence of the self altogether, is the only path that avails.[29]

When the system transcends and includes a binding pattern per-
petuating the original symptoms, the current Landscape transforms, a
different kind of Landscape emerges, and life is lived with reorganised
metaphors and perceptions. Because each client's way of evolving is
dependent on, and has to emerge from, their existing and unique
organisation, there can be no universal method of transcending and
including. Paradoxically it is the person-specific limitations and contradictions that *both* prevent *and* enable clients to transform.[30]

THE EFFECTS OF CHANGE ARE INDETERMINATE

Once a change has happened it will have effects which go on to trigger other changes, some of which will influence the part of the system that initiated the change. Because self-organising systems have these "circular (or more complex) chains of determination"[31] the full consequences of any change are not predictable. But because a change is specified by the organisation of the system it is not random: a change at "the lower [level] sets the possibilities of the higher; the higher sets the probabilities of the lower."[32]

It may not be obvious at first whether a change in a Metaphor Landscape is a translation or a transformation. Only later, in comparison with the past and in light of feedback can the client know for sure. As the 'butterfly effect' analogy illustrates, the full significance of any change can only be assessed retrospectively when the possibilities and probabilities have become actualities.

Transformations can occur very slowly over a long period or in a cataclysmic discontinuity, a defining moment. Either way, once a threshold is crossed, the system and the person can never be quite the same again.

The Five-Stage Therapeutic Process

The Five-Stage Therapeutic Process is a framework for facilitating clients to self-model the way their Metaphor Landscape is organised and evolves. The stages are introduced below with a full description of each given in Chapters 5 to 9. Although the five stages are presented sequentially, the process is not a linear procedure; rather it is an emergent, systemic and iterative way of conducting psychotherapy.

The Penguin Dictionary of Psychology defines psychotherapy as "any technique or procedure that has palliative or curative effects upon any mental, emotional or behavioural disorder." By this definition, psychotherapy is concerned with remedial change. For us, however, it also includes changes of a more generative and evolutionary nature; changes which broaden and deepen existing qualities, strategies and resources; changes which strengthen people's sense of identity, purpose and spirit; and changes which add new ways of perceiving and knowing.

To use Robert Dilts' analogy:

> Remedial change is like pulling weeds; generative change is like plant-
> ing new seeds; evolutionary change is like altering the landscape upon
> which the weeds and the seeds are growing.[33]

Although there are a multitude of ways to describe the psychotherapeutic process, most talking therapies work within a similar framework:

1. The process starts, in a more or less predetermined manner, with an
    intention by the client to change in a beneficial way.

2. This introductory phase is followed by a period when information is
    gathered, assembled, discovered, constructed or de-constructed.

3. Thereafter the information is viewed, reviewed and otherwise explored
    for connections, conclusions and other forms of pattern.

4. At some point the client experiences a change. Given how little is known
    about the process of how people change, probably the most accurate
    description of this stage is: 'and then a miracle occurs'.

5. Thereafter the aim of the process itself changes—from seeking change,
    to seeking to preserve, stabilise and maintain the changes. Eventually
    the new becomes old as the client continues their journey of personal
    development.

Different therapies have their own names for these five stages. In Symbolic
Modelling we call them: Entry, Developing Symbolic Perceptions, Modelling Symbolic Patterns, Encouraging Conditions for Transformation,
and Maturing (Figure 2.4).[34]

STAGE 1: ENTRY

The horizontal dashed line in Figure 2.4 denotes a threshold between
two worlds: below the line is everyday narrative, conceptual description and dialogue; above the line is embodied metaphor, symbolic
perceptions and trialogue. During Stage 1 clients become aware that
their verbal and nonverbal expressions, as well as objects and events in
the physical environment, can be perceived metaphorically. This
requires only the merest shift of attention from commonplace recounting
of events to engaging with a world of personal symbolism. *Entry* into
the symbolic domain can happen spontaneously, or it can be facilitated
by a clean question.

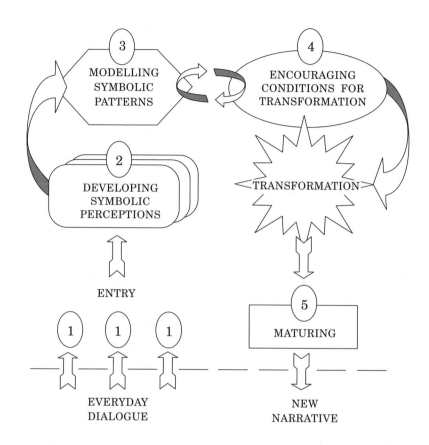

FIGURE 2.4 Symbolic Modelling's Five-Stage Therapeutic Process

STAGE 2: DEVELOPING SYMBOLIC PERCEPTIONS

A symbolic perception encompasses a unit of symbolic time which need have little obvious relation to 'clock' or 'remembered' time. It can be a moment, an event, a scene, a process, or even an entire lifetime. It allows an instant to be examined for hours or an aeon to be explored in a few minutes. Stage 2 focuses on developing *single symbolic perceptions*, one at a time. The client's desired outcome should be represented as one of these symbolic perceptions—preferably the first.

During Stage 2 clients individuate the components of each symbolic perception from the "undifferentiated information mass" they typically bring to therapy.[35] When the matrix of their experience differentiates into symbols which have an existence and an identity, each symbol's attributes and relationships with other symbols becomes apparent. As clients embody and engage with their symbols, a symbolic perception forms and comes to life—like a photograph emerging from developing solution. The client can then be asked to draw, or in some other way to physicalise the configuration of symbols and relationships.

STAGE 3: MODELLING SYMBOLIC PATTERNS

Clients make the transition to Stage 3 when multiple perceptions have been developed and a more complex Metaphor Landscape emerges. The Landscape creates a context in which *patterns across perceptions* can be identified and examined.

Patterns manifest as stable configurations, repeating sequences and recurring motifs (over space, across time and among attributes). Once identified, each pattern can be named, symbolically represented and explored. Thus the modelling process repeats at a higher and more inclusive level. As the organising logic of the Metaphor Landscape is revealed, the client discovers:

- The role of the configuration of symbols and relationships.
- The sequence in which thoughts, feelings and behaviours repeat time and time again.
- The significance of recurring motifs within the overall scheme.
- Resources which can beneficially influence the Landscape.
- Binding patterns whose organisation prevents change and maintains the status quo.
- How the system can evolve.

When, as a result of self-modelling, change occurs spontaneously, Stage 4 is bypassed and the change is matured in Stage 5.

STAGE 4: ENCOURAGING CONDITIONS FOR TRANSFORMATION

If change does not occur spontaneously, or if a change *translates* the 'present state' into another form without changing its essential nature (the classic 'jumping out of the frying pan into the fire'), a binding pattern of patterns, a double bind, will be maintaining the Metaphor Landscape's existing organisation. In these cases a *transformation* to a new form of organisation is required.

While transformations cannot be manufactured to order, Stage 4 encourages the *conditions* from which transformative change can emerge. We have identified six approaches which encourage clients to vary the way they attend to, and work with, the inherent logic of their Metaphor Landscape:

A. Concentrating attention on lower, more fundamental levels of organisation

B. Attending to higher, more significant patterns of patterns

C. Broadening attention to outside or beyond existing spatial boundaries

D. Lengthening attention to before or after a sequence of events

E. Identifying the logical conditions necessary for change

F. Introducing one symbol to another so that information or resources can be transferred or exchanged.

Changing attention in these ways tends to trigger expanded awareness and new perceptions—just the conditions required for the transformation of an existing conflict, dilemma, impasse or paradox.

STAGE 5: MATURING

When the form, location or function of a symbol changes, the effects of that change can be matured in Stage 5. *Maturing* is a process by which a newly changed symbol is evolved, developed and differentiated from its previous form, and the effects of the change spread to other symbols. When sufficient changes accumulate or a change of sufficient significance occurs, thresholds are exceeded, boundaries are crossed, defining moments occur and binding patterns transform. Then a new organisation emerges which transcends and includes the limitations of the existing Landscape. After further maturing, the new Landscape takes on a solidity and life of its own. Now the client can contemplate the changes which have taken place, become familiar with their new symbolic world and make new associations. As this happens cognition, perception and behaviour change correspondingly.

The Five Stages as one integrated process

The five stages are provided as a framework to guide *you* while accompanying a client on their unique journey of self-evolution. Your knowledge about where they are in the process will inform your choice of which clean question to ask and what to ask it of.

You may have noticed a correlation between levels of organisation and the Five-Stage Process. Stage 2 is about identifying component symbols and their relationships within a single symbolic perception. Stage 3 reveals patterns of relationships, patterns across perceptions and binding patterns. Stage 4 works with the inferential logic of the whole Landscape to encourage conditions for the transformation of binding patterns of organisation. Viewed in this way, the Five-Stage Process is congruent with, and a reflection of how self-perpetuating systems are organised and evolve.

While we have presented the five stages sequentially, the *transition* between stages is necessarily ill-defined because identifying and working with symbolic perceptions is an emerging, unpredictable, iterative and fuzzy process.[36]

Stage 1 does not happen just at the beginning, as the client may enter their symbolic world once or, more likely, several times during a session. Similarly whenever another symbolic perception appears, the form and relationships of its symbols are developed using Stage 2 processes. Equally, as soon as the client has a sufficiently well-developed Metaphor Landscape they can start Stage 3, modelling the logic inherent in the patterns across their perceptions. Self-modelling patterns is a recursive process which frequently produces spontaneous change. When it does the client progresses to Stage 5 where the change is evolved and spread to other symbols. Like all other stages, maturing is not a one-time event. It will involve a series of changes as the Landscape metamorphoses and a new organisation emerges. In cases where a binding pattern prevents change occurring, or when a change turns out to be another example of the same pattern repeating, Stage 4 is required to encourage conditions for transformation.

At any time during the five stages the client may return to everyday dialogue, bringing with them new perceptions and different feelings about those perceptions—with the resultant changed behaviour. The whole process can take place in less than an hour or it may require many iterative cycles. How the client cycles through the stages and how long each stage takes is dependent on the nature of their Metaphor Landscape—it takes as long as it takes, and no longer.

Principles of Symbolic Modelling

The salient features of the three frameworks within which Symbolic Modelling operates (the organisation of Metaphor Landscapes, how they change and evolve, and the Five-Stage Process) can be summarised as a set of operating principles designed to guide you when facilitating a client to self-model.[37] These are presented below.

AN INDIVIDUAL'S SYSTEM WORKS PERFECTLY AT DOING WHAT IT DOES

- It does what it does because it is organised to do so. It simply cannot do something it is not organised to do, no matter how desirable that may be. In other words, at every moment, people cannot not be themselves.

- Since the organisation of a client's metaphorical expressions is isomorphic with the organisation of their cognition, self-modelling their Metaphor Landscape allows them to explore and learn from the organisation of their cognition.

- Each component of a system performs a function which affects other parts of the system and contributes to maintaining the existing organisation. Therefore within the current setup each symbol will have adapted to and, to some degree, be dependent upon every other symbol's existence—even if that symbol is the meanest and most frightening symbol that ever existed.

- The processes that result in limitations and constraints are the same as those that generate creativity, learning and loving. It is not the processes themselves, but how they are organised and utilised that determines whether there is a problem or not.

METAPHOR LANDSCAPES EVOLVE AS APPROPRIATE CONDITIONS ARISE

- The process of a client self-modelling the organisation of their Metaphor Landscape—becoming aware of symbols, relationships between symbols, and patterns across perceptions—creates a context for change. Change itself is a by-product of self-modelling symbolically.

- While clients always have the capacity to change and evolve, when, how and why a particular Metaphor Landscape reorganises is inherently indeterminate. There are, however, conditions which increase the likelihood of significant change occurring. These principally involve the system learning about its own organisation.

- Binding patterns such as paradox, conflict, dilemma and impasse will be operating when a client has experienced repetitive unwanted symptoms over a period of time despite their desire and best efforts to change.

- A translation which reorganises the form of the existing Metaphor Landscape will, more often than not, satisfy the client's desire to change. When it does not, a new Landscape with a transformed pattern of organisation will be required.

FACILITATORS NEED TO OPERATE FROM A STATE OF 'NOT KNOWING'

- You can never know another person's experience or even fully understand their description of their perception, because to do so invokes your metaphorical constructs. What you can do is build a model which has a corresponding organisation (is isomorphic) with their Metaphor Landscape; but it will always be your model of their descriptions and behaviours.

- Symbolic Modelling involves working with emergent properties, fuzzy categories, apparently illogical causal relations, multiple levels of simultaneous and systemic processes, iterative cycles and unexpected twists and turns. In short, especially during the early stages, the client's information is intrinsically unpredictable and messy.

- Symbolic Modelling is a dynamic process and your model of the client's model will require continual revision as each new piece of information emerges—especially as their Landscape may well start changing before a comprehensive model has been identified.

- You can rely upon the intelligence and wisdom of the *whole* system (i.e. the combined conscious and unconscious mind-body-spirit that comprises you, the client, their metaphors and the immediate environment) to indicate what needs to happen at each and every moment in time. This requires you to stay true to the process, especially if you feel confused, lost, helpless or hopeless. In other words, when you do not know what to do, *the system knows*.

- Analysis and interpretation of the meaning of symbols *by the facilitator* is counterproductive because it distracts the client's attention from their own perceptions. Instead you can accept clients' metaphoric expressions as perfect examples of their patterns manifesting in the moment.

- You can facilitate clients to self-model their embodied symbolic perceptions by accurately referencing their verbal and nonverbal metaphors, and by asking clean questions within the inherent logic of their metaphors.

- Neither you nor the client can make, induce, trick, reframe or otherwise cause a transformation. While you are continually triggering responses in the client's system, all responses and changes are specified by the particular form and pattern of organisation of the system (not the trigger). Therefore there is no need for you to make something happen or to solve anything; rather your aim is to encourage the appropriate conditions in which change is the specified response. These conditions will exist within the inherent logic of the Metaphor Landscape.

Concluding Remarks

Part I of this book has presented the theoretical background of Symbolic Modelling. Chapter 1 introduced the symbolic domain of experience and the central role of metaphor in understanding, communicating and learning. We explained that metaphors and symbols can be expressed verbally, nonverbally, materially and imaginatively, and that an individual's embodied symbolic perceptions are part of a coherent and consistent Metaphor Landscape.

In Chapter 2 we described how each Landscape is both unique and conforms to self-organising patterns of existence, operation and evolution. These systems consist of a network of multi-dimensional and fuzzy relationships whose transformation is inherently indeterminate. Therefore traditional linear, formulaic and analytical approaches to therapy are incongruent with the nature of Metaphor Landscapes. Instead we provided an alternative, iterative and systemic Five-Stage Process for Symbolic Modelling.

The primary purpose of Symbolic Modelling is to facilitate an individual to learn about the organisation of their metaphors. In the process of becoming aware of the way their system works, conditions emerge in which change is a natural consequence. Change does not occur in a vacuum—it requires a context, a Metaphor Landscape. Once the context exists, simply using Clean Language within the logic of the client's metaphors and faithfully following the process as it unfolds, normally activates the change process.

As you will see next, it is the simple and well-specified structure of Clean Language that makes it easy to learn how to facilitate clients to self-model their symbolic perceptions.

II

THE HEART OF
SYMBOLIC MODELLING

3

Less is More: Basic Clean Language

A gentle genie has escaped from the lamp.
His name is David Grove and his magic is 'clean language'.
Ernest Rossi

Verbal communication is one of the defining characteristics of being human and the way each of us uses language in part defines us as individual human beings. Our language not only expresses who we are, it also allows listeners to peek into our private perceptual world. As the listener listens, a multitude of meaning-making processes are automatically activated. This happens so fast that they are unaware of what they have gone through to make sense of what they hear. In this way *all* language triggers reactions, only some of which appear in the listener's consciousness.

How therapists use language largely determines the way they conduct therapy. There can be few people who have spent more time in the thick of clinical interactions exploring the influence of language than David Grove, and the result is an outstanding contribution to psychotherapy: the concept, definition and application of Clean Language.

While Chapter 4 addresses how to use Clean Language with non-verbal metaphors, this chapter covers the basics of using Clean Language with clients' verbal metaphors. It introduces:

The Purpose of Clean Language
An Outline of the Components of Clean Language
A Client Transcript: Castle Door
The Function of Syntax
The Function of the Nine Basic Clean Questions
Utilising Vocal Qualities

The Purpose of Clean Language

In his book, *Resolving Traumatic Memories* (coauthored with Basil Panzer), David Grove is explicit about the purpose of Clean Language:

> The first objective is for the therapist to keep the language clean and allow the client's language to manifest itself. The second objective is that the clean language used by the therapist be a facilitatory language; in the sense that it will ease entry into the matrix of experience, and into that altered state that may be helpful for the client to internally access his experience. ... By asking clean questions we shape the location and the direction of the client's search for the answer. In asking a question we do not impose upon the client any value, construct or presupposition about what he should answer. ... The client is free to find an answer and may keep the answer to himself. It may not be necessary for the client to share his memories, thoughts or feelings. ... The questions are not asked to gather information or to understand the client's perspectives. We ask our questions so that the client can understand his perspective internally, in his own matrix. ... We want to leave our questions embedded in the client's experience. ... Our questions will have given a form, made manifest some particular aspect of the client's internal experience in a way that he has not experienced before.[1]

In other words, Clean Language has three functions:

- To acknowledge clients' experience exactly as they describe it.
- To orientate clients' attention to an aspect of their perception.
- To send them on a quest for self-knowledge.

Clean Language is an extraordinary language because *everything* that you, as the facilitator, say and do is intimately related to what the client says and does. Since each Clean Language question takes as its point of departure the client's *last* verbal or nonverbal description, there is minimal need for them to translate and interpret your words and behaviour. And because the client's response always informs your next question, the organisation of the client's information leads the therapeutic interaction. Thus the entire focus of the process becomes an exploration of the client's model of the world from *their* perspective, within *their* perceptual time and space, and using *their* words.

Of course Clean Language influences and directs attention — *all* language does that.[2] Clean Language does it 'cleanly' because it is sourced in the client's vocabulary, it is consistent with the logic of their metaphors and only introduces the universal metaphors of time, space and form. Facilitating clients to *self-model* using Clean Language requires that your attention be focused on the logic inherent in their information when, according to David Grove, "the I-ness of the therapist should appear to cease to exist."[3]

An Outline of the Components of Clean Language

In order to use Clean Language you need to understand the function of its essential components: the full syntax, the nine basic questions, and the vocal qualities. (A fourth component, nonverbal behaviour, is covered in the next chapter.) Although these components are interrelated, we introduce them separately to show the contribution that each makes to the Symbolic Modelling process; first as an overview, then as a client transcript and then in a detailed explanation.

Syntax

Syntax is the way that words are combined into sentences to achieve a purpose. The syntax of Clean Language is unusual in that it directs the client's attention to their own perceptions. The *full* syntax of Clean Language is made up of three elements:

And [client's words]. **And when/as** [client's words], [**clean question**]?

It is designed this way so that your language automatically acknowledges the client's description, then invites them to orientate their attention to an aspect of their symbolic perception and finally sends them on a search for self-knowledge.

The nine basic questions

In everyday conversation the quality of a question is judged by the information elicited and its usefulness to the *questioner*. With Clean Language the quality of a question depends upon how the client processes the question and its usefulness to *them*. A clean question sends the client on a quest. Whether they find the Holy Grail is less important than that they seek it, and in so doing learn about themselves along the way.

At the heart of Clean Language there are just nine questions. Our research shows that David Grove asks variations of these nine questions about eighty percent of the time, which is why we call them the *basic* clean questions:[4]

DEVELOPING QUESTIONS

And is there anything else about [client's words]?

And what kind of [client's words] **is that** [client's words]?

And that's [client's words] **like what**?

And where is [client's words]?

And whereabouts [client's words]?

MOVING TIME QUESTIONS

And then what happens?

And what happens next?

And what happens just before [client's words]?

And where could [client's words] **come from**?

When a question requires "client's words" this can be a single word, a phrase or everything the client has just said, depending on where you want to direct their attention.

How can so few questions invoke such a wide range and depth of responses and facilitate profound change? As you will see, the answer lies in their cumulative capacity to value what is, and to elicit what could be.

Vocal qualities

It may seem obvious that in every therapeutic encounter words are generated from two sources: the client and the therapist. But the difference between *the way* client-generated words are spoken and *the way* therapist-generated words are spoken is essential to the effective use of Clean Language. To reflect the difference between the two sources you need acute listening skills and the flexibility to alter your voice, so that:

- When using client-generated words, match *the way* they speak those words.

- When using therapist-generated words, s-l-o-w d-o-w-n your speed of delivery, and use a consistent, rhythmic, poetic and curious tonality.

To reiterate: the essential components of Clean Language are the syntax, the nine basic questions, and the vocal qualities you use to ask the questions. As soon as you have an understanding of these components you can begin practising and building the skill of working within clients' symbolic perceptions.

Client Transcript: Castle Door

The following transcript illustrates the basic facets of Clean Language. We recommend you read it out loud in order to familiarise yourself with the syntax, questions and vocal qualities. With the exception of personal pronouns, all the words that we introduce are shown in **bold** to distinguish them from client-generated words, *not* to signify emphasis. For simplicity we have not identified which one of us asked the questions. The client is female, in her late 30s. She responds to our opening question with:

C1: I'd like to have more energy because I feel very tired.

T1: **And** you'd like to have more energy because you feel very tired. **And when** you'd like to have more energy, **that's** more energy **like what**?

C2: It's like I'm behind a castle door.

T2: **And** it's like you're behind a castle door. **And when** behind a castle door, **what kind of** castle door **is that** castle door?

C3: A huge castle door that's very thick, very old, with studs, very heavy.

T3: **And** a huge castle door that's very thick, very old, with studs, very heavy. **And when** huge castle door is very thick, very old, with studs, very heavy, **is there anything else about that** huge castle door?

C4: I can't open it and I get very very tired trying to open it.

T4: **And** you can't open it and you get very very tired trying to open it. **And as** you get very very tired trying to open it, **what kind of** very very tired trying **is that**?

C5: Like I'm struggling on my own and not getting anywhere. It takes a lot of energy. I feel like I'm banging my head on a wall.

T5: **And** like struggling on your own, not getting anywhere, **and** banging your head on a wall. **And as** it takes a lot of energy banging your head on a wall, **what kind of** wall **is that** wall?

C6: A castle wall of thick granite and I get very frustrated and very angry.

T6: **And** a castle wall of thick granite and you get very frustrated and very angry. **And when** very frustrated and very angry, **where is that** very frustrated and **that** very angry?

C7: In here [touches solar plexus region].

T7: **And when** in here, **whereabouts** in here?

C8: Exactly in here. Hollow. Full of darkness.

T8: **And** exactly in here. Hollow. Full of darkness. **And when** hollow **is** full of darkness, **is there anything else about that** darkness?

C9: It's very dry.

T9: **And** it's very dry. **And when** darkness is very dry, it's very dry **like what**?

C10: It's dry like a desert.

T10: **And** it's dry like a desert. **And when** dry like a desert, **is there anything else about that**?

C11: It keeps me in one place and it doesn't let me move.

T11: **And** it keeps you in one place and doesn't let you move. **And** dry like a desert, hollow full of darkness in here **and** struggling on your own **and** very very tired trying to open huge castle door **that's** very thick **and** very heavy **and** very old. **And is there anything else about that** door you can't open?

C12: Yes. A great big circular handle that's all twisted around.

T12: **And is there anything else about that** great big circular handle that's all twisted around?

C13: It looks like twisted pasta. It's big. It's old. It's dull. It's metal, iron, black.

T13: **And when** great big circular handle looks like twisted pasta **and** it's old iron, black, **where could that** old iron **come from**?

C14: A spear.

T14: **And** a spear. **And what kind of** spear **could that** spear **be**?

C15: Like a Roman would use—I've a sense of a centurion standing with it.

T15: **And** you've a sense of a centurion standing with it. **And what kind of** centurion **could that** centurion **be**?

C16: [Smiles.] Big and broad with armour on and a spear.

T16: **And when** big, broad centurion with armour on **is** standing with a spear, **then what happens**?

C17:   He knocks on the door.

T17:   **And as** he knocks on the door, **what happens next**?

C18:   I can hear him but he can't see me and he goes away. And I can't get out. Then I get *very* frustrated. It gets almost too much to bear.

T18:   **And** it gets almost too much to bear. **So when** you're behind huge castle door with a twisted iron handle, **and** you get very very tired trying to open it, **and** hollow **is** full of darkness, **and** a big broad centurion with a spear knocks, **and** you can hear him but he can't see you, **and** he goes away, **and** you can't get out, **and** it gets almost too much to bear, [pause] **then what happens**?

C19:   [Pause.] Then I lose all my energy because I don't know what to do.

T19:   **And** then you lose all your energy because you don't know what to do. **And when** you lose all your energy because you don't know what to do, **then what happens**?

C20:   I sit in the corner and go to sleep.

T20:   **And** you sit in the corner and go to sleep. **And as** you sleep, **and** sleep, **what happens next**?

C21:   I have to find a way out. I try to open it again.

T21:   **And** you have to find a way out. **And** you try to open it again. **And what happens just before** you try to find a way out again?

C22:   [Looks up and squints.] I can see the sky—I never noticed that before—hope is on the outside [long pause]. It's very strong. It gives me determination and the ability to keep trying.

T22:   **And** you can see the sky. **And** hope is on the outside. **And when** it gives you very strong determination to keep trying, **whereabouts is** it **when** it's very strong?

C23:   I can feel it right in the middle—at the absolute core of my being.

T23:   **And when** you can feel it right in the middle, at the absolute core of your being, it's **like what**?

C24:   It's gold.

T24:   **And** it's gold. **And when** it's gold at the absolute core of your being, **what kind of** gold **is that** gold?

C25:   Absolutely pure. It's always been there.

T25:   **And** absolutely pure. **And** absolutely pure gold's always been there at the core of your being. **And is there anything else about that** absolutely pure gold?

C26:   It's incredibly strong but malleable. Powerful. You could shape it but you couldn't break it. An almost silent powerful.

T26:   **And** an almost silent powerful. **And is there anything else about that** absolutely pure gold **that**'s incredibly strong **and** malleable **and** almost silent powerful at the absolute core of your being?

C27:   It can move.

(See Part V for the completion of this transcript.)

An explanation of the components of Clean Language, and the role each plays in the transcript, follows.

The Function of Syntax

The distinctive syntax of Clean Language is a defining characteristic. Its dual role is to keep your language clean and to keep the focus of the client's attention on their symbolic perceptions. We analyse the function of syntax under three headings:

The full syntax
Using clients' terminology
Shortened syntax.

The full syntax

The full syntax of Clean Language has three parts: to acknowledge the client's way of perceiving, to orientate their perception, and to request them to examine that perception for new information:

> **And** [client's words]. **And when/as** [client's words], [**clean question**]?

The overall purpose of the syntax is to encourage the client to go through the process of generating and self-modelling their symbolic perceptions again and again (see Figure 3.1).

In the transcript, our use of the full syntax is clear from the outset:

C1:   I'd like to have more energy because I feel very tired.

T1:   **And** you'd like to have more energy because you feel very tired.
       And when you'd like to have more energy,
       that's more energy **like what**?

C2:   It's like I'm behind a castle door.

Using the full syntax acknowledges the client's description and orientates her attention towards what she would like, "more energy." The question invites her to notice the form of that energy. Her answer is overtly metaphoric.[5]

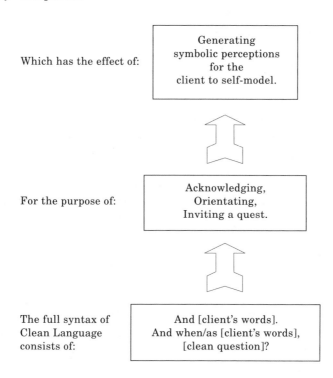

Which has the effect of: | Generating symbolic perceptions for the client to self-model.

For the purpose of: | Acknowledging, Orientating, Inviting a quest.

The full syntax of Clean Language consists of: | And [client's words]. And when/as [client's words], [clean question]?

FIGURE 3.1 The full syntax and its purpose

You may have noticed in the transcript that apart from the clean questions, the only words we introduce are *and, when* and *as*. And there are good reasons for using these little words.

STARTING WITH 'AND'

All clean language sentences start with the conjunction 'And'. Its function is to connect, to add, to continue. As well as being a gentle way of starting, 'And' signals that what is about to be said will not be a dialogue in which two minds compete for centre stage. Instead it says: 'What I am about to say is a continuation of what you have just said'. With repeated use, 'And' sends a mostly out-of-awareness message to the client: this whole interaction is to be conducted from *your* perspective.[6]

ABOUT 'WHEN'

Using 'when' invites the client to focus on either a *particular* moment when they experience what they are describing, or a *class* of experiences similar to that being described. Think of the former as viewing a single snapshot or video clip, and the latter as a number of snapshots or clips of similar events. In other words, 'when' asks the client to perceptually 'stop time' so that new information and insights have a chance to enter awareness. You can see how this operates in the following example:

C2:   It's like I'm behind a castle door.

T2:   **And** it's like you're behind a castle door. **And *when*** behind a castle door, **what kind of** castle door **is that** castle door?

C3:   A huge castle door that's very thick, very old, with studs, very heavy.

Here 'when' invites the client to attend to her perception of the particular time and place called "behind a castle door"—in preparation for the question that follows.

ABOUT 'AS'

Like 'when', 'as' encourages perceptual time to pause so that the client can focus their attention on a single event. In addition, 'as' acknowledges and orientates to the ongoing and dynamic nature of the client's perception. This can be indicated in a number of ways: by a metaphor (e.g. C5: "It *takes* a lot of energy"); by nonverbals (say, a repeated circular motion of the hand); and by verbs ending in '-ing' which presuppose a continuing process (e.g. trying, struggling, banging). The following illustrates the difference between using 'when' and 'as':

C3:   A huge castle door that's very thick, very old, with studs, very heavy.

T3:   **And** a huge castle door that's very thick, very old, very heavy. **And *when*** huge castle door is very thick, very old, with studs, very heavy, **is there anything else about that** huge castle door?

C4:   I can't open it and I get very very tired trying to open it.

T4:   **And** you can't open it and you get very very tired trying to open it. **And *as*** you get very very tired trying to open it, **what kind of** very very tired trying **is that**?

C5:   Like I'm struggling on my own and not getting anywhere. It takes a lot of energy. I feel like I'm banging my head on a wall.

If you compare C3 with C4 you will notice the difference between a static perception of "A huge castle door" and a dynamic perception of "trying to open it." Referencing "castle door" with 'when', and "trying" with 'as', honours the nature of each description.

To summarise, the formulaic nature of the full syntax of Clean Language is designed to keep your vocabulary and metaphors out of the client's perceptions. The words 'and', 'when' and 'as' are used for continuity and to encourage clients to attend to a single symbolic event. This enables them to more fully explore whatever they are perceiving at the time, and because they hear mostly their own words, their attention is not distracted from what they are perceiving. Equally, because you do not need to manufacture words of your own, more of your attention is available to watch what they do and listen to exactly what they say.

Using clients' terminology

Once a client enters the symbolic domain, words take on special significance and meaning. They are packed with information: they indicate the client's current patterns, they represent the organisation which keeps these patterns replicating and they hint at the means by which these patterns can transform. David Grove puts it succinctly: "Within the paradigm of the presentation of the problem also lies its solution."[7]

Your first priority when using Clean Language, therefore, is to preserve the client's terminology. Four ways of doing this are: *repeating* their words exactly, *selecting* words and phrases, *backtracking,* and *accumulating* a number of the client's descriptions.

REPEATING EXACTLY

In the full syntax of Clean Language the first 'And' is immediately followed by repeating *exactly* what the client has just said. Since every one of their words (and the order in which they say them) potentially contains vital information, it is only by reflecting their words exactly that you can be sure to faithfully acknowledge their experience.[8] An exception is the need, on occasion, to change personal pronouns (and any associated use of the verb 'to be'). For example in T1 the client hears a precise echo of their words, except 'you' has replaced 'I':

C1:   I'd like to have more energy because I feel very tired.

T1:   **And** you'd like to have more energy because you feel very tired. ...

In addition, short words can be as important as long ones, prepositions as important as nouns, adverbs as important as verbs, and repetition no accident. Therefore, when the client says:

C4:   I can't open it and I get very very tired trying to open it.

"very very tired" is likely to have a different connotation to 'very tired' since the repetition itself may be a container of symbolic significance. This is why our response honours the client's exact description:

T4:   **And** you can't open it and you get very very tired trying to open it.
       And as you get very very tired trying to open it, **what kind of** very
       very tired trying **is that**?

Even if the question sounds somewhat strange to you, it will not to the client because it is *their* description of *their* experience. Another reason for making a point of repeating "very very" is that the client has already used the word "very" six times in her first four sentences: a minimal clue to the significance of this word for her!

Once a client's exact words have been acknowledged, the determiners 'a', 'the', 'my', 'your' etc. are often not repeated in the related question. Referencing symbols without determiners helps to establish a personal name for the symbol, and once something has a name, it then has an identity and a uniqueness which distinguishes it from other things. For example, we say 'it's a deer' or 'it's the deer', but as there is only one Bambi, we say 'it's Bambi' and not 'it's a Bambi' or 'it's the Bambi'. (Chapter 6 gives more information on naming symbols.)

When you repeat back clients' exact phraseology, a number of things happen:

- They hear their own words delivered from a different source.
- They know that what they have said has been heard.
- They have extra time to examine their current perception and discover associations with other perceptions.

As a result, clients seem to recognise (unconsciously at least) that:

- Their experience has been affirmed.
- Their terminology will be the basis for the interaction.
- They are being invited to stay with their current perception.

Another, not insignificant reason for word-for-word repetition is that it helps *you* to model their descriptions and gives *you* time to consider which clean question to ask next.

SELECTING WORDS AND PHRASES

When clients give long descriptions or explanations, it may not be possible or desirable to repeat every word verbatim. In such cases you can recap key phrases in the order given. Metaphors, repeated or emphasised words or phrases, and idiosyncratic, unusual or ambiguous expressions, are good candidates for selection. This is not summarising in the traditional sense, as it does not introduce words from your vocabulary. Rather, it is *selective word-for-word* reflection, as this example from another client transcript shows:

C: A feeling that I've got to love her as much as I can because she's not going to be around for that long. It's like I've got to eat all the sweets today even though there will be plenty more tomorrow. "It's too good to be true." I don't believe it will be there tomorrow. I'm not meant to be happy, it's not for me. Love brings me happiness but I can't handle happiness and joy. It's as if I have to live my life in the darkness.

T: **And when** you've got to eat all the sweets today, **and** you're not meant to be happy **and** you have to live your life in the darkness, **is there anything else about that** darkness?

C: I don't ever remember having been happy.

We repeat a few phrases as a way of encompassing the whole experience, before asking the client to notice one aspect—the metaphor of darkness. And because our question utilises the client's *last* statement, the flow and direction of their perception is maintained.

BACKTRACKING

Once a client begins to examine one aspect of their perception, other aspects may remain unexplored—like going down one particular road to the exclusion of any other. It is possible to retrace steps, to *backtrack* to the point of departure, and then go in a different direction, on a road not yet travelled. You can assist the client to do this by using their words in reverse order to track back from their current focus to the 'point of departure'. For example:

C11: It keeps me in one place and it doesn't let me move.

T11:   **And** it keeps you in one place and doesn't let you move. **And** dry like a desert, hollow full of darkness in here **and** struggling on your own **and** very very tired trying to open huge castle door **that's** very thick **and** very heavy **and** very old. **And is there anything else about that** door you can't open?

We acknowledge the client's last description (C11), before referring to desert (C10), hollow full of darkness (C8), in here (C7), struggling (C5), very very tired trying to open (C4), and huge castle door (C3). It will now be natural for the client to answer a question about the door because it has become the focus of her attention.

ACCUMULATING DESCRIPTIONS

The effect of repeating clients' individual answers will be enhanced if periodically you recap several of them in one review. We call this *accumulating* because it collects together a number of client descriptions into one perception. In the following extract, we first acknowledge what is said and then recap some previous responses:

C18:   I can hear him but he can't see me and he goes away. And I can't get out. Then I get *very* frustrated. It gets almost too much to bear.

T18:   **And** it gets almost too much to bear. **So when** you're behind huge castle door with a twisted iron handle, **and** you get very very tired trying to open it, **and** hollow **is** full of darkness, **and** a big broad centurion with a spear knocks, **and** you can hear him but he can't see you, **and** he goes away, **and** you can't get out, **and** it gets almost too much to bear, [pause] **then what happens**?

C19:   [Pause] Then I lose all my energy because I don't know what to do.

Accumulating descriptions (especially using the client's intonation, rhythm and speed as described in Vocal Qualities below) is likely to have a number of effects. First, it is wonderfully reassuring. When one of our clients said "it's like you understand what it's like to be me. Thank God *somebody* can understand and I'm not going mad," they may not have appreciated how little we understood about the meaning of their metaphors, but they knew we were in rapport with their symbolic patterns and this resonated at a deep level.

Second, accumulating descriptions encourages clients to become aware of the embodied nature of their language, or, as David Grove puts it, "to make words physical." In this way clients' figurative and imaginative perceptions come to life.

Third, accumulating descriptions can bring together a number of symbols or a sequence of symbolic events which may have emerged piecemeal during the session. This gives the client an opportunity to check the description for accuracy and completeness, to identify and embody their pattern as a whole and to make new associations. Once this happens, there is often no need to ask a question. Just pausing invites the client to ask a question of themselves, which in turn they answer— the ultimate in Clean Language.

Shortened syntax

To recap, the full Clean Language syntax has three parts:

1   **2**   **3**

And [client's words]. **And when/as** [client's words], [**clean question**]?

There are many occasions, however, when one of the following shortened versions is more appropriate:

1   **3**

And [client's words]. **And** [**clean question**]?

T14:   **And** a spear. **And what kind of** spear **could that** spear **be**?

2   **3**

And when/as [client's words], [**clean question**]?

T7:   **And when** in here, **whereabouts** in here?

3

And [**clean question**]?

T12:   **And is there anything else about that** great big circular handle that's all twisted around?

You can use the shortened syntax when:

- The client is answering quickly with short answers and you want to respond in kind.

- The client has attended to one aspect of their perception for some time.

- The client's Metaphor Landscape is well developed.

- You want to be congruent with a metaphor that is moving or changing fast.

- You are using Clean Language conversationally—perhaps in a business coaching context, or with a new client, or at the beginning of a session.

- You are using certain 'strategic approaches' (see Chapter 8).

Summary of syntax

The syntax of Clean Language is designed to acknowledge the client's perception, to orientate their attention to the perceptual present, to prepare them to gather information about their symbolic perceptions and to establish a context for the question to perform its task.

Not only does the syntax remind the client that they are involved in something other than an everyday dialogue, it also acts as a discipline for the therapist. In ordinary conversation it is natural to introduce your own vocabulary, paraphrase the other person's language and make suggestions. When working within the symbolic domain of your clients' experience, it is the distinctive syntax of Clean Language that will help you change this habit of a lifetime.

The Function of the Nine Basic Clean Questions

Clean questions are the second essential part of Clean Language and almost all David Grove's communication with clients is via questions. We have categorised the nine questions he most frequently asks by the aspect of perception they invite into the foreground of the client's awareness. These aspects, or perceptual dimensions, correspond to the universal metaphors of form, space and time. We distinguish two categories of basic questions: developing and moving time.

Developing questions

The first five questions are referred to as the basic developing questions. They invite the client to *identify attributes of form*, to *convert to symbolic form* and to *locate symbols in perceptual space*.

IDENTIFYING ATTRIBUTES OF FORM

Symbols are identified and distinguished by their attributes, qualities, features, characteristics and functions. When a client identifies a specific attribute of a symbol it becomes tangible in a way that abstract concepts do not. Whereas concepts are formless, symbols not only have functions and interact with other symbols, they also have a history and a destiny. Notice the difference between the concept of 'door' in general, and "A huge castle door that's very thick, very old, with studs, very heavy." These attributes give this door its unique form.

The two clean questions which invite clients to discover information about a symbol's attributes, functions or relationships with other symbols are:

And is there anything else about {that/those} [client's words]?

And what kind of [client's words] **is that** [client's words]?

The salient word in the first question is 'else'. It can mean any or all of the following: in addition to, extra to, more than, other than, different from, supplementary to, further, over and above, greater than.

Asking 'And is there anything else about that X?' invites the client to consider how they represent 'X', and to notice other characteristics that they have not previously described. The words 'about that X' encourage them to concentrate on a *particular* 'X' and to distinguish it from any other 'X'.

In the full syntax of Clean Language, 'when' orientates attention to the particular *context* (time and place) while 'about' and 'that' direct attention to the particular *content* (form and location) to be attended to. These words act cumulatively to orientate attention to *one* perceptual aspect at a time (be that a symbol, a relationship between symbols, a metaphor, a pattern of perceptions or the entire Metaphor Landscape). For many clients, 'that' also encourages symbols to acquire an independence, an identity, and to be perceived as separate from the perceiver (see Chapter 6).

'And is there anything else?' presupposes so little that it can usefully be asked at any time. We call this question 'the therapist's friend' because if you do not know what question to ask next, you can ask this one.

During a training exercise one trainee spent 20 minutes asking only 'And is there anything else?' about a fellow participant's metaphor. The recipient went through several remarkable emotional experiences, including intense frustration, culminating in a significant insight about patience. When the time came for a debrief the recipient thanked her partner, and asked in an incredulous tone, "How did you know that just asking that one question would prove so perfect for me?" He looked rather sheepish and admitted, "I didn't know. I just couldn't remember any of the other questions."

In the family of questions called Clean Language, the sibling of 'And is there anything else about X?' is 'And what kind of X is that X?'. The key word in this question, 'kind', is derived from the Old English word for 'nature'. Thus this question asks 'What is the nature of X?'. There are three common types of response to this question. Clients will describe the qualities or function of 'X', or offer an instance or example of 'X', or give an analogous description of 'X'. In whatever way they respond, they will likely discover something more about 'X'. The following extract from the transcript illustrates how clients typically respond to these two identifying-attributes questions:

C2:   It's like I'm behind a castle door.

T2:   **And ... what kind of** castle door **is that** castle door?

C3:   A huge castle door that's very thick, very old, with studs, very heavy.

T3:   **And ... is there anything else about that** huge castle door?

C4:   I can't open it and I get very very tired trying to open it.

T4:   **And ... what kind of** very very tired trying **is that**?

C5:   Like I'm struggling on my own and not getting anywhere. It takes a lot of energy. I feel like I'm banging my head on a wall.

In C3 the client specifies that she is perceiving a castle door which has a whole string of attributes: "huge, very thick, very old, with studs, very heavy." In C4 she describes the relationship between the castle door and the symbolic perceiver behind it as "trying to open"—and by implication the door's current function, which is not to open. In C5, she switches from describing attributes to explaining the nature of "very very tired trying" using a number of metaphors: "struggling," "not getting anywhere," "takes a lot of energy," and "banging my head on a wall." The client has now established a detailed context, an intention, and the effect of not achieving that intention—and all from three simple questions.

The 'Anything else?' and 'What kind of?' questions direct the client's attention to one aspect of their perception at a time. Then they invite the client to identify the attributes of that aspect and by what name it is known. These two questions perform such a useful role that they can be asked at any time during the Symbolic Modelling process.

CONVERTING TO SYMBOLIC FORM

When clients use sensory or conceptual expressions they can be requested to convert their description into metaphor by asking:

> **And that's** [client's words] **like what?**

The essential ingredient in this question is the word 'like' which means: similar to, resembling, in the same ways as, equivalent to, analogous with, akin to, comparable to, corresponding to, etc. The prime function of the 'Like what?' question is to enable the inexpressible, abstract or voluminous to be expressed as a tangible, vivid and compact metaphor. Compare "Sometimes I'm so desperate I don't know what to do" with its metaphorical equivalent, "It's like I'm on a roller coaster." A roller coaster can stop and the passenger can get off, or maybe the track can level out and become a railway going somewhere. There are a multitude of options available in the metaphor that are unavailable in the conceptual word 'desperate'.

During the conversion to tangible metaphoric form, the client's attention shifts from one type of perception to a parallel, isomorphic perception. For example:

C1: I'd like to have more energy because I feel very tired.

T1: **And ... that's** more energy **like what?**

C2: It's like I'm behind a castle door.

The 'Like what?' question prompts the client to convert her everyday narration into symbolism. In the next example, the 'Like what?' question is used *within* the metaphor to help her discover a form for an undefined "it":

C23: I can feel it right in the middle—at the absolute core of my being.

T23: **And when** you can feel it right in the middle, at the absolute core of your being, it's **like what?**

C24: It's gold.

T24: **And** it's gold. **And when** it's gold at the absolute core of your being, **what kind of** gold **is that** gold?

C25: Absolutely pure. It's always been there.

T25:   **And** absolutely pure. **And** absolutely pure gold's always been there at the core of your being. **And is there anything else about that** absolutely pure gold?

C26:   It's incredibly strong but malleable. Powerful. You could shape it but you couldn't break it. An almost silent powerful.

T26:   **And** an almost silent powerful. **And is there anything else about that** absolutely pure gold **that's** incredibly strong **and** malleable **and** almost silent powerful at the absolute core of your being?

C27:   It can move.

Once the client has shifted into metaphor, the 'Anything else?' and 'What kind of?' questions further develop the form and potential of the symbol, "gold."

'And that's like what?' has a special place in the family of clean questions. It can be used to initiate the Symbolic Modelling process; to convert sensory description, abstract notions and emotions to a more concrete symbolic form; to give form to relationships and patterns within a client's Metaphor Landscape; and to translate abstract concepts such as forgiveness, trust, hope, safety, strength, power, knowing, understanding and love into tangible resource symbols which can be utilised for healing and transformation.

LOCATING SYMBOLS IN PERCEPTUAL SPACE

Space is to perception what water is to fish. Just as physical space is constituted by things having a location, so is perceptual space. Clients can be invited to notice the location of their symbols and therefore the spatial nature of their metaphors by asking:

> **And where is** [client's words]?
>
> **And whereabouts {is}** [client's words]?

For example:

C6:   A castle wall of thick granite and I get very frustrated and very angry.

T6:   **And ... where is that** very frustrated and **that** very angry?

C7:   In here [touches solar plexus region].

T7:   **And when** in here, **whereabouts** in here?

C8:   Exactly in here. Hollow. Full of darkness.

Initially the client locates "very frustrated and very angry" verbally by "in here," and nonverbally with a gesture. The 'Whereabouts?' question then requests her to further specify the location, which she refers to as "exactly in here." These two questions focus her attention on the location of "very frustrated and very angry" long enough for the symbol "hollow. Full of darkness" to become apparent. Further into the transcript there is another example of locating symbols in perceptual space:

C22: [Looks up and squints] I can see the sky—I never noticed that before—hope is on the outside [long pause]. It's very strong. It gives me determination and the ability to keep trying.

T22: **And** you can see the sky. **And** hope is on the outside. **And when** it gives you very strong determination to keep trying, **whereabouts is** it **when** it's very strong?

C23: I can feel it right in the middle—at the absolute core of my being.

You may have noticed we were not quite clean. The client said "Hope is on the outside. It's very strong," whereas we accidentally attached the attribute "very strong" to determination. Even so, the client still locates "it."

While both these examples are related to the perceptual space *inside* the client, there are numerous references to the location of symbols *outside* of the client's (or perceiver's) body:

C2: It's like I'm *behind* a castle door.

C5: I feel like I'm banging my head *on a wall*.

C11: It keeps me *in one place* and it doesn't let me move.

C20: I sit *in the corner* and go to sleep.

C21: I have to find *a way out*.

C22: [*Looks up* and squints.] I can see the sky ... hope is *on the outside*.

The 'Where?' and 'Whereabouts?' questions invite the client to establish the precise location of each symbol. One client (who had been diagnosed as anorexic) used the word "angry" so often that each time she said the word we began asking, "And where is that angry?" She discovered seven types of anger, each located in a different place in her body. Rather than having them lumped into one conceptual category, being able to locate and convert each type of anger into a metaphor allowed her to differentiate these 'angers'. Then she could recognise which type of anger she was feeling at any moment and learn to have a choice of responses more appropriate to each one.

Once the inherent spatialness of the client's symbolic perceptions is developed, it is easier for one symbol to be distinguished from another, for patterns of spatial relationships to emerge and for the overall configuration of the Metaphor Landscape to take shape.

Moving time questions

In the physical universe time marches onwards. There is no stopping time, no going back and no jumping forward. Not so in the land of symbolic perception where the laws of physics do not necessarily apply and where, in the blink of an eye, symbols from one time and place can interact with symbols from a completely different time and place.

The five basic developing questions invite the client to examine their current symbolic perception for long enough to identify the form and location of its component symbols. And because the word 'is' appears in each developing question, the client is invited to perceive an event as if it is happening now, rather than looking 'back on' or 'forward to' it. In other words, they are encouraged to 'stop time' and assume the *perceptual present*—the timeframe of the event being described. In the land of metaphor, the present is a perceptual event which may coincide with the actual present, with a memory, or with an expectation of a future event. Often the perceptual present is 'outside time' altogether in that it can symbolise a pattern which may have repeated in one form or another for decades. As one mystified client discovered, symbolic events can even coexist or coalesce: "I don't understand this but I am seeing myself at 3 years old playing with a toy I got when I was 6 in the garden of a house I moved to when I was 14."

In contrast to developing questions, the four basic time questions invite the client to attend to an event subsequent, or previous, to whatever was last referenced. In other words they *move time forward* or *back*. While we adhere to convention and refer to these as temporal questions, they are not really about time at all—in the sense of the client's past, present or future. They enquire about a *sequence of events*.

Events do not occur in a vacuum; they only make sense as part of a temporal sequence, a number of related events which follow one after another in a particular order. An event is as much defined by what happens *before* and what happens *after,* as it is by what happens *during* (see Figure 3.2).[9]

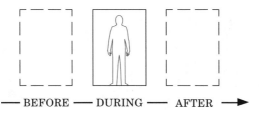

—— BEFORE —— DURING —— AFTER �

FIGURE 3.2 The perceptual present of a sequence of events

When repetitive sequences of thoughts, feelings and behaviours are unwanted, they are called bad habits, addictions, obsessions or compulsions. Yet some repetitive sequences result in a general disposition toward optimism, determination or persistence. Whether a client's sequence has three steps or dozens, and whether it takes a few seconds or many years to run through, each step can be symbolised by an equivalent event in their Metaphor Landscape.

Asking moving time questions to establish a sequence is like asking a client to use a remote control on a video to advance or reverse through a scene, one frame at a time. Through the skilful use of the four temporal clean questions, a complete sequence of symbolic perceptions can emerge and the client can recognise the underlying pattern. Once they understand how they 'do' the individual steps of a sequence, each step then becomes a choice-point, and hence an opportunity to change the pattern.

MOVING TIME FORWARD

The two basic clean questions which invite clients to evolve time, to describe the event subsequent to their current perception, are:

> **And then what happens**?
>
> **And what happens next**?

Whether the client's attention moves a fraction of a second within the current perception, or several years to another perception, or some unspecified length of symbolic time to an apparently unrelated event, will reflect the organisation of their Metaphor Landscape (see Figure 3.3).

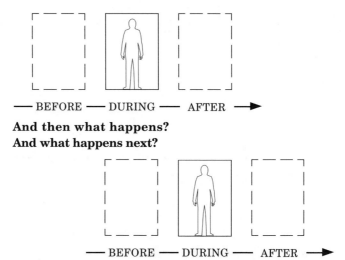

FIGURE 3.3 Moving the perceptual present to the next event

For example:

T15:   **And ... what kind of** centurion **could that** centurion **be**?

C16:   [Smiles.] Big and broad with armour on and a spear.

T16:   **And ... then what happens**?

C17:   He knocks on the door.

T17:   **And ... what happens next**?

C18:   I can hear him but he can't see me and he goes away. And I can't get out. Then I get *very* frustrated. It gets almost too much to bear.

T18:   **And ... then what happens**?

C19:   [Pause.] Then I lose all my energy because I don't know what to do.

T19:   **And ... then what happens**?

C20:   I sit in the corner and go to sleep.

T20:   **And ... what happens next**?

C21:   I have to find a way out. I try to open it again.

A sequence of events unfolds step-by-step until, as usually happens, the cycle repeats:

> A centurion knocks on the door (C17) -> he goes away -> she gets very frustrated (C18) -> she loses all her energy (C19) -> goes to sleep (C20) -> tries to open the door again (C21) -> *which will result in her getting tired (C4) -> and so on.*

MOVING TIME BACK

The basic clean questions which invite clients to explore preceding and antecedent events are:

> **And what happens just before** [client's words]?
>
> **And where could** [client's words] **come from**?

While the two evolving time questions are similar, there is a significant difference between the two 'pulling back' questions, as David Grove calls them.

'And what happens just before X?' asks the client to notice what occurs during the preceding event. The word 'just' plays an important role by directing the client's attention to the moment immediately before the one they have just described. It's like winding back a video recorder just one frame (See Figure 3.4).

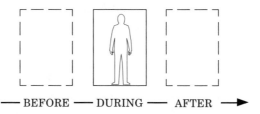

And what happens just before?

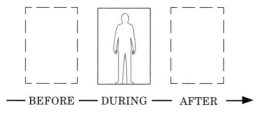

FIGURE 3.4 Moving the perceptual present to the preceding event

For example, the transcript continues when we ask the client to describe what happens *just before* she tries to find a way out again:

T21:   **And ... what happens just before** you try to find a way out again?

C22:   [Looks up and squints] I can see the sky—I never noticed that before—hope is on the outside [long pause]. It's very strong. It gives me determination and the ability to keep trying.

She discovers something new—that she can see the sky, that hope is on the outside, and that "it" gives her the determination and ability to keep trying to get out—and we can assume to repeat the sequence over and over.[10]

When 'And what happens just before?' is asked *repeatedly* it winds back a client's perception frame by frame to the beginning of a sequence, or even to the moment before the sequence starts.

Also, used in conjunction with the moving time forward questions, 'And what happens just before?' can invite the client to examine what occurs on either side of a threshold—at the beginning or end of a sequence for instance. This is especially useful when one side of the threshold is considered resourceful and the other unresourceful.

The other moving time back question, 'And where could X come from?' is a little more involved as clients generally give this question one of four meanings:

- What made 'X' possible (or caused 'X' to happen)?
- What was the location of 'X' before its present location?
- What or who had 'X' before?
- What is the source of 'X'?

For example:

C13: It looks like twisted pasta. It's big. It's old. It's dull. It's metal, iron, black.

T13: **And ... where could that** old iron **come from**?

C14: A spear.

We assume that the client opts for the last meaning and that her attention has moved to the source of the old iron—a spear before it was a door handle. Had the client given this question a different meaning she might have replied:

"A forge"	What made "old iron" possible.
"Underground"	Location of "old iron" before it was on castle door.
"My father"	Who had "old iron" previously.

To summarise, the principal function of the four moving time questions is to help clients notice how they punctuate their experience in a connected succession of perceptual events—a sequential pattern.

Repeated use of these questions enables the client to notice each step of the sequence. The word 'happens' appears in three of the moving time questions. This invites the client to attend to the perceptual present and describe events *as they happen*. Once a client has self-modelled a temporal pattern they are in a position to wonder how their metaphor might have a different beginning, middle or end, and how a change to a step in the sequence might result in a change to the overall pattern.

The basic clean question compass

David Grove's Clean Language questions are clean because they:

- Make maximum use of clients' terminology.
- Conform to the logic and presuppositions of clients' metaphors.
- Only introduce universal metaphors of form, space and time.
- Only use nonverbals congruent with clients' nonverbals (see Chapter 4).

Because of their universality they can be used in a remarkably wide range of circumstances. Although they leave clients free to process, respond and answer with whatever information they consider relevant, they, like *all* questions, presuppose a *perceptual orientation*.

To help you help your clients navigate their Metaphor Landscape, the nine basic questions are diagrammed in Figure 3.5 as a three-dimensional compass. The arrows indicate where each question invites the client to orientate their attention: to remain with the current perception and identify attributes; to convert the current perception into an isomorphic, symbolic form; to locate a symbol within the current perception; or to move forward or back in time to a subsequent or previous event.

Individually the nine basic questions may be simple, but when asked over a period of time, they have a complex, cumulative effect.

Each time a clean question is answered it sets up a feedback loop between the client and their symbolic perception. Describing these perceptions encourages further information to emerge, which can also be described, and so on. As this happens the client becomes the viewer-hearer-feeler of the symbolic content of their perceptions.

This intimacy establishes the existence of the key elements of their Metaphor Landscape.

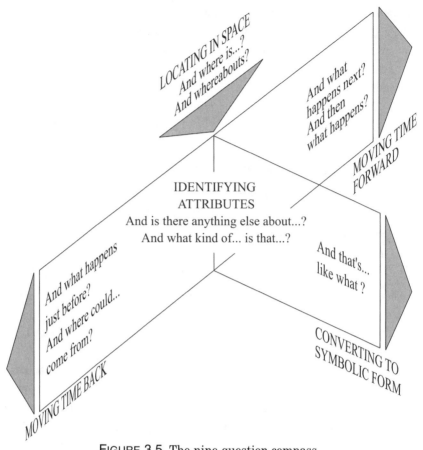

FIGURE 3.5 The nine-question compass

Utilising Vocal Qualities

The third essential component required to facilitate clients to self-model symbolically relates to how the questions are asked. David Grove's research has led him to use a particular combination of voice qualities when using Clean Language. The distinctiveness of his delivery is a result of:

- Matching the client's voice qualities when using their words
- The speed of delivery of his words
- The rhythm and tonality of his voice
- The consistency of his delivery.

Matching clients' voice qualities

People unconsciously personalise their speech by varying their tonality, volume, speed, pitch, rhythm, timbre, breathiness, etc. When you match the way clients express their words, you not only acknowledge their description, you gather impressions about how they use their body to produce those sounds. This can add to your model of their perceptions and enhance your intuition about which question to ask next. You are not required to mimic the client, only to adjust your voice to *more closely match* the emphases and changes evident in their speech. If a client speaks quickly and breathlessly, then when you *first* repeat their words you might need to speed up your delivery and add a little breathlessness to match them. Or a client may speak slowly and softly and emphasise one particular word—and so should you. There is no need to parrot, just to honour the way another person speaks by adjusting your way of speaking to correspond to theirs.

Speed of delivery

The golden rule of Clean Language when referring to any part of a client's experience is to use their words and phraseology as well as *their way of speaking those words*. However, it generally helps to s-l-o-w d-o-w-n the speed with which *therapist-generated* words are spoken. This gives the client's perception an opportunity to start forming, even before your question is complete. The speed of your delivery can drop to half or at times even a third of the speed of a typical conversation. You can slow your delivery by taking longer to say the words themselves or by pausing between words. As Mark Twain said, the right word may be effective, but no word is ever as effective as the right-timed pause.

Rhythm and tonality

You can convey curiosity about the client's answers if therapist-generated words are spoken with a somewhat poetic singsong rhythm, a smooth tonality and a slightly lower-pitch. Taken together, these voice qualities will encourage clients to wonder about their perceptions.

David Grove once told us that with Clean Language, sound, feel and rhythm take precedence over grammar, and that if we wanted to learn how to develop rhythmic tonality, we should listen to recordings of Dylan Thomas reading his work.

Consistency of delivery

Asking the same clean questions in the same manner—whether a client is describing their nail biting habit or sexual abuse—establishes a systematic and therefore predictable rhythm and format. The faithful adherence to a methodical delivery, regardless of the apparent magnitude of the client's experience, is one of the hallmarks of Clean Language. And since your questions are entirely focused on their information, there is little else for them to do but become intimately involved with their own perceptions (rather than react to the changes of emphasis and inflections in your voice). Clients may be surprised by *what* you ask about, but not by the way you ask it. They report that this consistency values *all* their experience and allows them to determine the significance of their symbolic perceptions for themselves.

It is particularly important to maintain a consistent delivery when working in metaphor because you may not appreciate the significance of a client's symbols or the correspondence to their 'real' life—and sometimes, to begin with, neither do they.

Another benefit of using a methodical and consistent delivery is that questions can be asked by more than one therapist working together, without distracting the client from their symbolic perceptions. Some clients report that when they are facilitated by both of us they lose track of which one is asking the questions.

Summary of vocal qualities

The syntax and delivery of Clean Language separates it from everyday conversation. While some people think they are overdoing the rhythm, tonality and slow pace when first using Clean Language, we usually recommend they make it even more pronounced. The combination of matching clients' voice qualities, asking clean questions with a tonality of implicit acceptance, curiosity and wonder, while using a slow delivery and a poetic rhythm, is a potent mixture.

As a result of self-modelling, many clients develop heightened states of self-absorption (trance) indicated by fixed focus of attention, slowed speech, negative and positive hallucinations, involuntary ideomotor mannerisms etc. David Grove explains:

> We do not maintain that clients need to go into trance. ... The structure of the questions induces the altered state [indirectly] ... Trance is often a prerequisite in finding the answer. Clients alter their state in going somewhere to get that answer. That somewhere is where we want to leave them, and that happens to be where they may develop in the trance. ... We normally do not want the client to be in a deep trance. ... We prefer our client in a state of conversational trance. ... Every time the client goes inside, as in a daydream, he is going into a trance. It can be very effective in therapy to use these facilitatory states in producing neurological changes. ...Questions couched in 'normal' language ask the client to *comment* on his experience. Every time he does that he comes out of a state of self-absorption to perform an intellectual task which interrupts the process we are working to encourage and to facilitate.[11]

While trance is a common result of using Clean Language, it is not a requirement. Nor is the use of overt metaphor. A number of our clients remain conceptual throughout therapy, with only brief forays into metaphor, yet they still derive enormous benefit from self-modelling.

Concluding Remarks

David Grove developed the precise formulation of Clean Language during many years of clinical practice. It is designed to evoke responses and information which bring a client's symbolic perceptions to life— uncontaminated by the facilitator's vocabulary, ideas, presuppositions and solutions.

With Clean Language you are not so much questioning the client as asking questions of their metaphors and symbols. In this way the client discovers something new about themselves. Therefore your job is to ask clean questions *on behalf* of the client's metaphors in a way that values their answers and enables them to become familiar with the hidden workings of their perceptual patterns. You do this by treasuring the metaphors embedded in their responses, and by asking clean questions in a consistent and methodical manner. The nine-question compass will help you to help the client navigate their Metaphor Landscape by orientating their attention to the fundamental dimensions of form, space and time. In the process the client will (consciously or unconsciously) model the organisation of their perceptions. It is this self-modelling that lays the foundation for a beneficial change in the configuration of their Metaphor Landscape, which in turn results in new patterns of thoughts, feelings and behaviours.

Clean Language governs what you say in relation to what the client says. It can also reference and utilise a client's nonverbal behaviour— and this is the subject matter of the next chapter.

4

Clean Language Without Words

We know more than we can tell.
M. Polanyi

While metaphors are traditionally thought of as verbal expressions, clients also use nonverbal, material and imaginative metaphors. These are embodied in movements, postures, sounds, objects, structures in the environment, mental images and feelings—*metaphors without words.*

In Symbolic Modelling all behaviour is considered "an outside view of the dance of internal relations of the organism."[1] In other words, there is a correspondence between whatever a client's body is doing and the organisation of their cognition. This means that when clients become aware of their repetitive nonverbal behaviour they can infer information about the embodied and spatial nature of their symbolic perceptions.

Chapter 3 described how Clean Language can assist clients to self-model their verbal metaphors. It covered what you, as a facilitator, say and how you say it. But how do you reference metaphors that have not been described in words? How do you orientate a client's attention to their nonverbal behaviour and enquire of its symbolism *cleanly*? How do you acknowledge the placement of symbols within a client's perceptual space?

The first thing to remember is that there are different types of metaphors without words. In Chapter 1 we identified four: two nonverbal metaphors and two related to the client's perceptual space. What distinguishes these is *where* symbolic information is located. With nonverbal metaphors—body expressions and sounds—the information is encoded in the *nonverbal behaviour* itself; whereas perceptual space contains material and imaginative metaphors which are *pointed to or indicated by* the client's nonverbal behaviour (Figure 4.1).

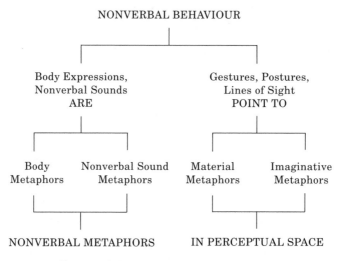

FIGURE 4.1 Types of nonverbal behaviour

When utilising Clean Language to reference a client's nonverbal behaviour, you use the standard syntax, questions and vocal qualities, *and* you use your nonverbal behaviour to refer to the client's:

Nonverbal metaphors, either by replicating, gesturing to, or looking at a body expression; or by replicating a nonverbal sound.

Perceptual space, with hand gestures, head movements and looks that are congruent with the client's perspective of the location of their material and imaginative symbols.

Hence the full syntax becomes:

And [replicate client's nonverbal or indicate to their perceptual space].
And when/as [replicate client's nonverbal etc.], [**clean question**]?

Nonverbal Metaphors

This section illustrates how both body expressions and nonverbal sounds can be addressed cleanly with the basic developing and moving time questions.

Body expressions

Nonverbal behaviour is often interpreted as unconscious communication, yet people involved in a telephone conversation will gesture, shift position, look around and make all sorts of facial expressions. Why do they do this when the other person cannot see them? Because these movements enable the speaker to sort out their feelings, keep their ideas straight and weigh up situations—they are unconsciously communicating with themselves.

This communication with one's self is amplified in Symbolic Modelling because the primary locus of the client's attention is with their metaphoric perceptions. We recommend therefore that you pay exquisite attention to clients' nonverbals, not as communication to you, but as potential carriers of information *for them*.

Clients use their body to express symbolism and metaphor in all sorts of ways:

Torso movements	leaning, bending, rocking, tics, shrugs, twitches, shudders, unusual breathing
Facial expressions	grimacing, pouting, grinning, frowning, blushing, mouthing, yawning
Interactions with own body	holding, rubbing, nail biting, thumb sucking, brow wiping, hair curling
Interactions with objects	rearranging clothing, cushion hugging, pen chewing, twiddling with jewellery

While clients are talking about their experience, their body is often enacting it. When this happens, words tend to express *what* they think and feel, and nonverbals *how* and *where* they are thinking and feeling. For example, a client doubles over and holds their head in their hands, or looks at the palm of their hand as if there is something on it, or adjusts the position of an object on a table.

Sometimes ideas and emotions can only be verbalised when they are spoken in conjunction with certain actions. At other times the body expresses that for which there are no words. As Isadora Duncan has said, "If I could tell you what it meant, there would be no point in dancing it."[2]

Just as every word or phrase used by a client represents the tip of an iceberg projecting above a submerged mass of interconnected ideas and meanings, so nonverbal behaviour can represent a vast amount of unseen knowledge.

While it is clear that touch, feelings, emotions and proprioception (position, movement, balance) encode information nonverbally, the body can also encode preverbal, preconceptual and idiosyncratic knowledge; unspeakable trauma; family lore, genealogical traits and cultural codes; spiritual connections and mystical experiences. David Grove explains that:

> In every gesture, and particularly in obsessional gestures and tics and those funny idiosyncratic movements, is encoded the entire history of that behaviour. It contains your whole psychological history in exactly the same way that every cell in your body contains your whole biological history.[3]

For example, a client periodically used the flat of her left hand to pat the arm of the sofa next to her. While she was in the process of patting, Penny asked:

> **And when** [fixed look at client's hand movement whilst nodding head to the same rhythm], **what kind of** [continue looking at hand and nodding] **is that** [continue looking at hand and nodding]?

The client looked at her hand as if it did not belong to her and watched it pat. After a while she replied, "It's how I keep my emotions down." Her out-of-awareness patting became an entry point into a Metaphor Landscape where she discovered she "buried emotions." Uncovering the precise sequence and the intricate mechanism of how she did this proved to be a vital step towards learning how she could express her emotions more appropriately.

To minimise the possibility of imposing your words and distracting the client's attention, you should only *verbally* reference their body expressions *after* they have labelled them for themselves.

In the above example there can be no doubt that the client's left hand was moving, yet to ask "And is there anything else about that *left hand?*" or "And what kind of *movement* is that *movement?*" would have attached our words to the client's experience. While this would have directed her attention to her hand or its movement, it may have been the arm of the sofa or a numbness in her shoulder that carried the most important information for her. Penny's use of a look and head movement enabled the client to determine for herself what was significant about the patting and to describe it in her own words, "keep my emotions down."

Another example is a client who, at his first session, delivered an unbroken hour-long description of his predicament. He ended with "So that's how it is" and looked expectantly at us. Penny replied, "And so that's how it is. And when that's how it is, that's how it is, like what?" He lifted his head, chin pointing up high. While he was considering the question his mouth started to open and close in a rhythmical fashion without sound. He was still deep in thought when Penny asked, "And [replicated angle of head and mouth movement]. And [repeated non-verbal] is like what?" The client repeated the mouthing movement and replied, "It's like I'm a goldfish in a deoxygenated pond having to come up for air." He had captured the essence of his dilemma in a single metaphor, and his body had acted it out before he knew what to say. Now he could work with the metaphor for the pattern rather than, as it appeared to us, swimming round and round, suffocating in the detail of his description.

Once a client recognises that their body, or parts of it, can be a metaphor, they can notice how it responds to each clean question. For example, by describing the reaction his body had to each of David Grove's questions, James connected with his 'sense of purpose'. By standing and attending to his body James discovered that his *head* looked to the right to what caught his attention and wanted to move in that direction; his *shoulders and trunk* faced forward in the direction his life was moving; and his *feet* wanted to move to the left toward his sense of purpose. Through doing this he was able to identify what needed to happen for all of him to be aligned and moving in the same direction. Over the next 18 months James took a number of important decisions to change direction—and one result is the book in your hands.

Nonverbal sounds

Sounds without words include sighs, in-breaths, throat clears, coughs, blows, clicks, groans, grunts, gurgles, giggles, snorts and expressions or exclamations such as oh-oh, ah, uhm-m, hems and haws, etc. David Grove recognised that these sounds can also be a source of, or a sign-post to, symbolic information which is outside the client's awareness.

A particular sound can become the focus of a question simply by replicating that sound as if it were a word within a clean question. Thus a client who preceded his answer with a big sigh was asked:

C: [Big sigh] I give up.

T: **And** [replicates big sigh] you give up. **And when** [big sigh], **what kind of** [big sigh] **is that**?

C: [Sigh] I'm not sure.

T: **And when** [sigh] you're not sure, **is there anything else about** [big sigh]?

C: I can't find the words.

T: **And** you can't find the words. **And when** you can't find the words **about** [big sigh] **is there anything else about** words you can't find?

C: They're locked away.

Acknowledging both the client's nonverbal and verbal answers validates them as equally appropriate and useful. Differentiating between 'sigh' and 'big sigh', and continuing to direct the client's attention to 'big sigh' means he discovers that he "can't find the words" and that "they're locked away." Later the client found a way to unlock the words so that he did not have to "give up" any more.

Moving time questions

So far we have given examples of using the basic developing questions with body expressions and sounds. Another way to utilise nonverbal metaphors is to regard them as temporal markers. You can ask questions which 'move time forward' or 'move time back' by using the client's non-verbal behaviour as a reference point. For example a client was fluently describing an event in metaphor when suddenly words deserted her:

C: The sky is filled with the wings of a giant eagle. She's gliding and scanning the ground and sees a boy. She swoops down and plucks out his eyes.

T: **And** giant eagle is gliding and scanning the ground and sees a boy. **And when** she swoops down and plucks out his eyes, **then what happens**?

C: [Skin goes pale, she doubles over and is still and quiet for a while.]

T: **And when** [takes up similar body position and sits quiet], **what happens next**?

C: [Pause. Sits up straight.] She's free.

We were surprised when the eagle plucked out the boy's eyes and had no idea what was happening during the client's long silence. When it became clear that the client's posture and silence *were* her answer, asking a clean question utilised this nonverbal response. In this case, a moving time forward question encouraged the sequence to unfold, and then the client had words available again.

Just as a body expression can be regarded as a temporal marker, so can a nonverbal sound. The following example demonstrates pulling time back with a client who periodically sucked air through her teeth. This made a small suction-like sound which in and of itself was not particularly noticeable. Over a period of time, however, the sound caught our attention, so we asked:

T: **And** [replicates sound]. **And when** [sound], **where could** [sound] **come from**?

C: [Long pause.] My God, that's the sound my grandmother used to make when she was angry and her teeth became loose.

T: **And** that's the sound your grandmother used to make when she was angry and her teeth became loose. **And is there anything else about** that sound?

C: It was terrifying. I used to stand behind my mother.

Although this habit of making a sucking sound had been pointed out by others, she had never before made the connection to her grandmother's long-forgotten false teeth. She discovered it symbolised her pattern of "hiding from confrontation" with others as well as from an aspect of herself. With this awareness, whenever she made this sound she could ask herself 'What am I hiding from?' and take appropriate action.

Given the opportunity, clients can usually translate their nonverbal behaviour into a verbal description which then can be explored in the standard manner. However, if no words are forthcoming, the entire process can be conducted by asking clean questions of body postures, movements and sounds without the need for the client to use words.[4] Either way, the result will be the formation of a psychoactive Metaphor Landscape within which change can take place.

Perceptual Space

As well as enacting nonverbal metaphors, clients also point to where their symbols are located in perceptual space, in what direction they are moving and how they interact. They do this mostly out-of-awareness, by positioning and moving their whole body, through gestures (with hands but also with feet, head, elbows), and by lines of sight (the direction of gaze and point of focus). You can think of clients as having a perceptual space around and within themselves which contains both their material and imaginative symbols. It is the *relationship* between the client and their symbolic perceptions that prompts their body to dance within its perceptual theatre. Such is the rhythm, precision and elegance with which the body utilises surrounding space that David Grove refers to it as 'choreography'. This symbolic marking out of space is crucial to the self-modelling process because of its direct correspondence with the configuration of a client's Metaphor Landscape. As Edward Hall noted, "Space speaks."[5]

Once clients become 'a-where' of the location of symbols in their perceptual space they begin to interact with them directly. They get curious about their function, relationship and configuration. In other words, they self-model. For clients to enter into a wondrous and trusting alliance with their Metaphor Landscape requires that you do so too. As David Grove says, "space will become your co-therapist if you pay it due regard."[6] The rest of this chapter explains how to pay due regard to:

- Aligning to clients' perceptual space
- Physical and imaginative space
- Lines of sight
- Physicalising perceptual space
- Metaphor Maps

Aligning to clients' perceptual space

Since you want to keep the client mindful of their symbolic perceptions it is important that your marking out of space aligns with the configuration of *their* perceptual space and not yours. Therefore you need to notice how clients nonverbally indicate the location of symbols so that you can refer to them as if they exist in those places. You refer to the location either by motioning or looking to where the symbol exists for the client when it is *outside* their body, or by replicating the way they nonverbally reference the symbol when it is *inside*, or a part of their body. For example, suppose the client gestures to a location outside their body:

C: It's out to get me.

T: **And** it's out to get you. **And when** it's out to get you, **where is** it?

C: [Pause, gestures down and to his right.]

T: **And when** it's [points down to client's right], **whereabouts** [points down to client's right]?

C: Down there.

T: **And** down there. **And when** down there, **whereabouts** down there [looks 'there']?

C: A couple of feet away.

T: **And** a couple of feet away. **And when** it's down there, a couple of feet away **and** it's out to get you, it's out to get you **like what**?

C: Like a boa constrictor.

When the client indicates that there is a symbol inside their body, you can use your gaze to mark its location or you can reference it as follows (the therapist is sitting opposite the client):

C: I can't speak my mind [touches neck with left hand].

T: **And** you can't speak your mind. **And when** [touches own neck with *right* hand], **whereabouts** [touches neck with *right* hand]?

C: [Clasps neck with left hand.]

T: **And when** [clasps neck with right hand], **whereabouts** can't you speak your mind [looks at client's neck]?

C: Inside.

T: **And** inside. **And whereabouts** inside?

C: In the middle.

T: **And when** inside, in the middle, **what kind of** middle **is that**
        middle, **where** you can't speak your mind?

C: [Makes a round shape with both hands.]

T: **And when** [replicates gesture] **is** inside [touches neck], in the
        middle, **is there anything else about** [replicates gesture]?

C: The words get stuck in my throat.

If the therapist was sitting *beside* the client they would have used their *left* hand to touch their neck, rather than mirror the client's gesture as in the example above. The general rule is, make your movements congruent with their perceptual space from their perspective. And as these examples show, once clients have described a symbol in words it is preferable to use their verbal description as its name, even if you continue to address its location nonverbally.

Accurately referring to the location of imaginary symbols is especially important when a Landscape first emerges because it encourages symbols to "lay claim to their own patch of perceptual real estate," as David Grove sometimes refers to it.[7]

Once a Metaphor Landscape is established, symbols tend to remain in the same place between sessions. This means you can assist clients to reconnect with their Metaphor Landscape by nonverbally orientating their attention to wherever their symbols were last located. If you remember any gestures or nonverbal sounds connected with them, so much the better. Should a symbol have relocated since the last session your references will give the client an opportunity to notice the change and update you.

Physical and imaginative space

Given the opportunity, clients unconsciously orientate themselves to their physical surroundings in such a way that windows, doors, mirrors, ornaments, furniture, shadows, etc. correspond to the configuration of their Metaphor Landscape. Generally, you know that a client has attached symbolism to a physical object or to a structure in their surroundings when they tell you or when they start interacting with it. In the first case you simply use their words when referring to the object, and in the second you refer to the *interaction,* using the methods described throughout this chapter. For example, if a client suddenly grabs a cushion and clasps it tightly to their stomach you might ask, "And when [look at cushion] what kind of [replicate clasping] is that?"

So revealing is the relationship between a client's perceptual space and their physical surroundings that David Grove gives clients an opportunity to align the two at the outset of each session. He asks them to sit where they want, to rearrange the furniture and to position him. Clients naturally place themselves where it is most appropriate for them to explore their symbolic world.[8]

When James asked a client where she wanted him to sit, she said "Anywhere but there [pointing directly in front of her]." Her presenting problem was a fear of heights and "a magnetic force pulling me to jump in front of trains." Exploring the characteristics of the magnetic force led her to identify what was pulling: "A shadowy something [she traced a shape in the air with both hands]. It's the same shape as that fire extinguisher there [pointing directly in front of her]." She instantly remembered a recurring childhood apparition where her deceased father came to her bedroom and beckoned her to join him. For the first time she realised that her childhood feelings of being drawn towards him were the same as the magnetic force pulling her to jump from heights and train platforms. Her fear transformed into comfort when the shadowy figure moved behind her and put his hands on her shoulders. She later reported that the magnetic pull had disappeared ("all that's behind me now"), and that she felt safer generally. What is noteworthy about this example is how the client positioned James in the room. Had he sat in the chair in front of her he would have blocked her view of the fire extinguisher which, at the very least, would have intruded on her symbolic perception.

Lines of sight

The last example shows that where clients sit and where they want you to sit is often determined by their dominant *lines of sight.* This particular nonverbal behaviour requires special explanation.

David Grove's clinical research suggests that the direction, angle and focus of a client's eyes can indicate an out-of-awareness, notional pathway which correlates with the location of material or imaginary symbols within their Metaphor Landscape. These lines of sight are probably formed as part of state-dependent memories or imprints.[9] Think of a child who, having just been beaten, looks up in vain to search a mother's face for a sign of love. The upward line of sight becomes encoded as an habitual part of the client's symptomatic behaviour. From then on similar feelings of being unloved may invoke the same posture and line of sight. Conversely, replicating the line of sight may lead to reaccessing the memory and feelings.

With a body expression the source of the symbolism is the nonverbal behaviour, whereas the symbolic information indicated by a line of sight is out in perceptual space. Lines of sight are most easily observed when the client fixes their eyes in one particular direction (such as staring out of a window), or at one particular object (a mirror, book, door handle), or is transfixed by a pattern or shape (a spot on the carpet, wallpaper motif, shadow), or gazes de-focused into space. Investigating these lines of sight can give the client direct entry to an area of their Metaphor Landscape seldom, if ever, visited.[10]

While waiting to begin a session with David Grove, Penny sat staring mindlessly at a box of tissues on a nearby table. She was vaguely aware that her reason for being there was to become comfortable speaking in front of large groups. When David Grove asked her a question about her line of sight she replied, "I'm looking at that box of tissues, at the part that stands out from all those triangles, the part with the frame around the words 'Peel off Label'." (She was thinking "What on earth am I doing talking about a box of tissues?") However a few questions later the frame began to look like a cinema screen. On the screen emerged a geometric shape which reminded her of the maze at Hampton Court. Further examination of the maze revealed a lost child alone and stuck, eternally attempting to get out by "pushing through the bushes backwards." (In retrospect Penny recognised this as symbolic of her inclination to step back when presenting until she was almost hidden by the flip chart.) As the metaphor evolved the child found resources that enabled her to move forward and find her way home. It is fascinating to think that asking clean questions of a stare at a box of tissues resulted in Penny comfortably presenting to 400 people six months later.

Although stares and repeated gazes most obviously indicate clients' lines of sight, even a momentary glance into a corner or over the shoulder is unlikely to be a random or meaningless act, but rather a response to configurations and events of their symbolic world. Clients also orientate their bodies and view to *avoid* looking at a particular space. This occurred when a client entered our consulting room, sat at the right-most end of the sofa, crossed his legs and angled them to his right. His shoulders were inclined right as well and for much of the session he had his left hand beside his left eye, like a horse's blinker. At one point, while pondering a question, his hand dropped away and he glanced down to his left momentarily. Immediately he was asked "And what happens just before [replicates hand movement and glance]?" He looked down and to his left and let out a massive sob. When he recovered his breath he said "Oh God, there's something down there (glance to left) and I don't know what it is. I haven't been down there in a very long time. If I look down there I will be trapped and it will be compulsive viewing." He discovered "down there" was a fog which symbolised confusion and feelings of abandonment. Further exploration revealed a symbolic scene of a younger self on a hilltop watching his father leave home, never to be seen again. The adult's "down there" line of sight was the same angle and direction of that little boy watching his father walk away. Later he realised that wherever possible—in meetings, walking down the street and at home—he would arrange to have people on his right to avoid looking at the space on his left. When that patch of perceptual real estate transformed, not only could he look "down there" and feel secure, but for the first time he could be confident he would not abandon his own family.

Physicalising perceptual space

Some clients' relationship with their perceptual space is such that they prefer to explore it by moving around rather than by sitting and visualising it. They may want to occupy the location of symbols and enact symbolic events. By *physicalising the space* these clients gain an understanding of the structure of their symbolic world. One colleague described the result of moving around his Metaphor Landscape as:

> I discovered the 3-dimensional nature of the landscape, the 3-dimensional nature of the elements within it and the spatial relationships between them all. I also discovered that some elements moved with me and some remained still, some modified in shape and some retained their shape. A lot happened![11]

One of our clients symbolised an important decision in his life as like having to choose between (on his left hand side) "a dark tunnel" and (on his right hand side) "a featureless white plain." By standing up and moving to where the tunnel was located he was able to experience and to describe this choice as "depleted, unhappy, blocked, trapped." On the other side of the room he wandered around the featureless plain and realised that although it represented "openness, lightness, freedom, relief, easy breathing" it was also "empty of meaning" offering "the illusion of freedom." No wonder he was incapable of making a decision when all his attention was on choosing between the tunnel and the plain. But what was in the space *between* left and right? When he occupied this space, he discovered "A vertical dividing line ... a place I've never been before." Several weeks later he wrote: "The place ... was remarkable to me in that it was a place of no expectation, a sense of underlying faith in events, acute senses, fully focused concentration, wide open attention, a sense of being fully present in my situation (not spectating). It was a discovery in its own right and it started to seem that here was the freedom I was so desperate for."[12]

In addition to utilising the space of the consulting room, David Grove also utilises the physical environment outside. He has held sessions on hill tops, beside lakes and at every time of the day or night in order to synchronise the client's imaginary and physical terrains. In one instance he conducted a session late on a summer's evening at sunset so that the client could physicalise their metaphor of "the sun going down" on their relationship with a close friend who had recently died. After the sun had finally disappeared behind a mountain David asked, "And what happens to a sun that sets?" It was a beautiful moment when the client realised that from the sun's perspective, it never sets.

Metaphor Maps

A Metaphor Map is a type of material symbolic representation that merits special attention (examples are shown in Figures 4.2 and 7.5). Asking clients to draw a map of the configuration of their symbols, either during or between sessions, is an integral part of Symbolic Modelling. Although other means of representing Metaphor Landscapes can be used, a map can conveniently depict symbolic shapes, colours, numbers of things and especially spatial patterns.

If you want to refer to any part of a client's Map the rule is the same—use their word if they have given one; if not, use nonverbals which correspond to the way they have nonverbally referenced it. If you have neither, and it seems important that the client consider an unreferenced symbol, then you can improvise. For instance, if a client produces a Metaphor Map with two symbols 'X' and 'Y' and they talk about the attributes of 'X' but never mention 'Y' you might say, "And when [attributes of X], is there anything else about [point to symbol Y]?"

FIGURE 4.2 Example of a client's Metaphor Map

Concluding Remarks

Clean Language can help clients recognise that a gesture, a body posture, a repetitive grunt, a pattern on a carpet or a piece of jewellery may symbolise an unacknowledged emotion, a relationship, an obsession, a childhood memory—or anything else.

Asking clean questions of a client's nonverbal behaviour invites them to become aware of the form, location and significance of the symbol, in relation to the rest of the Metaphor Landscape. This means more than simply copying a client's nonverbals. It means referencing their non-verbal behaviour in such a way that they continue to attend to the content and flow of their perceptions. Directing questions to nonverbal behaviour and perceptual space is an unusual procedure and may take clients by surprise. Your purpose is for them to become self-aware, not self-conscious.

In addition, it is far easier for clients to self-model when there is only one configuration of perceptual space to contend with—theirs. For this to happen you need to direct your questions to the space around or inside the client, and to adjust your nonverbal behaviour so that it is congruent with the location of symbols from the client's perspective. In this way the configuration of their Metaphor Landscape is preserved.

The relationship between the client and their perceptual space is as intimate as between a mother and her unborn child and forms one of the most important aspects of Symbolic Modelling. Once clients are aware of this relationship, their space becomes psychoactive and will continue to influence and inform them long after they walk out of your consulting room.

III

THE FIVE-STAGE PROCESS

5

Stage 1

Entering the Symbolic Domain

In oneself lies the whole world,
and if you know how to look and learn,
then the door is there and the key is in your hand.
Nobody on earth can give you either that key or the door to open,
except yourself.
Krishnamurti

The ability to process metaphorically and symbolically seems to be innate. It is not *if* someone can operate from a metaphoric perspective, but rather under what circumstances and in what manner are they consciously perceiving symbolically.

The Five-Stage Therapeutic Process was summarised in Chapter 2 (pages 39–44). This chapter examines Stage 1: how to start a Symbolic Modelling session by facilitating clients to begin self-modelling their metaphors. We describe how to initiate the process with the 'standard opening' question, or use an 'entry' question in response to one of six verbal and nonverbal 'cues'. We then give several examples of which entry question to ask in response to each type of cue. In short, this chapter provides:

> The Purpose of Stage 1
> How to Start
> Entry Questions
> Entry Cues

The Purpose of Stage 1

In the beginning of the Symbolic Modelling process your task is to use Clean Language to support the client to become aware that their metaphoric expressions have a correspondence with their life experiences.

At some point during the client's narrative, something they say or do will prompt you to select an entry question which invites them to switch from everyday perception to, as Caroline Myss calls it, 'symbolic sight'.[1] The question you select will depend on the logic of the information supplied by the client in relation to their outcome, their metaphors and their behaviour at that moment. With clients who are less aware of their use of metaphor, you may need to ask a number of entry questions for them to become familiar with the symbolic nature of their language and perception. These clients may cross the line from everyday narrative to consciously using metaphor many times before they settle into, stay with, and model their symbolic perceptions. On the other hand, for some clients, speaking metaphor is their mother tongue.

How do you recognise when a client has started to perceive symbolically, to engage with their metaphors and to self-model? There are a number of indicators, the most obvious being the client's use of overtly metaphoric language. More subtle are the nonverbal indicators which vary from client to client: marking out the location of symbols in perceptual space, enacting events within the metaphor, and entering a contemplative state. In addition, when a client meta-comments with "this is weird" or "I don't know where this is coming from but ..." or "it's difficult to put into words," they are usually indicating a transition to a consciously symbolic perception. Sometimes it is patently obvious when a client becomes aware of the symbolism inherent in their descriptions; at other times it takes acute observation to detect whether they have made the transition. For example, a client may dip into symbolism for just a few seconds, or they may be talking conceptually while seeming to express nonverbal metaphors with their body. It is vital that you calibrate the indicators to each client because, just as people exhibit differing degrees of emotion, so the range of behaviours which reflect their degree of awareness and involvement with their metaphors varies.

There are also indicators of when a client is not perceiving symbolically. These include repeatedly:

- Making eye-contact with you
- Asking you questions
- Meta-commenting or analysing
- Giving examples from everyday life
- Replaying events and dialogues, 'He said ... and she said ...'

Keep in mind, however, that *any* repetitive behaviour may itself be symbolic of an unconscious pattern to the client's perceptions.

How to Start

We begin the first session by asking the client where they would like to sit and, when they are settled, where they would like us to sit. Then we take a short personal history and ask them to define an overall outcome — a contract for therapy. This builds rapport, allows us to assess the client's level of self-awareness and to note the metaphors they use during the conversation. Then we ask entry questions of their metaphorical, sensory or conceptual expressions so that they begin to self-model.[2]

When to initiate self-modelling

You can start modelling symbolically from the first contact with the client, be that by telephone, letter or face-to-face. From the client's perspective, the process starts when you ask a clean question which invites them to consider their verbal or nonverbal expressions symbolically. How they respond will indicate whether, or to what degree they accept the invitation. While there are no cast iron rules for when to begin, there are two key factors to consider: your degree of rapport with the client, and their level of self-awareness. Studies have shown that how the client and therapist relate is one of the most important aspects of a successful therapeutic encounter, regardless of the type of therapy.[3] In this respect, Symbolic Modelling is no different to any other therapy, except that Clean Language is inherently rapport-building. By self-awareness we mean the client's ability to introspect, to self-reflect, to describe their own experience and to define a personal outcome. The greater the rapport between the two of you and the more the client is aware of their metaphors and patterns, the sooner the self-modelling process can begin.

The standard opening question

The standard opening question requests clients to specify their desired outcome for therapy and invites them to begin self-modelling.

And what would you like to have happen?

Although we did not make it explicit in Chapter 3, you have already seen an example of a response to this question:

T0:   **And what would you like to have happen**?

C1:   I'd like to have more energy because I feel very tired.

T1:   **And** you'd like to have more energy because you feel very tired. **And when** you'd like to have more energy, **that's** more energy **like what**?

C2:   It's like I'm behind a castle door.

After just two questions the client has defined an outcome, the problem and accepted the invitation to work in metaphor. Our second question orientates the client's attention to what she wants—"more energy"—and at the same time invites her to become aware of the nature of her outcome. Because she responds with an overt metaphor, a Stage 2 exploration of her symbolic perception can begin.

Whether you begin with the standard opening question or not, you start with a clean question. David Grove says:

> The first question is important because ... it is going to set the tone and the direction of how the session will go. This quality of direction is very important because it will direct the client's attention—[and then] he will direct our attention—to a particular location in his experience and to a particular orientation in time.[4]

If your objective is for the client to define an outcome for the session, then the standard opening question can be further specified by adding "during this session," "while you are here," or "during our time together today." It can also be used when, as is common, the client provides a detailed description of their problem. Then you can ask "And what would you like to have happen *instead of* [client's description of their problem]?" Asking the standard opening question has a number of benefits:

- Most importantly, it directs the client's attention towards what they want or need so that they describe whatever they think, feel or intuit will bring about the desired change.

- Even if the client answers "I don't know," they will still have *considered* the question, and in the process of considering they will have nonverbal responses.

- Whatever the client answers will provide information related to their beliefs about the process of change.

• Very often the client's response to this question is a microcosm of how they expect to resolve their issue in the future, or how they have tried (unsuccessfully) to solve their problem in the past, or how they are 'stuck' in their problem in the present.

Any of these responses give you an opportunity to begin constructing a model of their Metaphor Landscape. The client's response to the standard opening question inevitably carries significant information and usually more than you can comprehend in the moment. Therefore, we recommend you take *verbatim* notes of their answer (including pauses, nonverbal sounds, emphases, false starts and side comments). This allows you to refer back to it during this and subsequent sessions.[5]

Entry Questions

In addition to the standard opening question, David Grove uses eight common entry questions—the five basic developing and three specialist entry questions. During Stage 1 the function of these questions is to invite the client to cross the bridge from everyday narrative to a world of personal symbolism.

The basic developing questions

In many situations, one of the five basic developing questions described in Chapter 3 can be used to encourage a shift to symbolic self-awareness:

And [client's words]. **And when** [client's words] ...

  ... **is there anything else about that** [client's words]?
  ... **what kind of** [client's words] **is/could that** [client's words] **be?**
  ... **that's** [client's words] **like what?**
  ... **where is** [client's words]?
  ... **whereabouts** {**is**} [client's words]?

While these questions are used throughout the Five Stages, your purpose in asking them during Stage 1 is to invite perceptual time to stand still so that the client pays attention to the symbolism in their everyday language and behaviour.

When you are new to Symbolic Modelling we recommend you do not use the moving time questions in Stage 1 because they invite attention to shift to another time frame. The developing questions offer more opportunity for the client to notice and embody their experience by concentrating on a single symbol, event or place.

Specialist entry questions

In addition to the five basic developing questions, there are three specialist entry questions, each designed to respond to a particular type of cue presented by the client—an abstract concept, a line of sight or a symbolic object:

Entry via an abstract concept:

> **And** [client's words]. **And when** [abstract concept], **how do you know** [abstract concept]?

Entry via a line of sight:

> **And when you go there** [gesture and/or look along line of sight], **where are you going, when you go there** [gesture and/or look along line of sight]?

Entry via a symbolic object (e.g. Metaphor Map):

> [Look at object.] **And where are you drawn to**?

The function of each specialist question is introduced below. How they are applied follows in the section on Entry Cues.

AND HOW DO YOU KNOW?

The 'And how do you know X?' entry question invites the client to go beyond the label 'X' and search for evidence or signs that they had, or are having, the experience they call 'X'. Although many clients start therapy unable to differentiate and describe their perceptions, they have to have ways of distinguishing one feeling from another, one thought from another, the past from the present from the future, and so on. (If they do not, this may need to become part of their outcome for therapy.) Suppose a client says 'I want confidence'. How do they know they *want* it? In order to answer the question they must somehow represent this particular want to themselves in a way that enables them to distinguish it from other experiences (such as: need, have to have, choose to have, require). They will quite likely describe their want with a mixture of sensory-based language and metaphor, such as 'I feel a pull inside'.

When clients convert an abstract concept like 'want confidence' to metaphor or sensory description, they tend to embody what they are talking about. These see-hear-feel perceptions enable them to distinguish one experience from another. To encourage this you may need to ask the 'And how do you know X?' entry question two or three times before they get a clear sense of what they call 'X'.

'And how do you know?' goes directly to the client's epistemology because it asks them how they know that they know something. What and how they answer will depend on the organisation of their perceptions, the distinctions they make and the vocabulary they have available to describe them.[6] Surprisingly, clients' descriptive powers seldom have much to do with familiarity. Some clients have had the same symptoms for decades, yet cannot find more than a few words to describe them. Whatever their response the question has value, because in considering it they will have begun to model their perceptions.

AND WHERE ARE YOU GOING WHEN YOU GO THERE?

The last chapter explained how clients' lines of sight—the direction of their gaze either before they speak or as they answer a question—often indicates the location of their attention at that moment. Lines of sight suggest a client is perceiving (though not always by visualising) what is 'out there' in their Metaphor Landscape.

A client will not be aware of a line of sight until your entry question directs their attention to it. The specialist entry question "And when you go there [gesture and/or look along line of sight], where are you going, when you go there?" acknowledges that the client's attention is somewhere, invites them to become conscious of that somewhere, and asks them to give that place a name or an address. The question also requests the client's attention to remain where it is, so that whatever they are attending to can be identified and described. Should the client look at you when you ask this question, simply direct their attention back to the source of the information by gesturing along their line of sight with your eyes, head or hand and repeat the question.

AND WHERE ARE YOU DRAWN TO?

Sometimes we ask a client to bring two drawings to the first session: one of their current situation and the other of how they would like it to be. More often we ask the client to bring a Metaphor Map to the second and subsequent sessions. Occasionally a client will bring a photograph, memento or other item which has symbolic significance for them. In all these cases you can begin by looking at the object and asking the question, "And where are you drawn to?" Their search for an answer will either initiate the self-modelling process or connect them with a previously established Metaphor Landscape.

Use of 'you' in specialist entry questions

The standard opening question, "And what would you like to have happen?" and the three specialist entry questions, are the only Clean Language questions which introduce the word 'you'. This is permissible at the entry stage because the client is still engaged with their every-day narrative and perceptions. But once they have entered the symbolic domain the introduction of 'you' may distract them from considering their Metaphor Landscape and bring them back to ordinary dialogue. This is why all other clean questions only use 'you' in response to the client having said 'I' or 'me'.

Entry Cues

Every one of the client's words, sounds or body expressions is a potential entry cue. We distinguish three types of *verbal* entry cues depending on whether the client's language is metaphoric, sensory or conceptual. As explained in Chapter 1, while these categories may be fuzzy, they usefully distinguish the ways in which people make sense of their experience. We tend to initiate the process via verbal entry cues until a client becomes familiar with self-modelling. Thereafter we also invite entry through nonverbal cues or symbolic objects.

Just as there are no hard and fast rules about when to start, there are few rules about which cues are the most appropriate to start with— it all depends on the client's outcome, the logic inherent in their metaphors, and their verbal and nonverbal emphasis. In practice, whatever entry cue or question you choose is less important than following the guidelines for Clean Language.

The rest of this chapter describes the six most common entry cues presented by clients with examples of questions you can ask in response to each type of cue:

- Overt metaphors
- Embedded metaphors and sensory expressions
- Abstract concepts
- Body expressions and sounds
- Lines of sight
- Material metaphors and symbolic objects

The relationship between the most common entry questions and each of the entry cues is summarised in Figure 5.1.

Stage 2: DEVELOPING A SYMBOLIC PERCEPTION

CLIENT'S RESPONSE

| Anything else? What kind of? Like what? Where is? Whereabouts? | How do you know? That's like what? | What kind of ... could that ... be? | Where are you going when you go there? | Where are you drawn to? |

| Metaphor or Sensory | Abstract concepts | Sound or Gesture | Line of sight | Metaphor Map |
| **Verbal** | | **Nonverbal** | | **Material** |

CLIENT'S RESPONSE

Stage 1: ENTRY

And what would you like to have happen?

FIGURE 5.1 Guidelines for entry questions

Entry via overt metaphors

The simplest and most obvious entry cue is via an overt spoken metaphor. When a client uses overt metaphor they are making use of their symbolic voice, symbolic sight or symbolic feelings. The "What kind of?" or "Anything else about?" questions invite the client to develop the form of their metaphor. For example:

T: **And what would you like to have happen?**

C: Life to be as easy as a smooth flowing river.

T: **And** life to be as easy as a smooth flowing river. **And when** as easy as a smooth flowing river, **is there anything else about that** smooth flowing river?

C: It has a rocky bottom.

T: **And** it has a rocky bottom. **And when** it has a rocky bottom **what kind of** smooth flowing river has a rocky bottom?

C: Deep, deep, deep.

The client's answers demonstrate the use of symbol and metaphor to self-model so they have progressed to Stage 2.

Entry via embedded metaphor and sensory expressions

Chapter 1 defined sensory expressions as words and phrases which describe objects, behaviours and sensations that can be seen, heard, felt or in some way sensed. While people can easily describe physical objects and behaviours in sensory terms, it is rare that they use sensory-based language for sensations that occur within their body. More commonly they use embedded metaphors—those out-of-awareness metaphors hidden in everyday language. Sensory expressions and embedded metaphors either directly reference or imply a *form* for, and a *location* of, what is being sensed. Take as an example these common descriptions for five types of feelings:

I'm *touched* by her kindness.	Tactile
I'm *holding* myself together.	
I'm *hot*.	Environmental conditions
I'm *under pressure*.	

My *gut reaction* is 'yes'. My *heart aches*.	Visceral (internal organs)
The feeling *comes and goes*. It starts in one place and *spreads out*.	Proprioception (movement)
I'm *off balance*. I'm *going round* in circles.	Vestibular (equilibrium and orientation)[7]

All of these expressions presuppose that certain sensations occur somewhere inside, on the surface or outside a sensing body.

Any of the five basic developing questions asked of a sensory cue will likely result in the client becoming more aware of their sensory experience. The 'What kind of?' and 'Anything else about?' questions invite the client to be aware of the qualities of their sensations; the 'Where?' and 'Whereabouts?' questions will direct their attention to the location of the sensations; and the 'Like what?' question will invite them to convert their description to an overt metaphor. For example:

T: **And what would you like to have happen**?

C: I don't want to be in pain any more.

T: **And** you don't want to be in pain any more. **And when** you don't want to be in pain any more, **what kind of** pain **is that** pain you don't want to be in?

C: A tightness.

T: **And** a tightness. **And when** a tightness **where is that** tightness?

C: Around my head.

T: **And** around your head. **And when** tightness around your head, **whereabouts** around your head?

C: Here [touches sides of head with both hands].

T: **And when** tightness around head, here [touches own head with both hands] **that's** tightness around head **like what**?

C: Like a vice.

This example illustrates the value of allowing time for the client to consciously embody their feeling by identifying its form and location *before* requesting an overt metaphor.

While clients often use overt metaphors to describe their symptoms and problems, they are more likely to use embedded metaphors to define their outcomes. A client may say "I need to stand back from the chaos" without realising the metaphorical and embodied nature of "stand back."

T: **And what would you like to have happen**?

C: I need to stand back from the chaos.

T: **And** you need to stand back from the chaos. **And when** you need to stand back, **is there anything else about that** stand back from the chaos?

C: I wish I could, but I seem to be attached to it.

T: **And when** you wish you could stand back from the chaos, but you seem to be attached to it, **what kind of** attached **could that** attached **be**?

C: It's chained to me.

The client has begun to self-model their metaphors, so they can proceed to Stage 2 where the nature of 'stand back', 'chaos' and 'chained' can be explored and developed.

Although the above examples describe feelings, the same principles about form and location apply to metaphors related to visual, auditory and olfactory senses. The following client refers to their visual sense:

C: I see nothing but difficulties in my life.

T: **And** you see nothing but difficulties in your life. **And when** you see nothing but difficulties in your life, **where do** you see **those** difficulties?

C: They're blocking my way.

T: **And when** difficulties are blocking your way, **what kind of** blocking **could that** blocking **be**?

C: Hurdles to get over.

T: **And** hurdles to get over. **And when** hurdles are blocking your way, **whereabouts could those** hurdles **be**?

C: In front of me [pointing with left hand].

T: **And when** hurdles in front of you [point to the same place] are blocking your way **what would you like to have happen**?

C: To have a clear bright future to look forward to.

By now the client has enough awareness of the symbolic nature of their perception to develop the attributes of the "hurdles," how they are "blocking" and, equally important, the client's "way."

In the next example where an auditory representation is used as an entry point, we keep asking questions about location until the client pinpoints the source of a hurtful voice:

T: **And what would you like to have happen?**

C: A voice says the most hurtful things, and I want it to be quiet.

T: **And** a voice says the most hurtful things, and you want it to be quiet. **And when** voice says the most hurtful things, **where could that voice be?**

C: In my head.

T: **And when** voice in your head says the most hurtful things, **whereabouts** in your head **is that** voice?

C: At the back.

T: **And** at the back. **And when** voice in your head **is** at the back, **whereabouts** at the back?

C: Just to the right-hand side.

T: **And when** voice in your head **is** at the back, just to the right-hand side, **is there anything else about that** hurtful voice?

C: It seems like it's hiding.

When you ask questions which connect a client with the form and location of their experience, you are inviting them to become aware of the embodied nature of that experience. If a metaphor does not emerge or if the client's responses indicate they are not yet ready to engage with their symbolic perception, you have a number of choices: continue to ask about their embedded metaphors; wait for an overt metaphor; or ask a question from another entry cue.

Entry via abstract concepts

If a client does not respond in metaphor or sensory-based language they will be using conceptual expressions. Given that a client's response may include dozens of conceptual words, you will need to direct your entry questions to those words which seem to have the most significance for them. These words or phrases will unconsciously be marked out by repetition, tonal emphasis, changes in physiology and gestures. In the Jubilee Clip transcript in Chapter 7 for example, we ask an entry question of the word 'vulnerable' after it had been used for the fourth time.

Clients generally begin by describing their symptoms in conceptual terms (e.g. angry, grieving, scared, confused, doubtful, depressed, lack of confidence, not enough love, don't want, too responsible, can't trust). These states of mindbody usually bear fruit as entry cues because, according to David Grove, "symptoms are metaphors waiting to be born."[8] The following are examples of responding to conceptual cues to initiate the self-modelling process. They make use of the basic developing questions and the specialist entry question:

> **And when** [abstract concept], **how do you know** [abstract concept]?

EXAMPLE 1

C: I get frightened.

T: **And** you get frightened. **And when** you get frightened, **how do you know** you get frightened?

C: Because I'm scared.

T: **And** because you're scared. **And when** you get frightened because you're scared, **where is that** scared?

C: I feel it inside.

T: **And whereabouts** inside?

C: In my stomach.

T: **And when** you feel scared inside, in your stomach, **is there anything else about** your stomach?

C: It turns.

T: **And** it turns. **And when** you get frightened because you're scared **and** you feel it in your stomach, **and** your stomach turns, your stomach turns **like what**?

C: A whirlpool.

Our first question asks the client to describe the behaviours, thoughts, and feelings they associate with the label "get frightened." In this case they answer with another concept, "scared." We acknowledge this and repeatedly (three times) direct them to attend to the location of this sensation. The client says that when they feel scared and frightened their stomach "turns" (an embedded metaphor that presupposes location, force, movement and direction). So we ask for an overt metaphor with 'Like what?'. Their answer, "A whirlpool" suggests they have accepted the invitation to shift to symbolism and have taken the first step towards constructing a Metaphor Landscape.

EXAMPLE 2

T: **And what would you like to have happen**?

C: I can't answer that question.

T: **And** you can't answer that question. **And when** you can't answer that question, **how do you know** you can't?

C: I don't know [pause]. I can't answer that question either [pause]. I've gone blank.

T: **And when** you've gone blank, **what kind of** blank **is that** blank **when** you can't answer?

C: A familiar one.

T: **And** a familiar blank. **And when** you can't answer, **and** you've gone blank, **where is that** familiar blank?

C: It fills my head.

T: **And when** blank fills your head, it fills your head **like what**?

C: Like a sponge.

As often happens, the client says "I don't know" in one breath, and gives an answer in the next.[9] Question by question we encourage them to become more aware of the experience labelled "can't answer" and "don't know." In this case the client uses an embedded metaphor "gone blank" before converting it into an overt "sponge" metaphor.

EXAMPLE 3

T: **And what would you like to have happen**?

C: I want my faith back.

T: **And** you want your faith back. **And when** you want your faith back, **is there anything else about** your faith you want back?

C: Life has no meaning any more.

T: **And when** life has no meaning any more **how do you know** life has
      no meaning any more?

C: I'm empty.

T: **And** you're empty. **And when** you want your faith back, **and** life has
      no meaning, **and** you're empty, you're empty **like what**?

C: A void.

T: **And** a void. **And is there anything else about** a void?

C: It's a bottomless pit.

These three examples follow the same Stage 1 process of asking
questions that invite the client to explore their perception until they
can identify and describe it in a graphic or embodied form.

Not all clients move from conceptual to symbolic descriptions after
so few clean questions—some take considerable time. If a client does
not immediately accept your invitation to perceive symbolically, it
probably means one of the following:

- The client is not ready yet—so continue to honour the way they are
  expressing themselves and ask questions which increase their awareness of the logic inherent in their abstract concepts.

- Your questions are not directing the client to attend to the embodied
  nature of their perception—in which case ask clean questions of
  their embedded metaphors.

- You have yet to find an appropriate entry point. Keep trying others
  (including the nonverbal cues which follow) until you find one to
  which the client can respond.[10]

Entry via body expressions and sounds

Chapter 4 explained how clients' gestures, movements, coughs, sighs
and other nonverbal expressions can either be symbols in their own
right, or pointers to information within perceptual space. When you
infer a particular movement or sound is symbolic, you can directly and
cleanly ask an entry question of the nonverbal expression. Whether the
expression is a sound, movement or posture, the same format applies:

And what kind of [replicate nonverbal] **is that** [nonverbal]?

Since clients' nonverbal behaviour is generally outside of their awareness, it is important that you direct their attention to it during or immediately after the behaviour. One of our clients responded to the "And what would you like to have happen?" question with an unbroken narrative for over 15 minutes when we noticed they were repeatedly tracing a horizontal figure eight (∞) in the air with their right forefinger. We asked:

T: **And** [replicate finger movement]. **And when** [finger movement], **what kind of** [finger movement] **is that**?

After a long pause while reproducing the finger movement a number of times the client replied:

C: I move forwards only to then move backwards, from one disaster to another, desperately trying to hold to the midpoint.

An exploration of the finger movement while it was happening revealed it symbolised a pattern that was "a major part of my life that has existed as long as I can remember."

In Chapter 4 we gave several examples of asking basic clean questions of nonverbal expressions such as a repetitive patting with the hand, a goldfish-like facial expression, a pointing hand, a touch of the neck, a big sigh, and a suction-like sound. All these examples can be considered as illustrations of entry via nonverbal expressions, even though they may have occurred well into the modelling process.[11]

The only exception to these general guidelines for entry via nonverbal behaviour is for a line of sight.

Entry via lines of sight

In Chapter 4 we explained how a line of sight is created by the direction, angle and focal point of where a client looks when they 'go somewhere' to retrieve or contemplate information. Lines of sight differ from other nonverbal cues in that the locus of attention is not with the body; it is with whatever is at the 'end of' or 'along' or 'related to' their gaze — regardless of whether that is located in physical or imaginative space, or both simultaneously. As the Zen master who pointed to the moon said: 'Do not be interested in my finger, be interested in what my finger points to'.

When you ask the specialist line of sight question, you facilitate the client to begin to notice and engage with whatever their eyes 'point to' at that moment:

> **And when you go there** [gesture and/or look along line of sight],
> **where are you going, when you go there**
> [gesture and/or look along line of sight]?

Whether clients fixate on something in the physical environment, briefly attend to somewhere in perceptual space, or just defocus, you ask the same entry question:

T: **And what would you like to have happen?**

C: [Gazing off into space.]

T: **And when you go there** [gesture to the space], **where are you going, when you go there** [gesture to the space]?

C: Out the window.

T: **And** out the window. **And when** out the window, **whereabouts** out the window?

C: Far far away.

T: **And when** far far away, **whereabouts** far far away?

C: Continents away.

T: **And** continents away. **And when** continents away **is there anything else about** far far continents away?

C: Oh, it's Africa [gasp].

The line of sight now has a direction, "out the window," an address, "Continents away," and a name, "Africa." The client has begun to build a model of where they go to access this information so they have made the transition to Stage 2.

Another client suddenly stops in mid-sentence while staring into a corner:

T: **And when you go there** [look to the corner], **where are you going, when you go there** [look to the corner]?

C: Oh, nowhere [looks at therapist].

T: **And** nowhere. **And when** nowhere [look to the corner], **where are you going, when you go** nowhere [continue looking to corner]?

C: Just over there [looks to the corner and pauses]. There's a shadow.

T: **And** just over there. There's a shadow. **And when** shadow, just over there, **is there anything else about that** shadow, just over there [continues looking to the corner]?

C: Funny, but it seems to go back a long way.

T: **And** it seems to go back a long way. **And when** shadow goes back a long way, **whereabouts** back a long way?

C: Strange, I remember standing in a passage in the dark and being scared stiff.

Here we encourage the client to stay with the line of sight until symbolic information becomes conscious. Although the client is describing a memory, the comments "funny" and "strange" make it a fairly safe bet that they realise this memory is charged with symbolism.

Entry via material metaphors and symbolic objects

Although Metaphor Maps are an obvious type of symbolic object, when clients bring a photograph or some other personal item to a session, you simply look at their map or object and ask the specialist entry question:

And where are you drawn to?

For example:

T: [Looking at the client's map] **And where are you drawn to?**

C: The fact that [points] they're all red.

T: **And is there anything else about** the fact that they're all red?

C: Intuitively I know they're all connected.

At this point we could invite the client to develop their 'intuitive knowing' into a resource symbol, to explore the attributes of the metaphor "connected," or even to cultivate the characteristics of the "I" that knows.

Concluding Remarks

The purpose of Stage 1 is to facilitate the client to become aware of the metaphors and symbolism inherent in their language, behaviour and perception—and thereby to start modelling themselves. One way of doing this is to choose an appropriate moment to ask the standard opening question and follow this with one or more of the five basic developing or three specialist entry questions. These questions are designed to respond to a variety of verbal and behavioural cues presented by the client: overt metaphors, embedded metaphors and sensory expressions, abstract concepts, nonverbal sounds and body expressions, lines of sight and symbolic objects.

Entry is not a one-off event as most clients will dip in and out of their symbolic world over the course of a session. When they do, you use the same entry questions to guide their attention back to their Metaphor Landscape.

The boundary between Stage 1 (Entry) and Stage 2 (Developing Symbolic Perceptions) is not always well defined. However, as soon as a client has indicated that they are aware of the metaphorical and symbolic nature of their language, behaviour or perception, they have begun to self-model and have automatically progressed to Stage 2. It is in Stage 2 that they develop each of the symbolic perceptions which constitute their Metaphor Landscape.

6

Stage 2

Developing Symbolic Perceptions

*The entire landscape comes alive, filled with relationships
and relationships within relationships.*
Frank Herbert

A Metaphor Landscape has to have a form before it can transform. Once a client has entered the symbolic domain (Stage 1), the more they attend to and engage with the symbols in their perceptual space (Stage 2), the more they establish the foundations of a Metaphor Landscape within which patterns can emerge (Stage 3), the more they create a context in which the conditions for transformation can arise (Stage 4). During this process the client discovers they have a special relationship with certain 'resource' symbols which can have a beneficial influence on other symbols.

Your role in Stage 2 is to facilitate the client's symbolic perceptions to develop *one at a time;* that is, for the client to identify and locate component symbols and to specify how they function and relate to other symbols within that perception. A new symbolic perception may emerge anywhere within the Five-Stage Process. When it does, it can be developed with Stage 2 questions. To facilitate this you will need an understanding of:

A Symbolic Perception
Developing the Form of Symbolic Perceptions
Resource Symbols
Specialist Developing Questions

A Symbolic Perception

A perception is a set of thoughts, feelings and behaviours that is regarded as a single unit. In other words, experience is punctuated so that a particular event (or events), moment (or period of time), place (or places), and symbol (or group of symbols) appear as a gestalt. Clients arrive with a stream of perceptions in which problems, solutions, outcomes, causes and effects are likely to be poorly differentiated. When they slow this stream down, their symbolic perceptions can be identified, separated, deconstructed and attended to long enough for each of them to develop a form.

How do clients know their symbolic perceptions exist? Because their physical and imaginative eyes see, ears hear, skin feels and body registers sensations. One of our clients spoke for many when he described his first taste of symbolic self-modelling:

> As I tried to verbalise what was just an intangible state of things I realised that I could in fact 'see' and 'feel' this experience within my mind. The more I talked and investigated, the more real it became. The struggle to put the whole experience of this intensely emotional time into words, into communicable concepts, actually formed images in my consciousness. Images I could feel, or feelings I could see—I'm not sure which.[1]

For a symbol to exist, it must be located somewhere in perceptual space. This space acts like a theatre in which symbolic events can happen. A perceptual space can include any combination of:

- The physical environment around the client
- The surface or inside of the client's body
- An imaginative space operating in the here and now
  (which can be inside and/or outside the client's body)
- An imaginary place elsewhere in space and time.

When clients experience these spaces as alternative and compatible ways of representing symbolic information they realise that any and all of their surroundings, language, thoughts, memories, emotions, sensations and imaginings may be symbolic of the patterns that comprise who they are and the kind of life they lead.

Symbolic perceptions come to life when the client responds as if their metaphors are happening to, around and inside them. When they experience their symbols moving, changing size, exploding, softening or releasing, they have reactions to their own imaginative representations: their eyes orientate to symbolic space, their body enacts imagined events, their hands, feet and head gesture to the location of symbols, and their face changes expression and skin colour. As this occurs, they are often taken by surprise and report an awareness of things happening without apparent reason. One wide-eyed client suddenly said, "Man, where did that vulture come from?" Another said, "The muscles are rippling all down my back and I haven't the faintest idea why." The embodied nature of the relationship between the client and their symbolic perception means that when their symbolic perceptions change, so do they.

Although symbolic perceptions are perceived as a whole, they are composed of parts:

- The content (whatever is perceived)
- A context (within which the content exists)
- A perceiver (with a point of perception and a means of perceiving the content and context).

The perceiver and the perceived may be separate but they cannot operate independently, nor can they operate outside of a context. It is this unique combination of content, context and perceiver that enables the client to distinguish between perceptions. Figure 6.1 shows a schematic of a single symbolic perception.

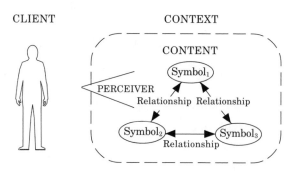

FIGURE 6.1 Schematic of a single symbolic perception

Next we describe the component parts of a symbolic perception and then explain how to facilitate clients to bring these to life.

Symbolic content

Every thing, entity or person identified within a symbolic perception can be considered a symbol. Symbols have a form that the client can see, hear, feel or in some other way sense, detect or perceive. No matter how abstract or vague a symbol is, if it exists it will have distinguishing attributes, it will be located somewhere in perceptual space, and it will interact or have some association with other symbols.

In mediaeval times people were named by reference to their distinguishing characteristics, as in 'Big John the Blacksmith', and located by reference to nearby landmarks, such as 'next to the bend in the river'. Likewise, in the land of metaphor, symbols are *named* by reference to their attributes, located by their relative perceptual *address,* and connected by their *relationships.*

SYMBOL NAMES

Anything that identifies a symbol qualifies as an attribute and provides a reference or name for that symbol. Names can be:

- What is seen (size, shape, colour, movement, number)
- What is heard (volume, tonality, rhythm)
- What is felt (temperature, pressure, texture)
- What is done (behaviours, reactions, emotions)
- How it is done (skills, manner, method)
- Why it is done (purpose, function, role).

SYMBOL ADDRESSES

Any reference that locates a symbol gives it a perceptual address. Addresses can be:

- A relative location ('over there', 'ten feet away', 'behind a door')
- A place ('inside', 'in a cage', 'Africa')
- A nonverbal indicator (pointing, a look, a body expression).

RELATIONSHIPS

Symbols do not exist in isolation—in fact they only exist in a network of relationships with other symbols. By 'relationship' we mean any interaction, connection, association, or way of relating between two symbols. Relationships are usually expressed nonverbally, or verbally by:

- Verbs, e.g. metaphors of behaviour (to open, to struggle, to bang), of possession (to have, to get, to take, to keep, to let), of perception (to feel, to look, to hear) and of existence (to be)
- Spatial metaphors (behind, on, in, outside, middle)
- Temporal metaphors (before, since, always).

Symbols are made up of component symbols and simultaneously constitute parts of other, larger symbols. A symbolic door may contain studs and a handle, and at the same time be part of a wall which itself is part of a castle. There are always symbols within symbols within symbols, and relationships within relationships within relationships.

Symbolic context

Context is the environment, the situation, the setting, the circumstance or the timeframe within which things happen. It can be as sensory as 'this room', as conceptual as 'a friendship', as symbolic as 'a golden wedding anniversary'; as specific as 'three o'clock in the afternoon', or as general as 'everywhere'. Context is a very fuzzy notion, yet without it meaning free-floats.[2] Context helps to punctuate experience into manageable pieces by establishing boundaries (separators or markers) which are defined by *time* (everything between the beginning and end), *space* (everything within a container), *form* (everything with a similar motif) or *function* (all the parts of something that work together). In the following example an unspecified symbol, a blur, is set in a well-specified context:

> Everything that happened that night [time] when I was 9 [time] in my bedroom [space] after the light was turned off [time] and it was so dark [form], is just a blur.

Once a context is defined, certain possibilities disappear and certain probabilities remain. If a client says they are trapped, then how they are trapped—in a cage, in a dungeon, in a bedroom, in a vice, in quicksand, in space, in a time-warp, by rising inflation, by their genes, by their history, by their beliefs, by glue, by the bogey man—makes all the difference. These examples show how context can be the surrounding environment in which events happen, or the cause of events, or both. When the context changes—the client unlocks the cage, breaks out of the dungeon, absconds from the bedroom, releases the vice, escapes the quicksand, finds Earth, goes through the time-warp, reduces the pressure, compensates for their genes, utilises their history, updates their beliefs, dissolves the glue, befriends the bogey man—they will not be trapped any more and then they will be free to make other choices.

Symbolic perceiver

There seems to be no limit to where, when and in what form a perceiver can exist. Sometimes the perceiver is synonymous with the client describing their here and now experience—while on every other occasion it is not. Although the client may be sitting in front of you, a symbolic perceiver may be floating above and just behind them, or intensely involved in reliving an incident from childhood, or interacting with an abstract representation made up of nothing but blobs of colour.

To perceive something requires a perceiver with a *form*, who is doing the perceiving from somewhere (the *point of perception*), and who is perceiving by some *means*. And just to make life interesting, clients can have *multiple perceivers*.

PERCEIVER'S FORM

Whoever or whatever is doing the perceiving can itself be regarded as a symbol which may take the form of:

- The client in the here and now
- The client at a younger or older age
- A body part
- Another person, real or fictitious (mother, teacher, Merlin)
- Living things, real or fictitious (animal, flower, unicorn)
- Inanimate objects, real or fictitious (rock, cloud, magic wand)
- Notional objects (point, line, circle).

POINT OF PERCEPTION

A perception will be perceived *from* somewhere, such as:

- The physical environment
    Structures (windows, walls, corners, doors)
    Patterns (on wallpaper, carpets, shadows, clothes)
    Objects (books, furniture, ornaments, pictures, mirrors)
    Nature (trees, ground, sky, sun).

- The body

  The extremities (hands, feet, head)

  Sense organs (eyes, ears, skin)

  Internal organs (heart, chest, stomach).

- Imagined places

  Openings, gaps, reflections

  A location relative to the client (above, below, in front)

  In a memory (of a bedroom, toy box, school, playground)

  Any place or time other than here and now (Heaven, Planet Zog).

MEANS OF PERCEIVING

Whatever or whoever is perceiving will have some means of doing so, such as:

- Seeing, hearing, feeling, smelling, tasting
- Intuiting or 'just knowing'
- Detecting apparatus (radar, compass, divining rod).

MULTIPLE PERCEIVERS

It is common for a client to have more than one perceiver within a perception. Each perceiver will either inhabit a different form, do the perceiving from a different place or have a different means of perceiving. The presence of multiple perceivers is often presupposed in the client's language:

> Part of me wants ... and part of me wants ...
>
> I'm not myself today.
>
> I need to pull myself together.
>
> I told myself ...
>
> I can't get in touch with my feelings.
>
> I saw things from their perspective.
>
> Why do I do it when I know it's no good for me?
>
> I'm beside myself with anger.

Multiple perceptions can also be indicated by nonverbal behaviour. A client may enact the posture and expression of a perceiver's body while simultaneously describing the scene from an entirely different position. They say "A boy's about to be hit" while simultaneously ducking as if the event is happening now. Their body is enacting the event from the boy's perspective, but their narration is about what is happening to "a boy" from the position of an observer. When such multiple perceptions occur they usually indicate important symbolic relationships which merit exploration.[3]

Adopting multiple perceivers and locations is a naturally creative faculty of the human mind and in itself is not dysfunctional. The important question is not 'does a person occupy multiple points of perception?' but 'how much choice do they have about where they perceive from, when, and for how long?'[4]

Regardless of how many perceivers there are and whatever form, location and means of perception they adopt, you can be sure that these will correspond to the way the client lives their life. And yet these aspects of perception are usually out of their awareness—until you ask the appropriate developing questions.

Developing the Form of Symbolic Perceptions

During Stage 2 your job is to use Clean Language to invite the client to attend to a single event, time or place long enough for the form, location and function of each symbol, and the relationships between symbols to develop. But how formed does each perception need to be? In principle a perception is 'well-formed' or 'well-developed' when:

- Each symbol is identified and named
- Each symbol's attributes and function are defined
- Each symbol's location has an address
- The relationships between symbols are specified
- The context within which the symbols relate is specified
- Each perceiver's characteristics are distinguished.[5]

In practice, these conditions are far from mutually exclusive since a symbol's location can be its identifying attribute, and its relationship to another symbol can be its name. And because symbols have varying significance for the client, not every symbol, relationship, context or perceiver needs to be fully developed.

The word 'develop' originally meant 'to unwrap'. Thus developing questions facilitate the client to unwrap perceptions one at a time so that their metaphors can emerge (often blinking and somewhat dazed) into the light of awareness. Developing questions hold time still and stop perceptions racing from one to the next to the next. This gives the client an opportunity to explore a moment, a place or an event in greater detail. Whether developing the form of a symbolic perception takes a few seconds or a few sessions, you ask the same developing questions:

And when/as ...
> ... **is there anything else about that** [client's words]?
> ... **what kind of** [client's words] **is that** [client's words]?
> ... **that's** [client's words] **like what?**
> ... **where is that** [client's words]?
> ... **whereabouts** [client's words]?

The following is an example of how developing questions establish the name, attributes, address and function of three symbolic rocks each of which represent a different kind of fear:

C: I have a fear.

T: **And** you have a fear. **And when** you have a fear, **what kind of** fear **is that** fear?

C: It's like a rock.

T: **And** it's like a rock. **And when** fear **is** like a rock, **what kind of** rock, **is that** rock?

C: A hard rock.	C: A sharp rock.	C: A porous rock.
T: **And** a hard rock. **And when** a hard rock, **where could that** hard rock **be?**	T: **And** a sharp rock. **And when** a sharp rock, **where could that** sharp rock **be?**	T: **And** a porous rock. **And when** a porous rock, **where could that** porous rock **be?**
C: Right in my way.	C: On my skin.	C: Deep inside.
T: **And** right in your way. **And when** hard rock is right in your way, **is there anything else about that** hard rock?	T: **And** on your skin. **And when** sharp rock is on your skin, **is there anything else about that** sharp rock?	T: **And** deep inside. **And when** porous rock is deep inside, **is there anything else about that** porous rock?
C: It's indestructible.	C: It tears my flesh.	C: It soaks up pain.

FIGURE 6.2 Developing three symbols' names, addresses and functions

The questions in these examples make extensive use of 'when' and 'that'. Generally, 'when' invites the client to consider a single event, and 'that' directs their attention to a particular component. Compare:

And you have a fear. **And what kind of** fear?

with:

And you have a fear. **And *when*** you have a fear, **what kind of** fear
is *that* fear?

Using 'when' and 'that' invites the client to attend to *a* time *when* they are experiencing *that* specific fear and to search for the distinguishing characteristics which make it *that* fear, and no other.

Each time a new symbol makes an appearance you can ask the client to consider its form, location and function. Although not every symbol needs to be fully specified, neither you nor the client can know in advance which symbols and which features of these symbols will be involved in the change process. Therefore it is advisable to spend some time developing each new symbol's characteristics so that the client discovers which are the most significant. When numerous symbols emerge in close succession, let your questions be guided by the client's *emphasis* (nonverbal marking, verbal repetition, emotional response). If you are unsure, simply ask about whatever the client refers to *last*. In the unlikely event you direct their attention away from a symbol or feature that is fundamental, rest assured it will reappear sooner or later—how could it not?

After a number of symbols and their relationships have been defined, the client can be requested to further develop the form of their symbolic perception by drawing a Metaphor Map. As they spatially and graphically represent what they already know, they are likely to add details, fill in gaps and notice new relationships. Some clients prefer to represent their symbolic perceptions by sculpting, building models, keeping a diary, writing poetry, making music, etc.

Developing a single symbolic perception is not a one-time process; rather it is a one-at-a-time process. You use the five basic developing questions, the syntax and mapping to facilitate the client to specify symbols, relationships, contexts and perceivers each time they consider a different perception. By the time a number of perceptions have been developed an overall Metaphor Landscape will have emerged and the client will have progressed to Stage 3.

Review of Castle Door transcript

To see how Stage 2 works in practice we return to the beginning of the Castle Door transcript. In Chapter 3 we used this transcript to explain the fundamentals of Clean Language. Here it demonstrates how the cumulative effect of developing questions encourages a single symbolic perception into being.

C1:   I'd like to have more energy because I feel very tired.

T1:   **And** you'd like to have more energy because you feel very tired. **And when** you'd like to have more energy, **that's** more energy **like what**?

C2:   It's like I'm behind a castle door.

T2:   **And** it's like you're behind a castle door. **And when** behind a castle door, **what kind of** castle door **is that** castle door?

Once the client accepts the invitation to respond in metaphor she is invited to attend to the particular symbolic event "when behind a castle door." Then the question "what kind of castle door is that castle door?" asks her to consider that particular door, and by presupposition, what distinguishes it from all other doors. She replies:

C3:   A huge castle door that's very thick, very old, with studs, very heavy.

T3:   **And** a huge castle door that's very thick, very old, with studs, very heavy. **And when** huge castle door is very thick, very old, with studs, very heavy, **is there anything else about that** huge castle door?

C4:   I can't open it and I get very very tired trying to open it.

The number of attributes describing "huge castle door" indicates its importance for the client, so we ask her to continue attending to it. Her reply shifts from describing the door to describing the *relationship* between it and the perceiver "I" behind the door. Her first four responses identify:

Three symbols (names):	'I', 'energy' and 'huge castle door'
A relative address:	I is 'behind' castle door
A context:	A 'castle'
Relationships of:	I 'would like to have' more energy
	I 'feel' very tired
	I 'can't open' and 'get very very tired trying to open' castle door

Our next question uses 'as' to acknowledge the ongoing nature of "trying" and invites the client to develop the form of "very very tired trying":

T4: **And** you can't open it and you get very very tired trying to open it. **And as** you get very very tired trying to open it, **what kind of** very very tired trying **is that**?

C5: Like I'm struggling on my own and not getting anywhere. It takes a lot of energy. I feel like I'm banging my head on a wall.

The client responds by describing her predicament with a number of new metaphors ('struggling', 'not getting', 'takes', 'banging' and 'on') and symbols ('anywhere', 'head' and 'wall'). Faced with an abundance of options, we ask about 'wall' because it is the last symbol mentioned and to clarify whether it is part of the castle context:

T5: **And** like struggling on your own, not getting anywhere, **and** banging your head on a wall. **And as** it takes a lot of energy banging your head on a wall, **what kind of** wall **is that** wall?

C6: A castle wall of thick granite and I get very frustrated and very angry.

The client confirms that the wall is a castle wall and describes its attributes. She then switches attention to her "very frustrated and very angry" emotional *response* to the situation. This indicates the existence of at least one new symbol. So we continue the developing process by enquiring about its location:

T6: **And** a castle wall of thick granite and you get very frustrated and very angry. **And when** very frustrated and very angry, **where is that** very frustrated and **that** very angry?

C7: In here [touches solar plexus region].

T7: **And when** in here, **whereabouts** in here?

C8: Exactly in here. Hollow. Full of darkness.

T8: **And** exactly in here. Hollow. Full of darkness. **And when** hollow **is** full of darkness, **is there anything else about that** darkness?

C9: It's very dry.

T9: **And** it's very dry. **And when** darkness is very dry, it's very dry **like what**?

C10: It's dry like a desert.

T10:   **And** it's dry like a desert. **And when** dry like a desert, **is there anything else about that**?

C11:   It keeps me in one place and it doesn't let me move.

By maintaining attention on the location of "very frustrated and very angry" (which in this case seems to be one symbol), the client identifies its perceptual address, "in here" and some attributes of that place, "hollow" and "full of darkness." Enquiring about the "darkness" reveals two metaphors: "it's dry like a desert" and "it keeps me in one place and it doesn't let me move." The latter appears to have a similar function to the "can't open" of castle door. To acknowledge this similarity and to give the client time to consider the key symbols identified so far, we backtrack to the door:

T11:   **And** it keeps you in one place and doesn't let you move. **And** dry like a desert, hollow full of darkness in here **and** struggling on your own **and** very very tired trying to open huge castle door **that's** very thick **and** very heavy **and** very old. **And is there anything else about that** door you can't open?

C12:   Yes. A great big circular handle that's all twisted around.

T12:   **And is there anything else about that** great big circular handle that's all twisted around?

C13:   It looks like twisted pasta. It's big. It's old. It's dull. It's metal, iron, black.

The client's attention is drawn to a new symbol, a handle, so we ask her to further describe its attributes and develop its form.

While the client has not described every symbol's attributes, nor defined every symbol's location, nor identified all the relationships between symbols, it is clear that this metaphoric perception is coming alive. From now on, we can expect any new information about the client's problem and outcome to relate to the symbols in the context of the castle. If a symbol emerges which is outside of this context it would indicate a new symbolic perception which we would then seek to develop with Stage 2 processes.

Thus far the client has identified eight symbols (assuming all the I's, my's and me's refer to the same perceiver) and numerous relationships, all within a single symbolic perception. These are summarised in Figure 6.3.

SYMBOL	RELATIONSHIP	SYMBOL
[1] I	would like to have	[2] More energy.
I	feels	[3] Very tired.
I	is behind can't open [is] trying to open	[4] Castle door—huge, very thick, very old, with studs, very heavy.
		[5] Circular handle— great big, all twisted around (looks like twisted pasta), old, dull, metal, iron, black.
I	struggling, not getting	[6] Anywhere.
My head	banging on	[7] Castle wall— thick granite.
I	get	[8] Very frustrated and very angry—
Me	[kept] in one place [isn't] let move [by]	in here [solar plexus], hollow full of darkness —a very dry desert.

FIGURE 6.3 Symbols and relationships in Castle Door

We return to the Castle Door transcript in the next section, and use it to illustrate how to develop a resource symbol.

Resource Symbols

A resource is a symbol (or attribute of a symbol) that a client regards as having value, use or goodness in its own right, or in relation to another symbol or context. Clients experience resource symbols as empowering, uplifting, redeeming, problem-solving, mystical, balancing, grounding, protective, enlightening, etc. — depending on their preferred metaphor.

When a resource symbol is present and its function fulfilled, it will have a beneficial influence on other symbols (including the perceiver). A resource symbol such as a key may simply unlock a door, or it may resolve a double bind which transforms the whole Metaphor Landscape.

There is no such thing as a universal resource. The word 'love' may be regarded as inherently positive, but what about a 'smothering love'? Is that negative? And if the client says, "It's a wonderful, smothering love I've wanted for a very long time," is that positive? Only the client knows for sure. Given that all resources are subjective and relative, it is vital that you give precedence to the client's judgment over your own and to the logic inherent in their metaphors. For example, our stomachs turned at a client's macabre description of maggots eating the eyes of a corpse, yet the client reported feeling strengthened by the experience and released from the corpse's evil gaze. In this metaphor, and for this client, the maggots were a resource.

Since all symbols have attributes, and all attributes have functions, and all functions serve a purpose, all symbols are *potentially* useful somewhere, somewhen or under some conditions. At any particular moment a symbol may be:

- An *overt resource,* whose potential is known by the client, even if its function has yet to be determined.

- A *latent resource*, whose potential is not revealed until another symbol or context is discovered that requires it.

- A *to-be-converted resource,* that needs to be released or in some way changed before its usefulness becomes available.

The rest of this section looks at overt resources—how they manifest and how to facilitate the client to develop them. Chapters 7 and 8 examine latent and to-be-converted resources respectively.

How overt resources manifest

Resources, like all other symbols, enter a client's awareness as a word or phrase, an image, a feeling, a movement, a memory, as something in their environment, or as just a vague sense. However the moment an *overt* resource makes an appearance, the client will know it has a positive potential or a beneficial effect. You, on the other hand, only know *when the client tells you* directly, when they indicate it *via accompanying nonverbals,* or *by developing a symbol's function.*

WHEN CLIENTS TELL YOU

The simplest way to know that a symbol has been recognised as a resource is when the client meta-comments with statements such as "This is important," "Something just shifted," "I feel better" or "It's amazing." At other times the modifiers and adjectives that clients use to describe a symbol indicate the presence of a resource. For example:

> I have a *lovely* warm feeling in my stomach.
> Freedom is *paramount*.
> *Wow*, it's like a bird's-eye view.

For some clients the symbols of a warm feeling, freedom and a bird's-eye view might be problematic. Here the use of 'lovely', 'paramount' and 'wow' indicate they are resources.

VIA ACCOMPANYING NONVERBALS

When clients connect with a resource symbol, you will probably notice accompanying physiological and vocal changes. When the symbol represents their sense of identity or spiritual beliefs, the change in the *quality* of their response is as palpable as a change in the atmosphere just after a storm. Since there is no universal 'body language' which signals the discovery of a resource it is advisable to check your intuitions with a clean question or two (as described in Chapters 4 and 5).

BY DEVELOPING A SYMBOL'S FUNCTION

Often clients know straight away whether a symbol represents an empowering aspect of themselves (or a benevolent power within or beyond themselves). Sometimes however, the resourceful nature of a symbol only becomes apparent when its attributes are developed; when, as David Grove says, it "confesses its strengths."[6] We spent a long time asking developing questions about a toy racing car before the client realised there was a "glint on the window that's a part of me I'd forgotten existed."

Sometimes resources appear as abstract or apparently insignificant symbols without much obvious value—until they are developed and their function becomes clear. For one person an arc ten feet away from their body turned out to be a longtime safety mechanism. For another, a thin grey line running vertically through the middle of their body developed into a sense of "my true self, who I really am."

Example of developing an overt resource

In the Castle Door transcript the client indicates that a number of symbols have resourceful potential: "energy" because "I'd like to have more" of it (C1); "centurion" because he is "big and broad with armour on and a spear" and because the client's smile indicates a friend rather than a foe (C16); and:

C22: [Looks up and squints.] I can see the sky—I never noticed that before—hope is on the outside [long pause]. It's very strong. It gives me determination and the ability to keep trying.

Although "sky," "hope" or "outside" could have been developed, we invite the client to specify and locate "it" because this is what *gives* her the determination and ability to keep trying.

T22: **And** you can see the sky. **And** hope is on the outside. **And when** it gives you very strong determination to keep trying, **whereabouts is it when** it's very strong?

C23: I can feel it right in the middle—at the absolute core of my being.

T23: **And when** you can feel it right in the middle, at the absolute core of your being, it's **like what**?

C24: It's gold.

T24: **And** it's gold. **And when** it's gold at the absolute core of your being, **what kind of** gold **is that** gold?

C25: Absolutely pure. It's always been there.

T25: **And** absolutely pure. **And** absolutely pure gold's always been there at the core of your being. **And is there anything else about that** absolutely pure gold?

C26: It's incredibly strong but malleable. Powerful. You could shape it but you couldn't break it. An almost silent powerful.

T26: **And** an almost silent powerful. **And is there anything else about that** absolutely pure gold **that**'s incredibly strong **and** malleable **and** almost silent powerful at the absolute core of your being?

C27: It can move.

The full extent of gold's qualities emerge because the client attends to "it" long enough to reveal "it" as absolutely pure, always been there, incredibly strong but malleable, you could shape it but you couldn't break it, an almost silent powerful, and it can move. "Can move" is particularly noteworthy because its function contrasts with "keeps me in one place and doesn't let me move" (C11). A symbol with this many resourceful qualities will inevitably play a part in the evolution of the Metaphor Landscape.

There are clients who have spent so long examining distressing aspects of themselves that to embody an empowering quality can be a revelation. Sometimes a well-developed resource is all that is needed to set a change in motion. Therefore we recommend even more diligence than usual when facilitating clients to develop the qualities and functions of resource symbols. If no obvious change results, be patient. The time spent will invariably prove worthwhile later in the process. Once a resource has a name, an address, clearly defined attributes and the client has an embodied connection to the symbol, it will happily wait in the wings for an hour, until the next session or if necessary for months. As Chapter 8 shows, all it requires are the conditions to arise whereby it can fulfil its destiny.[7]

Specialist Developing Questions

In many circumstances the five basic developing questions will be all you need to help the client breathe life into their metaphors. However, there are some situations where a *specialist* developing question can more precisely invite attributional and locational information into the client's awareness.

When using any specialist question there is an important rule: your question must be congruent with the logic of the client's metaphors. In other words, the client must indicate that the appropriate conditions exist *before* the question is asked. They can do this directly, through presupposition and other forms of inherent logic, or by nonverbal behaviour, as the next example shows.

Client Transcript: Steel Shutter

The following transcript was chosen for its unusual density of specialist developing questions (shown in ***italics***). We begin the second session by asking "And what would you like to have happen in your time here, now?" The client replies:

C1: [Looking up and straight ahead.] I want to have a sense of purpose and more self worth and confidence.

T1: **And when** you want to have a sense of purpose and more self worth and confidence, **where are you going when you go there** [gestures along line of sight]?

C2: Over there [gestures with right hand in front and up high].

T2: **And** over there. And *how far* over there [gestures to same place]?

C3: [Looking out of window.] Way over, over the roof.

T3: **And** way over, over the roof. **And is there anything else about** way over, over the roof [looks out of window]?

C4: It would be quite hard to get to.

T4: **And when** it would be quite hard to get to, **what kind of** quite hard to get to **is that**?

C5: A whole lot of traps [right hand motions down, in front].

T5: **And when** a whole lot of traps, *how many* traps *could there be*?

C6: One big one with a lot of offshoots.

T6: **And when** one big one with a lot of offshoots **is there anything else about that** one big trap?

C7: It's a big steel shutter. And I can hear the 'clunk' when it goes shut.

T7: **And** a big steel shutter. And you can hear the 'clunk' when it goes shut. **And when** big steel shutter goes shut and you hear 'clunk', *does* big steel shutter *have a size or a shape*?

C8: Way out of the room [both arms outstretched].

T8: **And** way out of the room. **And when** big steel shutter shuts 'clunk', *in which direction does* big steel shutter shut?

C9: [Puts right hand in front above head and motions down.]

T9: **And** steel shutter shuts [replicates hand movement]. **And when** you hear 'clunk', **are** you *inside or outside* big steel shutter?

C10: Inside [shrinks down in chair, looks up and whispers]. And I'm scared.

T10: **And** you're scared. **And when** scared, *how old could* scared *be*?

C11: Very young.

T11: **And when** very young is scared, *what could* very young *be wearing*?

C12: I don't know [long pause]. My Fred Flintstone pyjamas.

In response to the standard opening question, the client identifies an outcome, "purpose and more self worth and confidence," and via a related line of sight indicates where that is located in perceptual space. Through a series of basic and specialist questions, the client develops a symbolic perception for what is between them and what they want. At C10 they indicate the presence of a second perceiver who is "scared." Thus far they have identified four symbols as shown in Figure 6.4.

SYMBOL	ATTRIBUTES	LOCATION
[1] I	Wants to have a sense of purpose etc.	[Unspecified as yet]
[2] Purpose, more self worth, confidence.	Quite hard to get to.	[In front, out window] Way over, over the roof
[3] Trap / shutter	One, big, steel, a lot of offshoots, 'clunk' when it goes shut, [size] way out of the room, [shutting direction: down].	[Down in front]
[4] Very young	Scared, [wearing] Fred Flintstone pyjamas.	Inside steel shutter.

FIGURE 6.4 Symbols in Steel Shutter

Following are the specialist questions which invite the client to develop their symbolic perceptions by identifing attributes and locating symbols.

Identifying attributes

Apart from the two basic clean questions which identify attributes ('What kind of?' and 'Anything else?'), there are three clean questions which have the specialist functions of identifying a symbol's *size or shape*, the *number* of members in a group or the *age of a personified symbol*.

SIZE OR SHAPE

A characteristic of things is that they occupy an area and their boundary defines a shape. When clients refer to 'a thing' it is therefore reasonable to assume it has a size and shape about which you can enquire:

> **And does** [client's words for 'it'] **have a size or a shape?**

By asking about its size or shape, a symbol's form and existence in space is given prominence. In response to the client describing the symbol of a steel shutter we ask:

C7: It's a big steel shutter. And I can hear the 'clunk' when it goes shut.

T7: **And** a big steel shutter. And you can hear the 'clunk' when it goes shut. **And when** big steel shutter goes shut and you hear 'clunk', *does* big steel shutter *have a size or a shape*?

C8: Way out of the room [both arms outstretched].

In general this question encourages clients to discover information about a symbol's size and shape; to sharpen their representation of it—like adjusting the contrast on a TV screen; and to increase their engagement with the symbol (for instance using their hands to outline it). The question often proves valuable when the client's initial sense of a feeling or image is vague (for an example see T18 of the Jubilee Clip transcript in Chapter 7).

NUMBER

When the client's language or gestures indicate that attributes or symbols exist in multiples, you simply use their description to direct their attention to the group as a whole. The 'Anything else?' and 'What kind of?' questions will identify the group's distinguishing characteristics, and the 'Where?' and 'Whereabouts?' questions will elicit an address. The specialist question for directing the client's attention to the specific number in the group is:

And how many [name for group] **could there be?**

When the steel-shutter client says "A whole lot of traps," both the word 'lot' and the plural of 'trap' presuppose multiple traps:

C5: A whole lot of traps [right hand motions down, in front].

T5: **And when** a whole lot of traps *how many* traps *could there be*?

C6: One big one with a lot of offshoots.

The client responds with both a specific number "one" and a nonspecific quantity "a lot of." Whatever the client responds can be used to further develop the attributes of the group.

AGE OF A PERSONIFIED SYMBOL

When a client indicates the presence of a symbolic perceiver in the form of a younger version of themselves, it is appropriate to ask:

And how old could [name for symbolic perceiver] **be?**

And what could [name for symbolic perceiver] **be wearing?**

These questions are designed to develop the younger perceiver's body into a form which can then do things like run away, cry or have its needs met. Before these questions are asked the client should have clearly indicated the shift to a younger perceiver. They do this by using a personal pronoun or a proper name and the corresponding nonverbals. As always, you must refer to the younger perceiver by whatever name the client uses. This could be "he/she" or "little Johnny" or, as in the following:

C10:   Inside [shrinks down in chair, looks up and whispers]. And I'm scared.

T10:   **And** you're scared. **And when** scared, *how old could* scared *be*?

C11:   Very young.

T11:   **And** very young. **And when** very young is scared, *what could* very young *be wearing*?

C12:   I don't know [long pause]. My Fred Flintstone pyjamas.

Note that we did not ask 'How old could *you* be?' because that might have referenced the adult client and distracted them from their current perception. Instead we first used the name "scared" and then "very young" to direct attention to the perceiver. Once the form of the symbolic 'child within' emerges, you continue to develop its surroundings and its relationships, just as you would with any other symbol.

Locating symbols

The 'Where?' and 'Whereabouts?' questions will identify the address of a symbol, but they will not necessarily determine its *distance,* its *direction,* or whether it is *inside or outside* of a metaphorical container. There are three specialist developing questions which pinpoint these additional spatial characteristics.

DISTANCE

Whenever a client indicates that a symbol has a location in perceptual space, it must be at a distance from the perceiver (and from other symbols) and therefore you can ask:

And how far {is} [symbol's address]?

Directing the client's attention to the characteristic of distance solidifies the symbol's place in perceptual space. The client's response may not be in precise units of metres or miles; just as likely they will say "some distance," "it's quite close," "about that far [hands indicating the distance]," or:

C2:   Over there [gestures with right hand in front and up high].

T2:   **And** over there. And ***how far*** over there [gestures to same place]?

C3:   [Looking out of window.] Way over, over the roof.

DIRECTION

If a symbol moves, it must move in a direction relative to the perceiver, other symbols and its surroundings. The client can be invited to attend to this characteristic by asking:

And in which direction is/does [symbol's movement]?

In the transcript the client refers to a steel shutter shutting. This presupposes it must have an open position, a shut position and a movement between open and shut. Asking for the direction of the movement requires the client to consider all three. In this case, the client continues to answer nonverbally by motioning with their right hand:

C8:   Way out of the room [both arms outstretched].

T8:   **And** way out of the room. **And when** big steel shutter shuts 'clunk', ***in which direction does*** big steel shutter shut?

C9:   [Puts right hand in front above head and motions down.]

INSIDE OR OUTSIDE

One of the most common ways of conceiving of something is to regard it as being a container: the body contains feelings, the mind holds ideas, the heart is a receptacle for love, a house contains living space, a bank is a reservoir for money, a country is a territory for citizens, a club contains members, and so on. Container metaphors are one of the principal ways to conceive of 'togetherness', or conversely, 'separateness'.[8] And regarding the body as a container of our mind, thoughts, feelings, emotions and illnesses is so common we are apt to forget it is a metaphor.

By definition all containers have an inside, an outside and a boundary in between. Structurally it makes a big difference whether something is inside, or outside, or is the container itself. Is the wine inside or outside the bottle, is it inside or outside your glass, is it inside or outside your body?

The question that invites the client to identify whether the perceiver or another symbol is located inside or outside a metaphoric container is:

And is [symbol's name] {**on the**} **inside or outside**?

In the transcript the form of the container is not clear, but the boundary, a steel shutter, is. Therefore we ask:

C9:   [Puts right hand in front above head and motions down.]

T9:   **And** steel shutter shuts [replicates hand movement]. **And when** you hear 'clunk', **are** you *inside or outside* big steel shutter?

C10: Inside [shrinks down in chair, looks up and whispers]. And I'm scared.

These seven specialist questions are commonly used to invite the client to develop the form and location of a symbol, but they do not cover every eventuality. You may have to improvise a clean question in response to particular information given by the client. To do this and remain true to their metaphors, be sure the relevant conditions are presupposed *before* you design and ask your clean question.

Concluding Remarks

Whenever a client is conscious of attaching symbolic significance to an aspect of their experience, they form a symbolic perception—a multi-faceted yet unified representation of their knowledge. Like everything else, symbolic perceptions require a medium, a perceptual space, in which to exist.

The purpose of Stage 2 is for the client to become familiar with the form of each of their symbolic perceptions. They do this by identifying the characteristics and location of the component symbols. These must have unique attributes, otherwise how could the client distinguish them and how could they know they know *that?*

When symbols are named, located and the relationships between them become clear, the client establishes an affiliation with the whole perception. As they do, their body responds and reacts to what is happening in their perceptual space. To further embody their perceptions, the client can draw a map depicting each symbol's key features and relative location.

While some symbols are overtly resourceful from the moment they appear, others only reveal their beneficial qualities as they develop a form. Because clients have a special and idiosyncratic relationship with their resource symbols, only they can determine whether or not a symbol is a resource. And it is possible for a client to know a symbol is a resource but have no idea about its function—until more of their Metaphor Landscape emerges.

Developing the components of a symbolic perception is not something that only happens in the beginning of Symbolic Modelling; exactly the same process may be used once the client has progressed to Stages 3, 4 and 5. As the self-modelling unfolds, there is a transition from developing a single symbolic perception to considering multiple perceptions and patterns of relationships—the subject of the next chapter.

7

Stage 3
Modelling Symbolic Patterns

We are not stuff that abides, but patterns that perpetuate themselves.
Norbert Wierner

In Stage 3, the client uses information gathered in Stage 2 as the raw material for noticing relationships across multiple perceptions, and for detecting patterns in those relationships. These manifest as stable configurations, repeating sequences and recurring motifs—over space, across time and among attributes—as depicted in Figure 7.1.

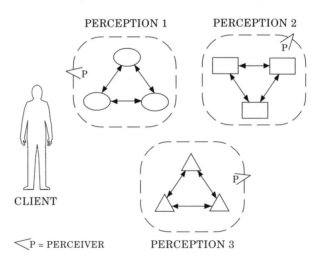

FIGURE 7.1 Schematic of multiple symbolic perceptions

Once identified, patterns can themselves be named and symbolically represented. Thus the modelling process repeats at a higher, more inclusive level of organisation. And because the client is the perceiver of their own perceptions, the *way* they notice patterns will also reflect (be isomorphic with) those same patterns. It is this wheels-within-wheels nature of the self-modelling process that means the system learns from itself and that changes in the Metaphor Landscape are reflected in changes in the client's thoughts, feelings and behaviour.

As Stage 3 unfolds, the logic inherent within the patterns can be explored. The client considers the function of each symbol in relation to the overall Landscape, the significance of the configuration of these symbols and the sequence of symbolic events which repeat time and time again. During this process the beneficial influence of resource symbols, the organisation of patterns that maintain the status quo, and the means by which the system evolves also becomes clear.

A change to a metaphor or symbol may spontaneously occur at any time in Stages 2 or 3. Whenever this happens, the change can be matured in Stage 5. If change does not occur, the modelling process continues in Stage 4, Encouraging Conditions for Transformation.

During Stage 3, your role is to support the client to notice relationships across symbolic perceptions and patterns of those relationships. In this way the client comes to recognise the organisation of their own system. To help you fulfil your role, this chapter provides information about:

> What is a Pattern?
> Latent Resources
> Specialist Relationship Questions
> Client Transcript: Jubilee Clip – Stages 1 to 3

What is a Pattern?

Despite what they say, people do not seek help from a therapist or counsellor because they have *a* problem. People seek help because they realise that, without intervention, the repetitive nature of certain thoughts, feelings and behaviours will continue over and over. This might be repeatedly having something they do not want (a symptom) or wanting something they do not have (an outcome). Either way, they

notice there is a *pattern* in their life which they do not like and do not
know how to change. Patterns are not 'wrong', 'bad' or 'diseased'. In
fact, the very patterns that no longer produce desirable, appropriate or
acceptable results will probably have made a major contribution to
whatever the client has achieved in their life.

But what exactly is a pattern? According to the *Collins Concise
English Dictionary* a pattern is "an arrangement of repeated or corresponding parts." This simple definition specifies three distinguishing
characteristics of all patterns. First, they are made up of 'parts' or
components which constitute the raw material out of which the pattern is fashioned. Second, there is an 'arrangement' such that the parts
are in relation to one another And third, the arrangement 'repeats or
corresponds' so there is some continuity, some non-randomness, some
predictability.

The dictionary definition, however, does not mention three other
fundamental requirements for a pattern to exist. Fourth, there has to
be *someone* to notice the pattern's existence—there has to be a perceiver.
Fifth, this someone must process the sensory input in a certain way,
one that requires the identification of similarities and differences
through comparative and contrastive analysis. And sixth, just as a
painter requires a canvas on which to paint, the process of perceiving a
pattern requires a medium (such as time, space or form) over which the
regularity can manifest.

Patterns exist because a perceiver notices a set of similar characteristics in contrast to other characteristics. The similarities which
constitute the pattern 'stand out' from the multitude of differences; the
signal is detectable from the noise. The pattern is not *in* the components, it
is *of* the components. It is what *connects* (links, unites) the components
by virtue of a noticed regularity. Magic Eye pictures are a good example. Looked at one way they are just a mass of random dots. Looked at
another, a figure emerges. The dots do not contain the figure. The
figure exists because of the *relationship* between the dots and the
perception of the observer. The same principle applies whether the
pattern is 'external' in the physical world or 'internal' in an imaginary
world. Beauty is said to be in the eye of the beholder. More generally
and less poetically, it can be said that patterns emerge from the interaction between the perceptual system of the perceiver and the attributes
of what is perceived.

Pattern detecting

In Symbolic Modelling there are *two* perceivers of pattern: the client, who detects symbolically significant patterns across their perceptions; and the facilitator, who notices patterns in the client's verbal and non-verbal expressions (see Chapter 2, Figure 2.1).

Information gathered early in the clean questioning process produces a symbolic 'sample' of the client's experience. As more information materialises, the sample size increases and patterns begin to emerge. Detecting patterns is an embodied experience that does not necessarily involve the intellect—the client may know that some symbols are related but not necessarily how or why.[1] Some of the ways clients detect patterns are when they become aware of:

Connections and coincidences	This is just like ...
Familiarity with what is happening	Oh no, not this again.
A sense of wholeness	So this is how it all fits together.
A repeating sequence	I'm going around in circles again.
The inevitability of their thinking	I can't conceive of anything else.
The unchanging nature of the past	Old dogs can't learn new tricks.
Isomorphism	I can think of dozens of examples of this in different areas of my life.
New ways of perceiving	I *know* all this, but I've never seen it this way before.

When clients first come face-to-face with the dominant patterns of their Metaphor Landscape, they may tell you explicitly: "This sums up my whole life" or "Now it all makes sense." Or they may be incredulous: "I don't believe this but ..." or "No, it can't be" or "This is wierd." Or they may be so engaged in contemplating their patterns that for long periods of time they say absolutely nothing at all. They may be fascinated by the intricacy and accuracy of their Landscape, or stunned by the apparent impossibility of resolving a double bind, or in awe of the beauty of a resource symbol. Meta-commenting as above and long contemplative pauses are frequently precursors of significant change.

Whether clients detect their patterns by contemplating, by examining their Metaphor Maps or by physicalising their imaginative metaphors, their system will be learning from itself and establishing conditions by which it can reconfigure and evolve.

Types of symbolic patterns

When clients model the relationships between and across their symbolic perceptions, patterns emerge. These patterns are made manifest as repeating relationships of *space, time, form, perceiver* and through *the emergence of inherent logic.*

PATTERNS OF SPACE

A pattern can emerge from the *spatial configuration* of symbols across perceptions. This can be a pattern of external shapes, of internal arrangements or of relative location. Spatial patterns can be dynamic (move in a consistent manner) or static (remain in the same place). On a seashore the *movement* of water in waves is dynamic, while the *shape* of the waves remains static.

Spatial patterns also derive from the relationships between perceptual spaces: the immediate physical environment, what is happening on the surface and inside the body, the imaginative space operating in the here and now, an imaginative environment happening somewhere and somewhen else. The client in Chapter 4 with the fear of heights is an example of how the shape and location of a symbol linked three perceptual contexts: the fire extinguisher in the physical environment, the shadowy figure she imagined during the session, and the memory of the apparition of her deceased father who visited her childhood bedroom.

PATTERNS OF TIME

In Chapter 3 we defined an ordered series of related symbolic events as a *sequence.* We described how the four basic moving time questions can help the client navigate backwards and forwards through events so that they discover temporal patterns. This proves useful because, despite experiencing the same set of symptoms for many years, most clients are unfamiliar with precisely how their symptoms start, progress and conclude—and how they repeat.

Just because a sequence is ordered does not mean that it has a linear structure with a definite beginning, middle and end. Other common forms of temporal patterns are: cyclical sequences which repeat over and over with no obvious start or finish, such as the seasons or the movement of the sun and moon through the sky; threshold sequences which progress to a distinct 'break point,' such as boiling, melting or volcanic eruptions; dialectical sequences that go through the stages of 'thesis, antithesis and synthesis', such as the development of ideas, sexual reproduction or the merging of competing corporations. These patterns of time are diagrammed in Figure 7.2.

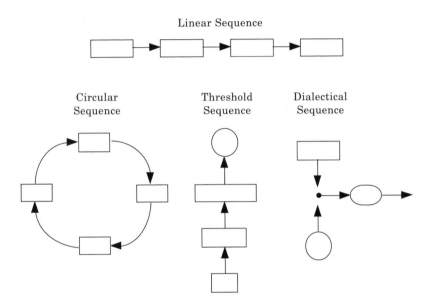

FIGURE 7.2 Four common sequential patterns

PATTERNS OF FORM

A *motif* is a symbolic feature that repeats. It comes from the Latin for 'motive'—that which moves or induces a person to act in a certain way. Thus a motif in a Metaphor Landscape is a recurring and distinctive feature which motivates the perceiver. When clients connect with a dominant motif they are moved—often to awe, sometimes to laughter, sometimes to tears.

Clients notice motifs when they either see, hear, or feel a particular form repeat in a number of their perceptions. This may be a recurring:

• Attribute

    Colour, number, shape

• Function

    Transporter of water: gully, gutter, river

- Consequence
  > Being inside something and not being able to get out:
  > trapped in a cave, lost in a fog, held in an oven

- Word or phrase
  > The multiple use of 'very' in the Castle Door transcript

- Word play
  > In synonyms, homonyms, etymologies, ambiguities, puns,
  > side comments and non sequiturs

- Gesture or movement
  > The hand patting example in Chapter 4 and the
  > 'figure eight' (∞) finger movement in Chapter 5.

For some clients a motif may be so pervasive and enduring that no imaginative symbolic representation is complete without it. Even *after* their Metaphor Landscape has transformed, something of the motif may well carry over to the new Landscape. For example, over a number of sessions a fearful client used numerous metaphors of "being on the edge of Lover's Leap," "having to leap into the unknown" and "dark thoughts leap to mind." At his last session, when his fear had transformed, he said his life was progressing in "leaps and bounds."

PERCEIVER PATTERNS

Patterns also result from regularities in *how* the perceiver perceives, *where* perceptions are perceived from, and *when* these shift. For example, every time a client needed to solve a problem he adopted a "bird's eye view" to watch a miniature version of himself acting out a scene from a play in which "tiny me" found a way of resolving a difficulty. Once his miniature self had successfully enacted the solution his "observing me" felt safe enough to try out the solution in real life. This strategy worked well for him until, no matter how hard he tried, "tiny me" could not solve one type of problem. Whenever the client thought about the problem he found himself "lost in a fog of not knowing," became depressed and withdrew from the world. When he discovered this pattern he realised three things: he was unlikely to see "tiny me" solving this particular type of problem from "here"; he needed to explore this problem from different positions (including from "tiny me's viewpoint"); and he could continue to participate in life while waiting to find a solution.

THE EMERGENCE OF INHERENT LOGIC

The primary focus of Stage 3 is for the client to discover relationships between, and patterns across, perceptions. Although we have described patterns of space, time, form and perceiver separately, they interrelate and operate as a whole. Through self-modelling, clients build an embodied sense of the rules and logic which organise their metaphors. As they do they discover:

- How each symbol's function relates to the overall Landscape

- How the configuration of symbols and relationships encode symbolic significance

- How sequences of unwanted behaviour and symptoms repeat

- How motifs point to an underlying pattern of patterns

- How conflict, dilemma, impasse or paradox maintain the status quo

- How resource symbols can beneficially influence the Landscape

- How the intention of symbols can be fulfilled

- How the system can evolve.

The rules by which things happen in the world of symbol may not conform to the laws of science but the logic of these rules will seem just as immutable to the client. And because symbolic logic differs from physical (cause-effect) and conceptual (propositional) logic, it allows the client to 'step outside' their perception of the physical and conceptual constraints which limit them.

After a pattern has been detected

When a client detects a significant pattern, a number of things can happen:

- They realise that their patterns are part of a higher, more significant pattern—a pattern of organisation—or that an unresolvable binding pattern is operating. In these cases the client is signalling the need to progress to Stage 4.

- They discover that a sequence can be reordered, a configuration reorganised, a motif can have an alternate function, or that a resource can be applied in another context. In these cases, changes can be implemented and matured using Stage 5 processes.

In other words, either there is more for the client to model, or their Landscape has started changing, and the effects of these changes can be evolved.

Latent Resources

A *latent* resource is a symbol or attribute of a symbol waiting to become an overt resource. A latent resource is one that does not reveal its beneficial function until another symbol or context manifests which requires it. Since it is impossible to predict the form or organisation of a client's Metaphor Landscape in advance, *all symbols are potential resources*. Latent resources become apparent in Stage 3:

> Through exploring existing relationships and patterns
> Through modelling inherent logic
> When new symbols or contexts appear.

These are presented individually and followed by an example transcript where a latent resource becomes overt and initiates a change.

Through exploring existing relationships and patterns

A symbol 'X' is a resource *in relation to* another symbol 'Y' if:

X can do something to benefit Y	A dolphin finds a mermaid's lost ring.
X and Y can do something together they cannot do alone	A 'he' and 'she' lion produce a cub.
The presence of X allows Y to do something	Heat from a fire releases feet glued to the floor so they can run.

Just modelling how symbols relate can induce latent resources to manifest, to reveal their true nature, to become overt resources. For example, one client had a sailboat metaphor for how he charted his life. Much to his amusement he discovered that his *backside* responded to changes in conditions of the sea and wind, prompting him to make micro adjustments to the tiller to keep himself on course. There were tears of laughter when he exclaimed, "I've often said I must have my brains in my arse but I never realised how accurate that was!" The resource was always there, but it was not until he explored the network of relationships between the water, sailboat, sailor, wind and destination that he discovered the resource was 'behind' him all the time.

Through modelling inherent logic

When modelling the client's information you may notice that latent resources are often suggested, hinted at, alluded to, or implied. Three common ways that clients indicate the existence of resources hidden within the logic of their Metaphor Landscape are *presupposition, complementary attributes* and *ambiguity.*

PRESUPPOSITION

Clients' language contains a wealth of information that is not in the words but is presupposed by sentence construction, implicit meaning or tonality. Presupposition is that which *has to be true* for a sentence to make sense.[2] It can point to latent resources as in the following examples:

CLIENT STATEMENT	PRESUPPOSES
The dog hasn't found its bone yet.	An ongoing activity of 'finding' and an expectation that the bone will be found.
The knife doesn't cut any more.	It did cut at one time.
I don't know what's beyond it.	There is a 'beyond' and that somebody or something else may know.

COMPLEMENTARY ATTRIBUTES

Metaphor Landscapes can be regarded as systems that continue to exist because they have balancing and homeostatic features which often appear as complementary symbols, pairings or processes. For example, a client may have a variety of symbols that push them around and make life chaotic, only to discover that the ground they are standing on is "firm and unyielding—solid as a rock." Generally, symbols that imprison also protect; where there is dark there will be light; what is below will have an above; if all the client's symbols are on their right, something will be on their left. Even those symbols which exert a 'negative' effect on the client will usually be complemented by symbols that have an opposite 'positive' effect: if "its been trying to strangle me forever," then something equally strong must have been preventing it from carrying out its intention of strangling.

AMBIGUITY

Homonyms, synonyms, puns and other plays on meaning make use of phonological and pictorial ambiguity and offer all sorts of possibilities for discovering latent resources. When a client notices a word has multiple meanings this can 'loosen' or 'expand' their perception, especially if humour is involved. For example, one of our clients symbolised his problem as an inability to climb a muddy river bank. During the exploration of the metaphor he realised that 'bank' can also mean 'certainty' or 'reliability'. This new-found understanding 'invested' him with the confidence he needed to climb the 'deposits' of mud so that he could 'save' himself.

When new symbols or contexts appear

The appearance of each new symbol or context creates an opportunity for *existing* symbols to fulfil their function or purpose. The classic example is a client who suffered childhood abuse resulting in symptoms of a knot in the stomach. Later, when a symbolic perpetrator appears, the knot comes out of the stomach, ties the perpetrator's hands and brings relief to the client. Once the perpetrator appeared, the knot became a resource because it could discharge its tying role in a new way—outside the body of the client.[3]

Within the Metaphor Landscape unresourceful symbols in one location or time can become powerful resources in another location or time. A horrible green slime from sessions ago might act as a fertiliser and rejuvenator for dry and barren ground which has just appeared in the Landscape.

When you are working with a client over a number of sessions we recommend that you, and they, keep a symbol inventory.

Example transcript: Still Circles of Light

Discovering and developing a latent resource often triggers a spontaneous change in another symbol, which can result in a change to a relationship, sequence, configuration, point of perception or means of perceiving. The client may receive comfort or hope from their discovery, they may take a more balanced view of their situation or themselves, or they may suddenly realise a new possibility where none existed before. The following example illustrates how developing a symptom in metaphor can reveal a resource symbol which can change the original symptom. A participant (C) on a training course for business people is standing around having just finished an activity called *Circles of Excellence*,[4] which "didn't work." James walks up to her and says:

J: How did it go?

C: It didn't work because the circles won't stand still.

J: **And** the circles won't stand still. **And when those** circles won't stand still, **what kind of** circles **are** circles that won't stand still?

C: Well, the light keeps moving [gestures high up with right hand].

J: [Continues looking to where gesture pointed to.] **And when** light keeps moving, **what kind of** light is **that** light [repeats gesture]?

C: [Talking increasingly fast.] It shines down and I can't catch up with it. Every time I attempt to step into the light it's not there—it's moved. I'm trying to catch up with it and—and I want to stand in peace and I can't.

J: **And** you can't stand in peace and you want to [pause]. **And when** you want to stand in peace, **what kind of** stand in peace **is that**?

C: I relax.

J: **And** you relax. **And what kind of** relax **is that** relax, **when** you stand in peace?

C: Deep.

J: **And** deep. **So when** you stand in peace, **and** relax, **and** deep, **then what happens**?

C: I stop.

J: **And** you stop. **So when** you stand in peace **and** relax, **and** deep, **and** you stop, **then what happens**?

C: The light shines on me [long pause]. It's not that I couldn't step into the light, it's that the light couldn't catch up with me!

J: **And** the light couldn't catch up with you. **And now** the light shines on you, **and** you relax, **and** a deep relax, **and** you stand in peace, **and** the light shines on you, **and then what happens**?

C: [Shakes head, eyes fill with tears, looks down.] It's amazing. I'm standing on a stage and a spot light is shining on me and I'm perfectly still—and I'm not saying anything—and there are people [gestures towards 'audience'] who have come to see me.

      [Long pause.]

J: **And take all the time you need to get to know what it is like now that** you're standing on a stage, **and** a light is shining on you, **and** you're perfectly still, **and** not saying anything, **and** people [gestures to same place] have come to see you, **and take all the time you need** [pause].

In the pause James walked away. For the remaining two days of the workshop the participant kept marvelling that it was years since she had felt so centred and relaxed.

There are a number of things to note about this transcript. First, it was conducted with conversational voice qualities outside of a therapy environment. Second, the situation was initially perceived as one of failure because "the light keeps moving." Third, the problem light became a resource when she discovered that by trying to "step into the light" she was preventing it catching up with her. Fourth, when *she* stopped moving, the light could perform its function as a resource. Fifth, only two clean questions were used.

Uncovering and developing a latent resource symbol may not produce an immediate spontaneous change. If it does not, it only means there is more for the client to discover. Be patient and continue facilitating the client to:

Determine the effects of having developed the resource	And then what happens?
Identify the source of resource [X]	And where could [X] come from?
Model the sequence used to (re)create the resource	As described later in this chapter.
Explore the resource's relationship to other symbols	See Specialist Questions in the following section.
Introduce the resource to another symbol or situation	See Chapter 8, Approach F.

Latent resources may be lurking around every corner, be staring the client in the face, or waiting patiently to be recognised and acknowledged. Even symbols which appear to have little to commend them may turn out to have been latent resources all the while—it is just that their value was hidden, embedded or implicit.

Developing a nose for potential latent resources is like a pig learning to snuffle out truffles—the end result is a prize of great value and well worth the effort.

Specialist Relationship Questions

Specialist questions are sometimes needed in Stage 1 to effect entry into the symbolic domain, in Stage 2 to develop the form of individual perceptions, and in Stage 3 to *identify relationships* between and across events, symbols and contexts. There are also specialist questions that identify and enact *intentional relationships*.

IDENTIFYING RELATIONSHIPS

Since these questions are about identifying the relational nature of form, time and space they will involve two symbols:

GENERAL	**And what's the relationship between** [X] **and** [Y]?
FORM	**And is** [X] **the same or different as/to** [Y]?
TIME	**And when** [event X] **what happens to** [Y]?[5]
SPACE	**And what's between** [X] **and** [Y]?

Relational questions can best be understood within the context in which they are asked, so their function will be explained as part of the annotation to the transcript which follows this section (see T15, T27, T40), and over the next two chapters.

INTENTIONAL RELATIONSHIPS

Intention in Symbolic Modelling simply means that a symbol has volition—a purpose, desire, choice or causal role. Intention is inherently relational. It is what links the intender to the intended. Clients indicate a symbol's intention by words such as: want, need, choose, have to, would like to, try to; must/mustn't, should/shouldn't; or by verbs of action—as someone or something must intend for the action to occur. There are a number of specialist questions for:

First, *identifying* intentional relationships
> **And what would** [X] **like to have happen/to do**?[6]
> **And would** [Y] **like** [intention of X]?

And then, *enacting* intentional relationships
> **And what needs to happen for** [X] **to** [intention of X]?
> **And can** [X] [intention of X]?

Examples of intentional relationship questions appear in the following transcript (see T22, T23, T30, T42). They can also play a large part in identifying binds and double binds, and in creating the conditions necessary to resolve them.

Client Transcript: Jubilee Clip – Stages 1 to 3

The following transcript is divided into segments to illustrate a variety of symbolic patterns and specialist relationship questions. After each segment we describe the client's emerging patterns and how these informed our questions. The first segment is an example of asking clean questions of a memory that was still symbolic for the client 30 years after the event. When a client models a memory, it is the organisation of their perceptions and how the memory influences them today that is important—not the memory's truth or accuracy.

The transcript begins 30 minutes into the first session. The client, a manager in his forties, had already used "vulnerable" three times when he responded to, "And what would you like to have happen?" with:

C1:   Total confidence in my own abilities. There is a colleague who has incredible self-belief. He believes he is going to succeed no matter what obstacles are put in his way. I became a senior manager by accident and now I feel vulnerable [touches chest with left hand]. It's like I'm waiting to be exposed and then people will say 'We're proved right'. I'm thinking, how can I disguise my weakness?

T1:   **And** you'd like total confidence in your own abilities and now you feel vulnerable. **And when** you feel vulnerable, **how do you know** you feel vulnerable?

C2:   Failure comes to mind. I failed the 11-plus exam.[7] I realised for the first time I wasn't invincible. I felt different about me.

T2:   **And** you realised for the first time you weren't invincible **and** you felt different about you. **And when** you felt different about you, **what kind of** felt different **is that**?

C3:   I see me as a young boy looking up at mother. She has a look of disappointment on her face. She's just read the letter saying I failed the 11-plus.

T3:   **And** she's just read the letter saying you failed the 11-plus. **And when** she has a look of disappointment on her face, **what kind of** look **is that** look?

C4:   Expressionless, drawn, eyes looking down, jaw set, a serious look of sadness. Almost a look of resignation.

T4: **And** when mother's read a letter saying you failed **and** mother has almost a look of resignation, **then what happens**?

C5: For the first time mother distances herself.

T5: **And** for the first time mother distances herself. **And as** mother distances herself, **then what happens**?

C6: He feels puzzled as it's never happened before. He knows something wrong has happened. Something has changed in the bond.

T6: **And what kind of** change **could that** change **be when** something has changed in the bond with mother?

C7: The child feels it's around love—it's not as strong.

T7: **And** it's around love **and** it's not as strong. **And when** love is not as strong, **then what happens**?

C8: A quietness. Mother goes about her housework but doesn't recognise the child in the same way.

T8: **And** a quietness, **and** mother doesn't recognise the child in the same way **after** she has read a letter. **And what happens just before** mother's read a letter?

C9: He can sense the affection between them. There is an air of expectancy, of success. He's happy.

T9: **And when** he can sense the affection between them, **and** an air of expectancy, **and** he's happy, **then what happens**?

C10: She completely read the letter. In fact I remember the moment—she completed reading the letter twice.

T10: **And** she completed reading the letter twice. **And she** completed reading the letter twice. **And what kind of** moment **is that** moment **when** she completed reading the letter twice?

C11: Not a pleasant moment. He doesn't want to repeat it.

T11: **And** he doesn't want to repeat it. **And when** he doesn't want to repeat it, **then what happens**?

C12: He feels that something is wrong with himself.

T12: **And when** he feels something is wrong with himself, **what kind of** feels something is wrong **could that be**?

C13: A bad feeling. He's hurt somebody, caused pain.

T13: **And** he's hurt somebody, caused pain. **And** a bad feeling. **And where does** he feel **that** bad feeling?

C14: Here [touches chest with left hand].

T14: **And whereabouts** here?

C15:   In the chest. In the upper chest.

T15:   **And** in the upper chest. **And what's the relationship between** a
       bad feeling in upper chest **and** vulnerability?

C16:   It's the same as an adult feeling of vulnerability.

The beginning of the transcript is an example of how to facilitate a
client to identify a temporal sequence. The combination of basic developing and moving time questions enables him to unpack his initial
answer (C2) to "How do you know you feel vulnerable?" As is common,
the client does not describe his perceptions in a neat linear fashion.
Rather the sequential nature of his pattern emerges out of the clean
questioning process. This sequence can be summarised as:

> The young boy is happy, expecting success in the 11-plus exam (C9).
>
> Until he sees the "look of disappointment" on his mother's face (C3).
>
> And then "For the first time mother distances herself" (C5).
>
> Then he knows "Something has changed in the bond" (C6) and "feels
> that something is wrong with himself" (C12).
>
> After that, mother goes about her housework (C8) and the defining
> moment has passed.

Figure 7.3 formats the client's words to emphasise the sequential
logic of the information. We recommend you read this diagram in two
ways: in the order the information was described by the client, and in
the sequence indicated in the columns 'before', 'during' and 'after'.

The three events 'during' show that "vulnerable" is a far more
complex mixture of emotions, realisations and conclusions than might
at first be obvious. Also note the defining moment: the boy's perception
of himself, his mother, and the bond (relationship) between them all
changed in the few seconds it took for her to react to the letter. The
exquisitely detailed description of a mother's look of disappointment,
"Expressionless, drawn, eyes looking down, jaw set, a serious look of
sadness. Almost a look of resignation" is indicative of the significance
of this moment. In addition, mother reading the letter *twice*, and the
client's perception of *distance* as a symbolic measure of the strength of
a mother's love, are (as you will see) early indicators of the emergence
of symbolic patterns of form and space respectively.

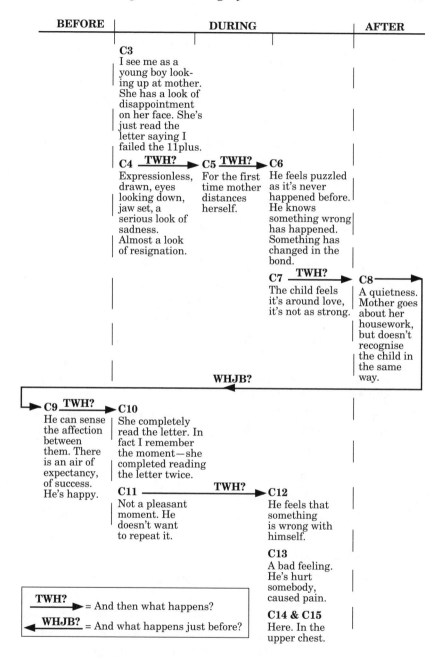

FIGURE 7.3 The organisation of a sequence of events

Because the client's gesture at C14 is the same as at C1, we assume that he has modelled a complete sequence (an operational unit) and is embodying what he is describing. T15 checks this assumption with the specialist question: 'What's the relationship between?'. The client confirms the connection between the young boy's bad feeling and the adult's vulnerability, so we continue to develop the attributes of the feeling:

T16: And it's the same feeling. **And is there anything else about** that feeling **when** it's the same feeling?

C17: Rapid, shallow breathing and a tightness.

T17: **And** rapid, shallow breathing and tightness. **And when** tightness, **what kind of** tightness **could that** tightness **be**?

C18: [Pause.] It's difficult to explain.

Notice how the client's language has changed from mostly conceptual to sensory to it being difficult to explain his experience. We ask the 'Size or shape?' specialist question to encourage "it" into form.

T18: **And when** rapid, shallow breathing and tightness, **and** it's difficult to explain, **does** it **have a size or a shape**?

C19: [Client holds left forefinger with right hand.] It's like a finger is grabbed and pressure is applied—I have a picture—it's of a jubilee clip tightening around a hose.

T19: **And** a jubilee clip tightening around a hose. **So when** jubilee clip is tightening around hose, **where does that** tightening **come from**?

C20: A screwdriver.

T20: **And what kind of** screwdriver **is that** screwdriver?

C21: Flat-bladed with a plastic handle.

T21: **And is there anything else about that** flat-bladed plastic-handled screwdriver **that's** tightening jubilee clip?

C22: The handle is yellow.

The client has developed a new perception, a detailed metaphor for his feelings of vulnerability involving three symbols—a jubilee clip, hose and screwdriver. These symbols are related by: screwdriver tightening jubilee clip, which in turn is tightening around hose. Furthermore a motif, a pattern of form, is beginning to emerge: "*around* love" (C7), "jubilee clip tightening *around* a hose" (C19), and, of course, jubilee clips and hoses are *round*, and a screwdriver tightens by going *round and round.*

At this point we direct two specialist questions to screwdriver:

T22:   **And** handle is yellow. **And when** flat-bladed screwdriver is tightening jubilee clip around hose, **what would** yellow plastic handle **like to do?**

C23:   Undo it.

T23:   **And can** it undo it?

C24:   There's a conflict.

T22 requests the symbol (not the client) to reveal its intention or desire. We ask the question of "yellow plastic handle" rather than screwdriver because, logically it is the movement of the handle that determines whether a screwdriver tightens or untightens. As soon as screwdriver's intention is known, the simplest of questions, "And can it?" enquires whether it is able to enact its intention.[8]

The client discovers that although screwdriver is causing the tightness and feeling of vulnerability and wants to undo jubilee clip, it cannot. This is valuable information because it indicates there are processes operating which maintain the status quo and keep the Metaphor Landscape from changing. When the client reveals "There's a conflict" he is describing a metaphor for the *binding pattern of relationships* between intentions—a higher level metaphor which encompasses both what screwdriver is doing and what it would like to do (which are in conflict). As a new metaphor has been introduced, we use standard developing questions to encourage the nature of the conflict into form:

T24:   **And** there's a conflict. **And when** screwdriver **would like to** undo jubilee clip **and** there's a conflict **what kind of** conflict **could that** conflict **be?**

C25:   There's a fear about undoing the clip. It's an unknown risk.

T25:   **And when** there's a fear about undoing the clip, **and** it's an unknown risk, **what kind of** unknown **could that** unknown **be?**

C26:   Is somebody going to be disappointed at the result?

T26:   **And** is somebody going to be disappointed at the result? **And when** there's a fear about undoing jubilee clip, **where could that** fear **be?**

C27:   In the chest again [touches chest with left hand].

T27:   **And** in the chest again. **And is that the same or different as** vulnerable in the chest?

C28:   No difference. They're the same.

The question "What kind of conflict?" reveals a fear *about* undoing the clip. This implies undoing the clip is not the problem, rather it is the fear associated with the risk of undoing the clip. But the risk is unknown, so how can he assess whether it is a risk worth taking? Furthermore, the client's response at C26 is a question to himself. He wonders "Is somebody going to be disappointed at the result?" As there is always a possibility somebody *might* be disappointed, there will always be a fear about undoing jubilee clip. It is these further 'turns of the screw' which make the conflict unresolvable.

A clear pattern is emerging: the fear of an unknown risk is the same as "vulnerable" which is the same as the 11-year old's response. So we accumulate descriptions to bring the logic inherent in the pattern to the fore, and then we ask, given all this, "What happens next?":

T28: **So** fear and vulnerable are the same. **And** screwdriver is tightening jubilee clip round hose. **And** screwdriver **wants to** undo jubilee clip, **and** there's fear of undoing jubilee clip—is somebody going to be disappointed at the result? **And as** screwdriver is tightening jubilee clip, **and** fear of unknown risk, **and** vulnerable in chest, **and** screwdriver is tightening, and screwdriver **wants to** undo jubilee clip, **what happens next?**

C29: A feeling of helplessness.

T29: **And** a feeling of helplessness. **And when** helplessness, **is there anything else about that** helplessness?

C30: [Shrugs shoulders.] No.

The result of the conflict is expressed by a feeling of helplessness. The way the client says "No" indicates he is helpless to answer the question, thereby manifesting the pattern in the moment and confirming the impossibility of solving this conflict within the current organisation of the metaphor.

We next ask a specialist question to direct his attention to the conditions necessary for the binding pattern to be resolved; in this case, for screwdriver to fulfil its intention to undo jubilee clip:

T30: **And** no. **And** helplessness. **So when** there's a conflict **and** helplessness, **what needs to happen for** screwdriver **to** undo clip?

Notice the question does not sidestep the problem, reframe it or impose a solution; rather it acknowledges the client's situation by asking what needs to happen *when* "there's a conflict and helplessness." The answer is:

C31: A person has to do it [pause]. And that person is me.

T31: **And** a person has to do it and that person is you. **And what kind of** person **is that** person **who** has to do it?

C32: Not afraid. Confident, comfortable with myself. Congruent. Well-balanced. Focused [pause]. In harmony.

T32: **And** not afraid, confident, comfortable with yourself. Congruent. Well-balanced. Focused. In harmony. **And when** in harmony **what kind of** harmony **is that** harmony?

C33: With people, with nature, with myself. With the good and bad things in life.

T33: **And when** harmony with people, with nature, with yourself, **and** with the good and bad things in life, **that's** harmony **like what**?

C34: A truly balanced person. It reminds me of a TV show and the Master from Kung Fu.

T34: **And** a truly balanced person, the Master from Kung Fu. **And what kind of** Master **is that** Master?

C35: He has answers to life. A deep understanding of himself, nature, his place in the world. He can be an example, a guide.

T35: **And** he can be an example **and** a guide. **And** he has answers to life, **and** a deep understanding of himself, **and** nature, **and** his place in the world. **And when** he has a deep understanding of himself, **where could that** deep understanding **come from**?

C36: A large part from himself. And some external. But mostly it comes from within.

T36: **And** some external but mostly from within. **And whereabouts** within **does** deep understanding **come from**?

C37: The head. The brain. And all the senses.

T37: **And when** deep understanding **comes from** the head, the brain and all the senses, **is there anything else about where** deep understanding **comes from**?

C38: It includes emotional things—I picture a heart.

T38: **And what kind of** heart **is that** heart?

C39: A mature heart.

T39: **And** a mature heart. **And is there anything else about the** mature **of that** heart?

C40: It's had lots of experience. It's red. It's a picture of a heart, but it doesn't look like a real one.

By repeatedly asking developing questions the client's attention is continually directed to the *form* of the emerging resource, the "me" who has to undo jubilee clip. The result is a new symbolic perception of a Kung Fu master with a mature heart. The 'Where come from?' questions are used to direct attention to the *source of the resource* — which is usually even more resourceful than the resource itself.

The client now knows that when "me" has these qualities he will be able to undo jubilee clip, even if there is an unknown risk of disappointing somebody. However, the last ten responses have all been in the land of 'what needs to happen' and not, what *is* happening. And why has he not already developed the qualities needed and applied them? Asking the specialist question 'When [event X] what happens to Y' directs his attention to where the answer lies — in the *current* relationship between mature heart and the person who has to undo jubilee clip:

T40: **And when** red mature heart has had lots of experience, **what happens to** a person who has to undo jubilee clip **that's** tightening?

C41: I feel like the pupil. I've not reached the level of maturity required.

T41: **And when** you feel like the pupil and you've not reached the level of maturity required, **is there anything else about** the level of maturity required?

C42: It's not to do with age. It's to do with upbringing and principles and thought processes. I don't think I've had the upbringing [pause]. I've only started to grow over the last few years.

"I feel like the pupil" suggests the client is beginning to recognise that three of the four perceptions identified so far — his recurring thoughts and vulnerable feelings about his work, his memory of being the 11-year old, and the metaphor of jubilee clip tightening — all symbolise the same pattern. Interestingly, the pupil has complementary attributes to that of the Master (a teacher), which constitutes a fourth perception.

You may also notice a spatial pattern. Compare: "I don't think I've had the *up*bringing" and "I've not reached the *level* of maturity required" with a Master who has "a *deep* understanding of himself," a mother's "eyes looking *down*" and "a young boy looking *up* at mother." This clearly indicates an up-down orientation to the Landscape.

The client's last statement C42 announces a new metaphor, "grow" — a naturally-changing process (with an implied up-down orientation) that may resolve his bind — so we ask a specialist question for him to identify the conditions under which he *can* grow to "the level of maturity required":

T42:   **And** you don't think you've had the upbringing **and** you've only started to grow over the last few years. **And what needs to happen** to grow **to** the level of maturity required?

C43:   I wonder if I can ever achieve it. There's an element of doubt. I'm looking for an external experience [laughs]. Like an exam!

T43:   **And** you're looking for an external experience to reach the level of maturity required. **And what kind of** exam **could that** exam **be**?

C44:   A very difficult exam.

T44:   **And** a very difficult exam. **And is there anything else about** a very difficult exam?

C45:   I haven't got the background to sit it. I'm inadequate to take the exam.

The client realises he is looking for an external experience so that he can reach the level required to undo jubilee clip, *but* he is in a paradox: although he needs to pass a very difficult exam, he does not have the background to sit it, so can never pass. It is the inherent logic of this paradox that keeps him going round and round (see Figure 7.4).

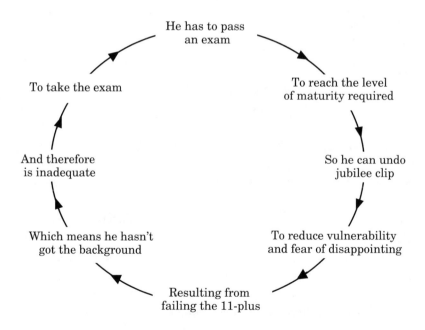

FIGURE 7.4   The organisation of a paradox

We continue by asking the client to self-model the paradoxical nature of the binding pattern:

T45: **And when** you haven't got the background, **and** you're inadequate to take the exam, **what kind of** inadequate **could that** inadequate **be**?

C46: My childhood upbringing. Not being exposed to intellectual stimuli. I didn't grow as fast as I might. Everything seems to come late.

T46: **And** everything seems to come late. **And when** you didn't grow as fast as you might, **is there anything else about** not growing as fast as you might?

C47: I'll have to prove myself more than once.

T47: **And when** you'll have to prove yourself more than once, **how many times** will you have to prove yourself?

C48: Twice, to be his equal.

T48: **And** twice, to be his equal. **And what kind of** twice **could that** twice **be**?

C49: It's like running round a track and I have to overtake him twice.

T49: **And** like running round a track and you have to overtake him twice. **And** running and running. **And** you'll have to prove yourself more than once. **And** you have to overtake him twice. **And as** you're running round **that** track and you have to overtake him twice, **what kind of** him **could** he **be**?

C50: My ideal me.

Not only is the client's background inadequate, he also discovers the bind has an additional constraint: he has to prove himself *twice*. (Remember his mother read the 11-plus failure letter twice.) By C49 the client has modelled enough of his binding pattern to specify the entire paradox in a higher-level 'running *round* a track' metaphor. His predicament is abundantly clear and the logic of the metaphor proposes the question, who is the "him" he has to overtake twice? T49 seeks to find out, and its formulation is worth noting. The question's repetitiveness honours the twice-ness and the running-roundness of the metaphor, further encouraging him to embody the whole binding pattern. His response only deepens the paradox: "him" turns out to be his "ideal me."

So far a number of interrelated metaphors have emerged: a change in the strength of the bond between the boy and his mother; screwdriver tightening jubilee clip while wanting to undo it but fearing disappointing somebody with the result; having to pass an exam without an adequate background to sit it; and having to run round a track to overtake his ideal self twice.

While all of this might seem like doom and gloom, there is great value in the client embodying his patterns. At one level of understanding none of this is new to him. At another, by symbolising his lifetime pattern he has never before seen himself so clearly. And as you will see in the next chapter, Kung Fu master and mature heart have yet to play their part.

FIGURE 7.5 Jubilee Clip's Metaphor Map

Concluding Remarks

Recognising patterns and making sense of them (modelling) is a universal human endeavour. Clients can learn to self-model by becoming familiar with the pattern of their metaphors and symbolic perceptions. Patterns come in all shapes and sizes, and how the client detects, recognises and relates to their patterns will be isomorphic with those patterns.

While clients usually have a few symbols that are overtly resourceful, every one of their symbols might be a latent resource—a resource-in-waiting. The client's most useful resource is often in the least expected place, at the most unexpected time, and in the most unlikely form. If the required resource were obvious, the client would have already applied it. Therefore to facilitate the client to discover and utilise their resource symbols you must go beyond your, and invite them to go beyond their, everyday thoughts about time, space and form.

As a Metaphor Landscape develops, the configuration and sequence of components, relationships and patterns may spontaneously reorganise —in which case you proceed to Stage 5. If they do not, continue facilitating the binding patterns to emerge into the client's awareness. This is a prerequisite for encouraging the conditions for their transformation (Stage 4), to which we turn next.

8

Stage 4
Encouraging Conditions for Transformation

Freedom does not mean escape from the world;
it means transformation of our entire way of being,
our mode of embodiment, within the lived world itself.
Francisco Varela, Evan Thompson and Eleanor Rosch

The stages of the Five-Stage Process are cumulative. In Stage 1 the client starts their journey into metaphor. During Stage 2 they name and locate symbols and identify the relationships within individual symbolic perceptions. In Stage 3 they recognise relationships across multiple perceptions and patterns in those relationships. This chapter describes Stage 4: how to facilitate the client to model the overall organisation of their Metaphor Landscape and how this can change and evolve. We address:

> The Nature of Change
> The Nature of Attending
> Resource Symbols as Change Agents
> Modelling the Organisation of Binds and Double Binds
> Client Transcript: Jubilee Clip – Stage 4
> The Six Approaches

The Nature of Change

Change is a strange beast. It is easy to recognise, but not so easy to define. It requires a perceiver to compare an event 'after' with an event 'before', and can therefore only be detected retrospectively. For change to be noticed it must somehow be embodied so that it can be seen, heard, felt, smelled, tasted or otherwise sensed. During Symbolic Modelling change can be:

SPONTANEOUS when the client notices a change in:

The *Metaphor Landscape* (with or without knowledge of how it happened).	• Oh, the key's just unlocked the lock. • I don't know what happened, but the door is now open.
Their *point of perception* or *means of perceiving*.	• Hey, how did I get outside the door? • I felt trapped but now I see the door is protecting me.

INITIATED BY:

The *client* suggesting a change could, should or may occur.	• The silver key can unlock the lock. • Maybe I could knock down the door.
The *therapist* asking a symbol for its intention which is then enacted, or introducing a resource symbol to another symbol (see Approaches E and F below).	• And when lock is locked, what would key like to do? • And would key be interested in going to locked lock?

Clients notice a change in their Metaphor Landscape when the attributes or location of a symbol changes. This change in form can embody a change to a relationship between two symbols, a change in the configuration of symbols, a change to a sequence of events, a change to a motif, or a change in the overall pattern of organisation. Thus change can happen at different levels of organisation.

Furthermore, each level has its own 'laws' or logic of change, and a change at one level influences the potential for change at other levels: "the lower sets the possibilities of the higher; the higher sets the probabilities of the lower."[1]

Not all changes are of the same magnitude or significance. Some happen on many levels simultaneously while others require time for the effects to cascade, percolate and ripple through the Landscape. Significant change is often marked by the crossing of a threshold—a space, time or form boundary.

There are two fundamentally different types of change: translation which occurs *within* a level, and transformation which takes place *between* levels.

Translation

When a symbol or a relationship between symbols changes without significant alteration in a pattern organising the Metaphor Landscape, a *translation*, rather than a transformation, will have occurred. A good example is someone who cycles through periods of being 'down in the dumps' followed by periods of 'feeling on top of the world'. If they come to you depressed and leave feeling better, at best this will be a translation—*unless* the down-up-down-up *pattern* changes.

Ken Wilber points out that it is a common mistake to interpret bigness, broadness or a large number of translations as transformation.[2] New and more are not necessarily better. People make huge changes in their lives, only to find they are repeating the same pattern in a new city, with a new partner, in a new job.

Chapter 2 described the effects of translation as rippling horizontally across a Landscape without transforming the nature of the Landscape itself. It is possible, however, for numerous translations to accumulate until they cross a threshold to transformation, like the straw that breaks the camel's back.

For many clients, translatory change is all they want. Why rebuild the house when all that is required is to move the furniture? Other clients want or need to make a more significant shift in their lives— to perceive, to be in, and to relate to the world in a different way. They may have undertaken many translatory changes before noticing that a larger pattern is operating. In these cases a qualitatively different type of change is required—a transformation.

Transformation

When evolution approaches a threshold, the conditions for transformation emerge. Transformations are discontinuities within a continuous process of evolution. They are the surprising and defining moments that 'shift' from one configuration to another, 'break' with the past, 'cross over' a threshold, or make an evolutionary 'leap' to the next more inclusive and more significant level of organisation.

According to Ken Wilber, transformation is characterised by a *re-organisation* such that the new organisation builds upon, preserves and encompasses the fundamental features of its component parts and predecessors—it transcends and includes. A new organisation emerges with additional properties that were neither in any of the parts, nor predictable from the relationships between the parts. Transformation requires 'vertical' change so that:

> whole new worlds of translation disclose themselves. These "new worlds" are not physically located someplace else; they exist simply as a *deeper perception* (or deeper registration) of the available stimuli in *this world* ... Translation shuffles parts; transformation produces wholes."[3]

Transformation is a change to a higher, more significant level of organisation. Higher and more significant "because more of the [client's] universe is reflected or embraced in that particular wholeness."[4]

Transformation is characterised by indeterminacy, unpredictability and novelty. You cannot know when, where, how or what form a transformation will take, until *after* it has occurred. Transformations involve an element of surprise.

Given that transformations encompass the above characteristics, how is it possible to make them happen during psychotherapy?

The answer is, it isn't. When appropriate conditions emerge, or as Buddhists say, 'arise', transformation occurs spontaneously. All you and your client can do is to work with what happens in such a way as to *encourage* conditions for transformation. This would be a random process were it not for the developmental, progressive nature of Nature, whose directionality is often represented by an arrow—an arrow that does not travel in a straight line, but one that spirals and meanders as it progresses.[5]

How do conditions for transformation materialise in a Metaphor Landscape?

When the Landscape gets complex enough, then a simpler, more inclusive pattern becomes apparent; when symbols, relationships and patterns are separated and distinguished enough, they become available for a new synthesis; when certain structures, processes or motifs are recognised as inherent, a new responsiveness and flexibility becomes possible; when symbols realise they will not be forced to change, they become prepared to relate in new ways; when symbols and patterns are perceived within larger contexts and purposes, then perception itself becomes ready to change.

The Nature of Attending

What is the role of the client in the transformation of the Metaphor Landscape? The Landscape is not a disembodied, stand-alone entity. Its existence, meaning and significance depend on the client, its creator. Changes in the client's attention and ways of perceiving are in "relational exchange" to changes in the Metaphor Landscape, and vice versa. Neither can evolve alone; they must "coevolve."[6] Therefore personal change is intimately linked to changes in the nature of attending. And surprisingly there are only a few ways in which the process of attending can change. It can shift from what is represented in perception to what is not, from narrow to broad (or vice versa), from single to multiples (or vice versa), from a lower level to a higher level (or vice versa), and from part to whole (or vice versa). These shifts in attention are massively overlapping, interdependent and relative; they can occur spontaneously, or may be prompted by your clean questions.

By developing individual symbolic perceptions, Stage 2 focuses on what is represented and invites the client to narrow their attention to one fundamental part at a time. Stage 3 is more about noticing what is not represented and the patterns across perceptions. This requires a broader, longer, higher, more holistic way of attending. Stage 4 goes further. It is less about single shifts and more about strategic and organisational shifts in attention.

Directing attention strategically and organisationally

In Symbolic Modelling your active involvement is confined to using Clean Language to orientate the client's attention. This chapter is about using clean questions strategically; that is, in combination and with the aim of encouraging conditions for change and transformation. We have identified six approaches, or practices, which do just this:

Concentrating Attention
Attending to Wholes
Broadening Attention
Lengthening Attention
Identifying Necessary Conditions
Introducing Resource Symbols

These approaches are not neatly packaged, self-contained techniques or procedures. Instead, they are general fuzzy principles which respect the indeterminate nature of change. They require you to honour each client's unique organisation, inherent logic and characteristic ways of perceiving. They offer the client an opportunity to transcend and include their existing organisation by cooperating with the idiosyncratic processes and intrinsic directionality of their unfolding evolution.

The Six Approaches were derived from observation and analysis of what happens when clients undergo change, release a binding pattern, recode their way of being, connect with a higher purpose, make new meaning of their lives, experience a defining moment, or in a thousand other ways perceive themselves and their world in a different way.

The Six Approaches are summarised below and Stage 4 of the Jubilee Clip transcript is used to illustrate how they operate in practice. Each approach is discussed in detail later in the chapter.

A. CONCENTRATING ATTENTION

By repeatedly directing the client's attention to a *single* aspect of their Metaphor Landscape you encourage them to concentrate on one form, one space, one time. This invites them to notice additional parts, additional attributes, additional functions and additional relationships—each with the potential for initiating change.

B. ATTENDING TO WHOLES

By repeatedly directing the client's attention to their Metaphor Landscape's *multiple* forms, places and times you encourage them to accumulate more and more perceptions into one simultaneous mindbody space. This invites them to identify patterns of relationships, patterns of patterns and patterns of organisation. As a result they recognise higher and higher levels of communion, of cooperation, of interdependency, of connection to something larger—the next inclusive whole.

C. BROADENING ATTENTION

By repeatedly directing the client's attention to the *edge*, to *outside* and *beyond* the boundaries of their Metaphor Landscape you encourage them to notice what is external, to discover new forms and relationships over a larger area, to widen contexts and to extend ranges—all in the service of a broader perspective.

D. LENGTHENING ATTENTION

By repeatedly directing the client's attention to either the origin or consequences of the symbolic event currently in their awareness, you encourage them to sequentially shift the locus of the perceptual present to *before* 'the beginning' or *after* 'the end'. This invites them to make historical connections, identify patterns which repeat over time, encounter new resources or (re)discover a sense of their purpose—any of which can lead to a reorganisation of existing perceptions.

E. IDENTIFYING NECESSARY CONDITIONS

By repeatedly inviting the client to discover what needs to happen for a change to take place in their Metaphor Landscape, you encourage them to find the *logical associations* between the first thing that needs to happen and all the subsequent things that need to happen for a desired change to occur. In this way a symbol's function can be enacted or its intention satisfied, and this inevitably influences other parts of the Landscape.

F. INTRODUCING RESOURCE SYMBOLS

By inviting a resource symbol to connect and form (or reform) a rela-tionship with another symbol—*introducing* one symbol to another—you offer the symbols an opportunity to commune; to transfer properties and information; for one to catalyse or activate the other; or for them to integrate into a new whole. Often this will initiate a reorganisation of the whole Landscape.

In summary, directing attention strategically is first and foremost a way of working with and within the inherent logic of your client's patterns. Secondly, it invites them to discover new information, make new connections, take a different perspective and have insights. And thirdly it is a way of encouraging conditions for transformation to arise.

Next we examine resource symbols and the role they play in the transformation of the Metaphor Landscape. Following this we turn our attention to the binds and double binds which prevent clients' Land-scapes from transforming spontaneously.

Resource Symbols as Change Agents

In Chapter 6 we explained how resources within a Metaphor Landscape exist in a variety of guises: overt, latent and to-be-converted.

Overt resources are symbols which the client values, even if their exact function has yet to be determined. They can appear at any time: at Stage 1 as a conceptual word or nonverbally; in Stage 2 as a symbol or attribute of a symbol; during Stage 3 as a relationship or pattern; and as a result of using the Six Approaches in Stage 4.

Latent resources are symbols which do not reveal their potential until a corresponding symbol or context appears which requires that resource (during Stages 3, 4 or 5).

To-be-converted resources are symbols that:

- Are overt resources that cannot fulfil their intention. They are in a binding pattern and need to be released from their current function or place in the Metaphor Landscape.

- Need to change before their resourcefulness becomes apparent or available. The blackest pit, the most frightening monster, the most painful trap are usually the last symbols the client expects to become a resource or to have a valuable purpose—until they have transformed.

Generally this releasing, converting or transforming takes place during Stages 4 or 5.

Discovering resources in Stage 4

Five of the six strategic approaches encourage the client to discover, or rediscover, additional resources by repeatedly directing their attention to:

Lower levels	A. Concentrating Attention
Higher levels	B. Attending to Wholes
Different spaces	C. Broadening Attention
Different times	D. Lengthening Attention
Logical connections	E. Identifying Necessary Conditions

Approach F, Introducing Resource Symbols, uses one resource to release or convert a less-than-resourceful symbol.

Applying resources

Resource symbols are no different from any other symbol except that they have the ability, power or function to initiate or create a positive change. They do this by interacting with other symbols in the Metaphor Landscape. This creates an opportunity for symbols to connect and form (or reform) a beneficial relationship, to transfer properties or information, to catalyse and activate each other, or to integrate into a new whole. A resource can fulfil its function in three ways:

- Spontaneously—an interaction just happens
- By the client initiating the interaction
- When the therapist enquires if a resource symbol's intention can be enacted (Approach E), or asks if the resource would like to be introduced to another symbol (Approach F).

Although a resource symbol may be identified in one session, or exist at one time or in one place, all symbols in the Landscape are part of a unified space-time. This means that once a symbol's resourcefulness becomes apparent it has the potential to form a relationship with any other symbol regardless of when or where either was discovered. When a resource's intention is known it can immediately be enacted, or it can wait in the wings to be used later in the process.[7]

Modelling the Organisation of Binds and Double Binds

Every living system has self-preserving processes which maintain organisational coherence and continuity, and which act to conserve the system's identity. That is, the system is able to change at one level in order to maintain itself at another, higher level. However the same processes that keep a system from dissolving or escalating out of safe bounds can also act to inhibit, brake, prevent, constrain, hinder and block development and transformation. We use *bind* as a generic term for any repetitive self-preserving pattern which the client has not been able to change, and which they find inappropriate or unhelpful.[8]

Although binds take many forms, there are four commonly occurring 'prototypical' binds—conflict, dilemma, impasse and paradox—which replicate unwanted symptoms, tie up resources and prevent resolution:

BIND	DEFINITION	EXAMPLE
CONFLICT	A struggle between equal and opposing forces (intentions).	Part of me wants to and part of me doesn't.
DILEMMA	A situation necessitating a choice between two equally (un)desirable alternatives (intentions).	I'm damned if I do and damned if I don't.[9]
IMPASSE	A situation in which (the intention to) progress is stopped by an insuperable difficulty (intention to block).	I keep banging my head against a brick wall.
PARADOX	A self-contradictory statement or statements (which include two contradictory intentions).	My head aches through trying to stop you giving me a headache.[10]

Binds can be expressed conceptually, metaphorically or nonverbally, and they come in all shapes and sizes. When expressed *conceptually* they may be simple one-line descriptions like that of Groucho Marx, "I don't want to belong to any club that will accept me as a member" or convoluted, recursive and multilayered conundrums, as this example from R. D. Laing's *Knots* demonstrates:

> I never got what I wanted.
> I always got what I did not want.
> What I want
>   I shall not get.
>
> *Therefore,* to get it
>   I must not want it
> *since* I get only what I don't want.
>
>   what I want, I can't get
>   what I get, I don't want
>
>   I can't get it
> *because* I want it
>   I get it
> *because* I don't want it.
>
> I want what I can't get
> *because*
>   what I can't get *is* what I want
>
> I don't want what I can get
> *because*
>   what I can get *is* what I don't want
>
> I never get what I want
> I never want what I get.[11]

Stripped of their narrative and drama, these schematised 'knots', as Laing calls them, are mindbendingly fascinating and frighteningly familiar. When clients express their binds in metaphor, however, it is usually much easier for them to see, hear and feel how their binds are operating and thus to model the organising pattern. As you will see, when the Jubilee Clip client says it is like trying to run round a track to overtake his ideal self twice only for the gap to widen the more he grows, it is obvious to him and to us that this is an impossible problem to solve within the current organisation. For students of binding patterns numerous other examples can be found in the transcripts at the back of this book.

A bind can only exist when there are two or more components which have complementary, yet opposing or contradictory *intentions*. It is the inherent balance of forces in a conflict, equality of choices in a dilemma, insurmountable blockage at an impasse, and self-contradictory nature of a paradox, which means binds *cannot* be resolved within their existing logic or organisation. This is why apparent solutions are either temporary (don't last), illusory (the way out just leads back in), or translatory (the form changes but not the pattern).

The inherent logic and organisation of a bind *compels* each component to fulfil its function in the service of maintaining the bind. This means that regardless of whether a symbol is bound, or is part of the binding mechanism, it is unable to fulfil any other function. A jailer restricts the freedom of a prisoner, and in so doing is himself restricted. However, it only takes *one* component to transform (not translate) for the existing organisation of the bind to dissolve, evaporate or extinguish. When this happens, what was bound and what was binding have an opportunity to use their attributes as resources in other ways and in other contexts.

Resolving a *single* bind is relatively easy. The client simply reformulates (reframes) the problem and moves on, or they accept its unsolvable nature and stop fighting, or they randomly decide between alternatives, or they choose a different route altogether, or they ignore the paradox, or a thousand other solutions. Paul Watzlawick uses one of Chaucer's *Canterbury Tales* to illustrate this point. A young knight is presented with a series of choices. Each time he chooses he is faced with yet another dilemma. Eventually he finds himself married to an old hag who, on their wedding night, says he can either accept her as she is and she will always be a faithful wife, or she will turn herself into a beautiful maiden who will never be faithful. The knight, after much thought, *refuses the choice itself*. At that moment the hag transforms into a beautiful maiden who is faithful to him for the rest of his life.[12]

But what if life is not that simple? What if, for some reason or other, *resolving* the bind is unachievable or unacceptable? What if the potential for transformation is itself bound? Then another pattern—*a double bind*—must be operating to preserve a larger organisation.

Gregory Bateson clarified the organisation of double binds. He noted that a secondary bind prohibits escape from the primary bind because it "conflicts with the first at a more abstract level" which if opposed or ignored would "threaten survival."[13] Thus, perfectly good solutions for the primary bind cannot be implemented because they would conflict with, or trigger, another binding pattern. Bateson points out that a common secondary bind involves the client being unable to speak about their predicament for fear of triggering the primary bind (e.g. "It would kill my mother if I told her the truth"). In more complex, and thankfully rare cases, the way out of the double bind may itself be constrained by yet another bind—forming a triple bind. One way or another, the client is bound by their own binds and the more they struggle, the more hopeless and helpless it seems.

How clients transform double binds

Although the organisation of each binding pattern is unique, we have observed a general flow to how double binds transform.

When a client identifies two or more symbols whose relationship is such that their intentions cannot be enacted or fulfilled, they have discovered a primary bind. As they explore the logic of the primary bind:

(a) The primary bind *translates* and repeats the same binding pattern, but in a different form, or

(b) A secondary bind becomes apparent, or

(c) The primary bind spontaneously *transforms*—it transcends its limitations and includes the creativity of the current organisation.

If (a) occurs, the client discovers whether the translation is useful and productive, or whether they are just 'going round the loop' again.

If (b) occurs, the client can identify the components of the secondary binding pattern, and specify its relationship to the primary bind so that the nature of the interlocking patterns which constitute the *double* bind become apparent. They will then be faced with the same three options—to translate, or in the case of a triple bind to continue modelling at an even higher level, or to transform—but at a higher, more significant, more inclusive level of organisation.

If (c) occurs, the client can proceed and discover the unexpected effects of the transformation. (See Figure 8.1)

As a client models the organisation of their double bind they inevitably start to experience and manifest its symptoms. Although they are unlikely to enjoy the experience, it is part of the process because as they embody the bind they shift from talking about it to modelling it happening in the moment. For many clients, truly acknowledging 'this is the way it is' and accepting 'current reality' is the first step on the road to transformation.[14]

Accepting current reality sounds simple, yet clients rarely face the unresolvability of their double bind without a struggle. Instead they experience frustration, angst, grief, anger or depression as they come to terms with and accept the fact that even their most tried and tested technique, their most successful method, their cleverest trick, their most beloved reframe, will *never* resolve this particular conundrum. In fact they often come to realise that these techniques, methods, tricks and reframes are part of the bind.

As clients become aware of their binding patterns they are faced with a stark choice: to be forever constrained to act out of the bind, or to transform it by venturing into that most fearful of places, the unknown. No wonder translation, disguised as transformation, is often a preferred option.

When binding patterns do transform, some clients report how strange the transformed pattern feels at first. Others become amnesic for the old problem. Mostly however it is through feedback that the significance of the change becomes apparent—when they notice themselves automatically responding in new ways to old situations, or their changed behaviour is pointed out by others.

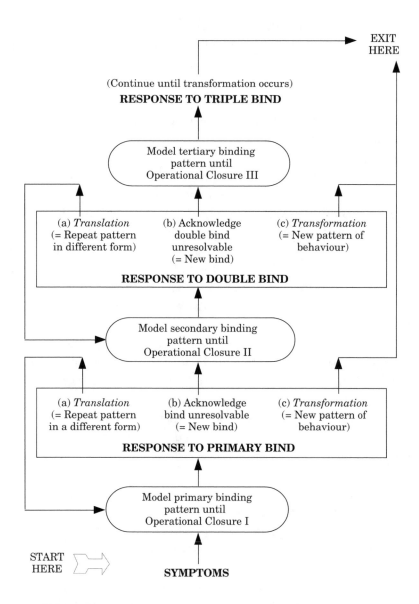

FIGURE 8.1 How clients can model and transform double binds

NOTE: 'Operational Closure' occurs when the pattern of relationships is well
enough specified that an operational unit manifests in awareness (see
p. 195, Approach B, for a fuller explanation).

Facilitating the client to model their double binds

In Symbolic Modelling it is not your job to resolve the client's bind. Rather your function is to facilitate the client to model their metaphors so that the organisation of their binding pattern becomes clearer and clearer to them. As a result, the conditions for transformation arise. The general process for facilitating clients to model and transform their double binds is summarised in Figure 8.2, followed by an example from the Jubilee Clip transcript.

---

1. When the client identifies two or more symbols whose intention or function cannot be enacted or satisfied, facilitate them to model the pattern preventing resolution and then to identify a metaphor for the primary bind.

2. Use the Six Approaches to facilitate the client to explore the primary bind's inherent logic until either:

    • a secondary bind appears (then go to step 3), or
    • it spontaneously changes (then go to step 5).

3. Facilitate the client to self-model the pattern of the secondary bind and its relationship to the primary bind, and identify a metaphor for the double bind.

4. Use the Six Approaches to facilitate the client to explore the inherent logic of the double bind, until either:

    • a tertiary bind appears (in which case continue modelling the whole organisation), or
    • it spontaneously changes (then go to Step 5).

5. Mature all changes as they occur (as described in Chapter 9) until either:

    • the binding pattern *translates* and repeats in a different form (i.e. you are back at either Step 1 or 3), or
    • the binding pattern *transforms*.

FIGURE 8.2 Facilitating clients to model and transform double binds

---

When you are modelling the client modelling their double bind, the chances are you will start to embody the client's binding pattern as well. At these moments you may feel uncomfortable, lost or stuck.

If this happens, it pays to know your own patterns so that you can be aware of the difference between the client's bind and yours. At this point it is also vital that you stay true to the Symbolic Modelling process. Doing anything else may send one of two signals to the client: either *you* cannot handle their experience, or you do not believe *they* can handle their experience. Either way you risk reinforcing their binding pattern.

Even after years of facilitating clients to self-model, we still find something magical and sacred about the moment when a binding pattern transforms and a Metaphor Landscape evolves. At these moments we are grateful to be working alongside the developmental and progressive arrow of evolution.

Client Transcript: Jubilee Clip – Stage 4

The next part of the Jubilee Clip transcript illustrates how binds and double binds manifest, how to encourage conditions for transformation, and how three of the Six Approaches—Attending to Wholes, Lengthening Attention and Introducing Resource Symbols—work together within the logic of the client's metaphors.

Two of the Six Approaches have been employed in the previous part of the transcript (Chapter 7): Concentrating Attention facilitated the emergence of the resource symbol of the Kung Fu master's red mature heart (T31–T39); and Identifying Necessary Conditions helped clarify the organisation of the binding patterns (T30 and T42). The client also began to discover the pattern of his binds, which can be summarised as:

- Screwdriver wants to undo jubilee clip. Yet because of a conflict (a fear of an unknown risk that somebody might be disappointed as a result), is actually doing the opposite.

- Not being able to resolve the conflict leads to a feeling of helplessness (which means he cannot have confidence in his own abilities and is vulnerable to being exposed).

- He feels like a pupil who has not reached the level of maturity required to become the person who has to undo jubilee clip. He needs to pass a very difficult exam, but he does not have the background to sit it. This is like running round a track trying to overtake his ideal self twice.

In Chapter 7 the transcript concluded with:

C49: It's like running round a track and I have to overtake him twice.

T49: **And** like running round a track and you have to overtake him twice. **And** running and running. **And** you'll have to prove yourself more than once. **And** you have to overtake him twice. **And as** you're running round **that** track and you have to overtake him twice, **what kind of** him **could** he **be**?

C50: My ideal me.

Although the client is clearly in a bind, there may be a way out. If he continues growing and running round the track, presumably he will eventually overtake his "ideal me" twice. Or will he? Our next few questions aim to direct his attention to the paradox and move time forward so that he discovers whether the potential resolution "grow" does in fact offer a way out:

T50: **And** your ideal me. **And as** you're running round **that** track **and** you have to overtake your ideal me twice, **what happens as** you grow?

C51: It changes the situation.

T51: **And as** you grow it changes the situation, **and then what happens**?

C52: The gap widens. The more I grow the more the gap widens.

T52: **And** the gap widens. **And** the more you grow the more the gap widens. **And** the more you grow the more the gap **with** your ideal me widens. **And** the more you're running round a track, the more the gap widens [pause]. **And then what happens**?

C53: It's a no-win situation.

T53: **And** it's a no-win situation. **And** is no-win situation **the same or different as** helplessness?

C54: It's the same.

Repeatedly asking 'And then what happens?' lengthens time forward (Approach D), giving the client an opportunity to consider the consequences inherent in the logic of the metaphor. He discovers this is no ordinary gap because the more he grows (which is his only chance of proving himself), the more the gap widens and prevents the possibility of him overtaking his ideal self and resolving the paradox. Thus the solution to the bind is prevented by a further bind—a classic double bind. (And notice the parallel between a gap widening and the memory of his mother *distancing* herself after she read the letter twice?)[15]

The formulation of T52 is a method David Grove developed for work-ing with conflicting intentions. By recapitulating the elements of the bind several times, the client is given time to embody the binding nature of the pattern as a whole. In this context, 'Then what happens?' means 'What are the effects of you being bound in this way?'. The client responds with the metaphor "It's a no-win situation." The result of this double bind is the same as the result of the previous unresolvable conflict—no-win is the same as helplessness.

By now the client has been round his pattern twice and is experi-encing his binds enough to be able to readily identify a metaphor that encompasses the *whole* organisation (Approach B):

T54:   **And** no-win **and** helplessness are the same. **And when** no-win is the same as helplessness, **that's** no-win **and** helplessness **like what**?

C55:   It's like I have to keep climbing a mountain that gets higher the more I climb.

Helplessness and no-win are names for patterns symbolised by the tightening jubilee clip and running around a track. 'Like what?' asks for a metaphor which includes both experiences. It asks for a metaphor for the pattern of these two patterns—a pattern of organisation. To be able to generate such a metaphor the client must perceive the whole and operate from a perception 'outside', 'meta to' or 'at a higher level than' his patterns. As the organisation of this metaphor transforms, so will the processes which have been replicating the pattern—and so will his experience.

In C55 the client says "I *have to* keep climbing a mountain" which is consistent with "I'll *have to* prove myself more than once" (C47) and "I *have to* overtake him twice" (C49) so we direct his attention to what motivates the repetitive nature of the metaphor, the *have to*:

T56:   **And when** you have to keep climbing a mountain that gets higher, **where did the** have to **of that** have to keep climbing a mountain **come from**?

C57:   Not wanting to see a look of failure. Wondering 'Am I good enough?' [Touches chest with left hand.]

By asking where his "have to" comes from we want him to identify the source of, the fuel for, or what drives the repeating pattern. "Not wanting to see a look of failure" (just like mother's look?) suggests his motivation is to avoid repeating a bad *past* experience; while his wondering 'Am I good enough?' doubts his ability to do anything else in the *future*. You may notice that an organisation based on avoiding failure and doubting himself will actively preclude him from ever achieving his outcome of "total confidence in my own abilities."

The client's last statements are ambiguous. Is he reporting from the perspective of himself as a child or himself now? Most likely the two perspectives are merging as he recognises they are equivalent. Also, maybe for the first time, he has a clear sense of current reality—the impossibility of resolving his predicament and the futility of trying to avoid the consequences of the double bind.

It is at these moments that conditions arise for a shift in perception to a new level of thinking which both transcends and includes the existing pattern of organisation. Therefore we ask whether "red, mature heart" would be interested in going to "young boy who's not wanting to see a look of failure"—the first step of introducing a resource symbol (Approach F):

T57: **And** not wanting to see a look of failure. **And** wondering 'Am I good enough?' [Pause.] **And would** red, mature heart **that's** had lots of experience and deep understanding **be interested in going to** young boy who's not wanting to see a look of failure?

C58: [Long pause.] Yes.

T58: **And** yes. **And can that** red, mature heart **go to that** young boy?

C59: Yes.

T59: **And as** red, mature heart **that's** had lots of experience and deep understanding **goes to that** young boy [pause], **what happens next**?

C60: He feels life again.

It is clear that something has changed, so it seems the introduction has been successful—even though no one can yet know its significance or its effect on other symbols. Is it a translation or a transformation? To find out, the change needs to be matured, which is the subject of the next chapter.

But before discovering the fate of jubilee clip, we present a full description of the Six Approaches and show how each approach uses clean questions in combination and over a period of time to encourage conditions for transformation.

The Six Approaches

A. Concentrating Attention

When a client concentrates, narrows or focuses their attention on a *single* aspect of their Metaphor Landscape—on one symbol (in a place at a time), or one relationship (between two symbols, places or times), or one pattern (involving many symbols, places or times)—they likely notice additional attributes, components, functions *within and about* the symbol, relationship or pattern.

Imagine a client has a symbol of a big wall which they see as an impenetrable barrier. As they attend to the wall they recognise it is composed of hundreds of small grey blocks held together by cement. And wait a minute—there's some ivy clinging to the wall. And what's that? There's a crack in the cement. At first there was just a wall with only one function: to be impenetrable. A few clean questions later there are hundreds of blocks, cement that is holding, ivy that is clinging, and a crack. Maybe that wall is not so impenetrable after all. Instead it has become part of a story. Those grey blocks, that ivy and that crack must have got there somehow and each will have a function to perform. By now the client will likely be making all sorts of connections and associations as they concentrate on the additional information about the wall—and every bit of extra information offers a possibility for change.

Having identified a component of a symbol, clients may be able to identify components of that component, and so on, at lower and lower levels of organisation. Usually at one, two or three levels lower, another symbol will appear with attributes which complement or contrast with the attributes of the original symbol. In the above there were small blocks in contrast to the bigness of the wall, living ivy in contrast to the inanimateness of the wall, and a crack in contrast to its impenetrability.

To facilitate clients to concentrate their attention, *repeatedly* ask questions which 'hold' their attention on a single aspect of their Metaphor Landscape, in particular:

What kind of [X] is that [X]?
Is there anything else about that [X]?

The other three basic developing questions (Where? Whereabouts? and Like what?) and relevant specialist developing questions also can be used.

Concentrating can be thought of as a strategic version of developing. When developing, your aim is to bring a symbol or metaphor to life. When concentrating, your aim is for the client to get to deeper and more fundamental levels of a symbol or metaphor's organisation. For example, in an early part of Jubilee Clip the client discovers that a person has to undo the clip. A *series* of developing questions (T31–T39) concentrates his attention long enough for him to discover that the Kung Fu master has a heart that is red and mature—just the resource required later by a young boy who is inadequate to take an exam.

By concentrating attention on a single aspect its multiple parts are revealed, each of which has the potential to influence, and therefore to change, the whole. The 'one' becomes the 'many' at a *lower* level of organisation which increases the range of possibilities available to the *higher* levels (upward influence).[16]

B. Attending to Wholes

In Chapter 7 we discussed the importance of supporting clients to discover patterns as an integral part of the modelling process. Once identified, a pattern can be represented symbolically, mapped and explored. When a number of patterns have been identified, they will necessarily be part of a larger pattern—a pattern of patterns—which itself can be represented symbolically, mapped and explored. In this way the modelling process continues at a higher, *more inclusive,* more significant level of organisation. Theoretically this process could continue forever but in practice does not, for two reasons. First, for many clients, simply recognising their own patterns, or pattern of patterns, stimulates the process of change. Second, patterns which represent the organisation of the whole Metaphor Landscape emerge eventually.

You can encourage clients to recognise patterns of greater and greater significance with application to wider and wider contexts by inviting them to pay attention to wholes instead of parts. Rather than focussing on a particular form, place, time or point of perception, they bring all forms, places, times and perceivers into one simultaneous perceptual space. Rather than concentrating on foreground components, they sense the background network of relationships and patterns. Rather than a number of individual 'ones' the client recognises the connectedness of the 'many' to something larger—the next inclusive whole.

Through exploring a metaphor which symbolises a pattern of organisation, the client has an opportunity to notice properties of the whole which are not contained in any of its constituent parts, and often this alone is enough for the Landscape to start to transform. Any changes at the higher level set the probabilities for changes in the organisation of the lower levels (downward influence) because the higher transcends and includes the lower.

Three ways to encourage clients to attend to more inclusive wholes are: *accumulating perceptions,* working with *Metaphor Maps,* and *physicalising* the Metaphor Landscape.

ACCUMULATING PERCEPTIONS

In Chapter 3 we introduced the idea of accumulating *descriptions* to support the client to embody a symbolic perception as a whole. Now we extend this idea to accumulating *perceptions* — comprising multiple forms, multiple places and multiple times — into one simultaneous perceptual space. This process is like creating a collage of photographs taken at various times and places and then describing the picture as a whole.[17]

To invite the client to accumulate more and more of their Landscape into awareness you ask:

And when [A], **and** [B], **and** [C] ...
 ... **what happens to** [X], **and** [Y], **and** [Z]?
 ... **is there anything else about** *all* **that**?

A, B, C ... X, Y, Z are the steps of a sequence, events in a story, nodes in a configuration or premises of a personal philosophy. These questions invite A, B, C ... X, Y, Z to share the same perceptual space.

Our question at T54 of Jubilee Clip is an example of referring to two patterns, "no-win" and "helplessness," as a way of encouraging the client to identify a metaphor which encompasses both.

When the client has accumulated sufficient perceptions, you can ask for a single metaphor which describes their experience of the whole pattern:

And that's [A, B, C ...] **like what**?

And [A], **and** [B], **and** [C], ... **and** *all* **that's like what**?

How do you know when the client has established sufficient metaphors and symbolic perceptions for them to be accumulated into a whole?

This is a tricky question to answer because it depends on so many factors. Fortunately, once clients have gathered sufficient information they often 'put it all together' themselves and spontaneously generate a metaphor for the whole, such as "I seem to be going round in circles" or "Here I am, stuck in the mire again." Alternatively, they might explicitly tell you in a meta-comment that they are contemplating wholes rather than parts. They might say "This is like my whole life" or "This is exactly what happens time and again." If none of the above happens, you can be on the lookout for 'operational closure',[18] that is:

- When no new symbols or patterns emerge and the client's descriptions add no further information about how an operational unit of their Metaphor Landscape works and fits together.

- When new symbols or patterns continue to appear but they are isomorphic (have the same organisation) as existing symbols or patterns.

- When the logic of the client's description encompasses an entire configuration, a complete sequence or a coherent set of premises (with no gaps).

METAPHOR MAPS

Whenever clients draw a Metaphor Map which includes more than one perception they have accumulated those perceptions into one drawing. This enables them to make connections and see patterns across time and space and in so doing to recognise more of the whole. When clients produce several Metaphor Maps you can ask them to arrange the maps on the floor, wall or wherever they want and then, with a sweep of the hand, improvise a clean question such as, "And what do you notice about all of these?" or "And all of this is like what?"

PHYSICALISING

For some clients the best way to experience the entirety of their Metaphor Landscape is to enact or physicalise it as described in Chapter 4. This allows them to move around their perceptual space, to describe their embodied sense of its configuration, and to discover how it works as a whole.

C. Broadening Attention

When clients concentrate their attention on a single aspect of their Metaphor Landscape (Approach A) they discover more about its composition—its internal organisation. An alternative approach is for them to broaden their attention to *outside and beyond* the edge or boundary of their current Landscape. This offers them an opportunity to discover external resources, to widen contexts, to extend limits and to expand connections—all in the service of a broader perspective.

To facilitate this you can ask about *the space outside* or an *outside perceiver.* Or you can invite them to *extend their Metaphor Map* and suggest they *research key words.*

THE SPACE OUTSIDE

Once a Metaphor Landscape is established, its boundaries, limits and edges become apparent by the use of 'limits of space' words (e.g. end, border, finish, frame, periphery, extent) and nonverbal indicators such as gestures and lines of sight. When a boundary or edge appears or is implicit in a Landscape, you can invite the client to focus their attention on the boundary itself by asking:

> **And how** [big / long / high / wide / broad] **could [X] be?**
>
> **And how far does** [X extend / go / continue]?

When the client's attention is at the boundary, then you can direct it beyond, outside, over the edge or to the other side by asking broadening-type questions:

> **And ... what's *(broadening word)*** [client's name for boundary]?
>
> e.g. And impenetrable wall, and when impenetrable wall, ...
> ... what's *beyond* impenetrable wall?
> ... what's *outside* impenetrable wall?
> ... what's *above (over, on top of)* impenetrable wall?
> ... what's *below (under, beneath)* impenetrable wall?
> ... what's *behind* impenetrable wall?

To remain clean your question must honour and be congruent with the inherent logic of the Landscape; that is, you only ask about a space outside that can be presupposed from the client's description. In the following example a client discovers that all of her symbols, including herself, are on one side of a wall which is blocking her moving forward:

C   All there is is a big impenetrable wall in front of me.

T   **And when** all there is is a big impenetrable wall in front of you, **how big is that** wall?

C   [Looks left and right.] As far as the eye can see in both directions.

T   **And** as far as the eye can see in both directions. **And when** big impenetrable wall is as far as the eye can see in both directions [looks left and right], **how** big [looks up and down] **is that** wall?

C   [Gestures up.] Just above my head-height.

T   **And** just above your head-height. **And when** big impenetrable wall is just above head-height, **is there anything else above** head-height?

C   Nothing I can see.

T   **And** nothing you can see, **and when** big impenetrable wall's in front of you, **what's beyond that** wall?

C   [Long pause.] Everything I've ever wanted but can't have [tears].

By repeatedly guiding the client's attention to the current limits of her perception and then beyond, much to her amazement she realised that rather than blocking her, the wall had protected her from the pain of seeing "Everything I've ever wanted but can't have."

Outside Perceiver

Sometimes a client perceives their Landscape from outside the scene. That is, their point of perception is not located within the boundary of the event being described. In such cases, a way to broaden their attention outside the limits of their Landscape is to enquire about the perceiver:

> **And where is** [perceiver] [perceiving-word] **{that} from?**

Where 'perceiving-word' is the *means of perceiving* used by the perceiver, e.g. seeing, viewing, watching, hearing, feeling, sensing, etc. For example, a client whose outcome for therapy was to "be more present during sex" said:

C: I can see myself making love to my husband.

T: **And when** you can see yourself making love to your husband, **where are** you seeing **that from?**

C: It seems crazy to say, but seven storeys up.

T: **And** seven storeys up. **And whereabouts** seven storeys up?

C: I'm on a balcony.

T: **And what kind of** you **is that** you, on a balcony seven storeys up?

C: A severed me.

The client's attention shifted from the scene of herself making love to an observing "severed me" on a balcony seven storeys up—a perspective she realised she had habitually adopted since being close to death in a car crash.

EXTENDING A METAPHOR MAP

David Grove has devised a remarkably simple and yet highly effective method for encouraging clients to broaden their perspective outside their existing Landscape. Once they have drawn a Metaphor Map he tells them to add more paper around it so they can draw whatever is beyond its edges. He does this when the client's drawing suggests that only a part of the Landscape has been represented. For example, a river may stop at the edge of a page, or a mountain peak is off the top of the page, or a child is running towards the edge of the paper but what the child is running toward is not represented. To remain clean, you simply gesture to a location off the paper and ask "And what's over here?" or assign them to: "Draw what's over there."

RESEARCH KEY WORDS

David Grove has recently introduced a novel way of broadening attention: he asks clients to research the etymology and alternative meanings of the words they use. He once asked James to research 'prevailing' from his metaphor of a "prevailing wind." James discovered that 'pre' means 'before' and 'vail' means 'service', and so, much to his surprise, 'prevailing' could mean 'before service'. This insight had a profound effect because it introduced a spiritual dimension into his metaphor.

Similarly David asks clients to research the properties of their key symbols; how they work, their historical development and any additional functions they have (or have had). David usually selects words or symbols which the client has emphasised (by repetition, tonality, gesture, etc.) and especially any idiosyncratic or ambiguous words or phrasings. When researched information resonates with the client (either supporting or contradicting their perception) it will in some way hold symbolic significance for them.

Whether you ask questions, have the client extend their map or research their words, when broadening attention the principle is the same: the client attends to what is outside their existing Landscape. What they discover may well trigger all sorts of changes, and there may even be a resource symbol or two lurking beyond the known in previously unexplored places.

D. Lengthening Attention

You can think of lengthening attention as the temporal equivalent of spatially broadening attention (Approach C) since it invites clients to discover what comes before and what comes after the current limits of their conscious knowledge. In previous chapters we have described how you ask 'moving time' questions in combination to facilitate the client to identify a sequence of events—the metaphorical beginning, middle and end of the way their symptoms manifest today. When using the lengthening approach, you *repeatedly* ask questions that either *move time back* or *move time forward*.

MOVING TIME BACK

By repeatedly directing the client's attention to the timeframe *before* what is in their awareness, you invite them to sequentially shift the locus of their perception back in symbolic time.

And where does [X] come from?

And what happens just before [X]?

If you continue to ask these questions the client eventually gets to a time before the origin of the current pattern. This may be back to childhood, back to the womb, to a parent's personal history, to ancestors, to social, cultural or historical factors, back to before civilisation, to before the evolution of humans, to before life, back to the beginnings of the universe, back to God (and before).[19] An extended example of moving time back can be found in the Lozenge transcript in Part V (T23–T33).

MOVING TIME FORWARD

By repeatedly directing the client's attention to the timeframe *subsequent* to what is in their awareness, you invite them to sequentially shift the locus of their perception forward in symbolic time.

And then what happens?

And what happens next?

If you continue to ask these questions the client eventually gets to after the end of the current pattern. This may be any time in the future including after the client's death, and anywhere up to and after 'forever'. Examples of lengthening by moving time forward appear in the Castle Door (T16–T20) and Jubilee Clip (T50–T52) transcripts.

During either the moving time back or forward process, the client may make historical connections, identify repeating patterns, encounter resources, have insights or (re)discover a sense of purpose. When they attend to a time and place which is far enough from the time and place of their symptoms, it usually reveals "a new cosmology"—a world organised around a fundamentally different paradigm—and a resource which David Grove terms a "redemptive metaphor." When a redemptive metaphor is introduced to other symbols within the Landscape it usually initiates a reorganisation of existing patterns, inspiring new ways of perceiving, being, and relating to the world.

When the client traces connections across multiple timeframes and a spontaneous change occurs, your role is to facilitate the change to mature (see Chapter 9). However, should the client cycle through the pattern without any noticeable change in its organisation, or should they discover a secondary bind which prevents them from continuing to move time back or forward (as happened in Jubilee Clip at C53), you can utilise the other approaches to:

- Concentrate their attention on the properties of the secondary bind (see Approach A)
- Attend to the repeating sequence as a whole (see Approach B)
- Broaden their attention spatially to outside the repetitive sequence or bind (see Approach C)
- Lengthen time in the opposite direction
- Investigate the conditions necessary for the repeating sequence or bind to change (see Approach E)
- Introduce a resource to the repeating sequence or bind (see Approach F).

Whatever approach you use will need to be decided intuitively in the moment based on the overall logic of the client's Landscape.

E. Identifying Necessary Conditions

If the resolution of self-preserving patterns (which keep unwanted thoughts, feelings, and behaviours replicating) were predictable and logical, clients would resolve them themselves and no longer be bound. Given that they are not able to do this, you can ask questions that identify the seemingly illogical conditions maintaining the bind and what is necessary for the binding pattern to reconfigure. One way to do this is to ask the *symbols* for their intention and what needs to happen for that intention to be enacted, fulfilled or satisfied. Figure 8.3 gives general guidelines about how this approach unfolds.

---

1. Begin with either the existing intention of a symbol, or ask:
    And what would [X] like to have happen/to do?

2. Ask for the conditions necessary to fulfil X's intention:
    And what needs to happen for [X] to [X's intention]?

3. When the client answers with one or more conditions, ask whether the condition(s) can be enacted or fulfilled:
    And can [necessary conditions]?

    (Note: If the client gives multiple necessary conditions, you can ask for the order in which the conditions need to be fulfilled: And when [A, B, C ...] what needs to happen *first?*)

4. If the client's response to "And can ..." is:

    *   "YES." Enact the necessary conditions and mature the changes (see Chapter 9) by asking:

        And as [necessary conditions] ...
        ... what happens next?
        ... then what happens?

    *   "SOMETIMES." You can ask:

        And what's the difference between when [X] can [necessary condition] **and when** [X] **can't** [necessary condition]?

    *   "NO" or "YES, BUT ..." either:

        Identify the *prior* necessary conditions by asking,
        And what needs to happen for [necessary conditions]?
        or
        Specify the bind preventing the conditions being fulfilled.

FIGURE 8.3 Using the Necessary Conditions approach

The second half of the Castle Door transcript (see Section V) contains an example of identifying and enacting necessary conditions. The client discovers a very fine gold thread that links to her. We continue:

T40:   **And** very fine thread. **And what would** very fine thread **that** links **like to do**?

C41:   To pour some more of the gold into me.

T41:   **And** very fine thread **would like** to pour some more of the gold into you. **And what needs to happen for** very fine thread to pour some more of the gold into you?

C42:   A tap needs to be turned on.

T42:   **And can** a tap be turned on?

C43:   Yes, but it doesn't come out quickly enough.

T43:   **And** a tap needs to be turned on, but gold doesn't come out quickly enough. **So what needs to happen for** gold **to** come out quickly enough?

C44:   To come out over the top of the vessel.

T44:   **And** to come out over the top of the vessel. **And what needs to happen for** gold to come out over the top of the vessel?

C45:   An unseen hand needs to tip it so it runs round the outside.

T45:   **And can** an unseen hand tip vessel so gold runs round the outside?

C46:   Yes!

T46:   **And as** unseen hand tips vessel and gold runs round the outside, **what happens next**?

C47:   Some of it gets into me [pause]. I get stronger as it goes down.

T47:   **And when** some of it gets into you, **and** you get stronger as it goes down, **then what happens**?

C48:   I feel much more calm and stronger.

T48:   **And as** gold goes down **and** you feel much more calm and stronger, **what kind of** calm **is that** calm?

C49:   I don't have to panic behind the door.

The transcript illustrates how unexpected symbols and apparently illogical events can have an influence: how did the tap, the vessel and an unseen hand appear on the scene? Maybe the client knows, and maybe they don't. What is more important is that these symbols had a beneficial effect on the Landscape and on the client.

Identifying the conditions necessary for symbols to fulfil their intentions may be enough to resolve single binds. If not, continuing with this approach can help reveal a secondary bind preventing resolution of the primary bind. For example in Stages 2 and 3 of the Jubilee Clip transcript:

- We ask for the intention of screwdriver (T22) and whether its intention can be satisfied (T23).

- Because of a conflict, screwdriver's intention to undo jubilee clip cannot be enacted. Once the characteristics of the conflict are known, we direct the client's attention to the conditions necessary for the conflict to be resolved, "What needs to happen for screwdriver to undo clip?" (T30).

- The client realises "A person has to do it. And that person is me" (C31). This person develops into a resource symbol of a Kung Fu master's mature heart (C32–C40).

- However before he can undo jubilee clip another condition has to be fulfilled: that the client reaches the level of maturity required (C41).

- By asking what needs to happen for this latest condition to be fulfilled (T42), the client discovers he needs to pass a difficult exam (C43–C44).

- Further investigation reveals a secondary bind: the client has not got the background required to sit the exam which he needs pass in order to grow to the level of maturity required to undo jubilee clip (C45–C46).

Through identifying intentions and the conditions necessary for their fulfilment, the client discovers how he is doubly bound by the inherent logic of his patterns. In Jubilee Clip, as is often the case, the transformation of a double bind required the assistance of other approaches. In this case, Approach F.

F. Introducing Resource Symbols

There is an important distinction between the first five approaches and the sixth, Introducing Resource Symbols. In addition to their other functions, Approaches A to E can be thought of as ways for the client to *discover* overt or latent resources, whereas Approach F *introduces* a resource to another symbol that will benefit from the attributes of the resource. For example:

- Kung Fu master's red mature heart, *goes to* a young boy who does not want to see a look of failure, and "He feels life again." (Jubilee Clip T57–C60).

- A sun that brings light, and love, and happiness, and calmness, *goes to* shackles on a baby's ankles, which melt and "A baby grows up to be a happy person and he can take his time" (see Lozenge in Part V, T35-C38).

Because you, not the client, invite the resource symbol to go to another symbol, the process is packed with safeguards to ensure that each symbol's intention takes precedence over yours.

Next we explain Approach F in terms of the *effects of introducing symbols, the process of introducing,* and *when to introduce.*

EFFECTS OF INTRODUCING SYMBOLS

When symbols are introduced and there is a point of contact between them, one of the following changes may occur:

- The bound or unresourceful symbol changes (exhibits new attributes), while the resource symbol retains its resourcefulness for further use—like a battery that starts a car, or an oven that bakes dough into bread. The battery and oven can be used over and over.

- Both symbols change in different ways—like water poured onto fire become steam and ashes.

- Two symbols integrate into a new form—like red and yellow combine to become orange, or slowly adding oil to egg yolks produces mayonnaise.

When an introduction is successful, one or both symbols change and become available to influence other symbols. Through a ripple or cascade effect, the entire organisation of a Metaphor Landscape may be influenced —like a new idea that spreads through and updates a body of scientific knowledge, or a mutation that leads to a new branch of evolution.

THE PROCESS OF INTRODUCING

David Grove has devised a precise set of questions which allow you to invite a resource symbol to be introduced to another symbol. These questions are designed to keep your language as clean as possible and to keep the locus of control firmly with the metaphor. The standard question which initiates introducing one symbol to another is:

> **And would** [resource X] **be interested in going to**
> [symbol / context Y]?

There are a number of ways the client can respond:

"Yes"   interested
"Yes but …"   interested, but cannot
"No"   not interested.

INTERESTED

If the client indicates "Yes" resource 'X' is interested in going to symbol or context 'Y', you ask:

And can [resource X] **go to** [symbol / context Y]?

If they again reply "yes" ask:

And as [resource X] **goes to** [Y], [pause] **then what happens**?

The first question tests the interest of one symbol to go to another symbol or context. It does not ask the symbol to move, it just elicits the *interest* and therefore the symbol's intention. Having established there is a desire, the second question finds out if it is *possible* to enact that desire. These questions give the resource symbol two opportunities to reject your suggestion.

When you say 'And as X goes to Y …' it is important to dramatically slow your delivery, and pause before asking '… then what happens?'. This allows time for the resource symbol to move and enact its function, and for the client to notice the effects on other symbols. The introduction of symbols in Jubilee Clip is a classic example:

T57:   **And** not wanting to see a look of failure. **And** wondering 'Am I good enough?' [Pause.] **And would** red, mature heart **that's** had lots of experience and deep understanding **be interested in going to** young boy who's not wanting to see a look of failure?

C58:   [Long pause.] Yes.

T58:   **And** yes. **And can that** red, mature heart **go to that** young boy?

C59:   Yes.

T59:   **And as** red, mature heart **that's** had lots of experience and deep understanding **goes to that** young boy [pause], **what happens next**?

C60:   He feels life again.

The client may take a while to respond, in which case you simply wait and watch. When they answer, pay particular attention to the congruence of their responses. A verbal "yes" and a nonverbal shake of the head may indicate an incongruence which you would probably want to address before continuing with the introduction (you can do this by using the entry and developing questions for nonverbal behaviour). If you have the slightest concern about the appropriateness of 'X' going to 'Y', you can give symbol 'Y' a chance to have its say by asking either:

And would [symbol / context Y] **like that**?

or

And is [symbol / context Y] **interested in** [resource X] **going to** [Y]?

You may also like to ask one of these questions if the answer to the invitation seems to come from the client's "I" or from some other symbol, e.g. "Well *I'd* like it to go" or "Yes it *should* go." If there is a conflict of intentions between 'X' and 'Y', you must honour either symbol's rejection of your suggestion to introduce them.

INTERESTED BUT CANNOT

When the client responds with some form of "Yes, but…" the resource symbol wants to go to the other symbol but for some reason cannot. This response presents an opportunity for the client to discover the nature of a preventing bind, the source of the bind, or what happens when the intention of the resource symbol cannot be fulfilled:

And when [resource X] **is interested in going to**
[symbol / context Y] **but** [client's negative response] …

NATURE OF BIND	… **what kind of** [client's negative response] **is that**?
SOURCE OF THE BIND	… **where could that** [client's negative response] **come from**?
SUBSEQUENT EVENT	… **then what happens**?

NOT INTERESTED

If your invitation ("Would X be interested in going to Y?") is inappropriate, the client will respond with some form of "No" or "No, but…":

"No"—A straight negative response is feedback that either these symbols are not meant to be together, or the timing of your question was inappropriate. If you have misread the situation you may receive an angry or amazed response. A client once said to us, "Would what?! There's *no way* that rock wants to go to that pool. There'd be no bloody peace left if that happened!" We responded with "And there's *no way* that rock wants to go to that pool. And what *would* rock like to do?" Further examples of questions to a negative response are:

> **And** no. **And when** [X] **is not interested in going to** [Y], ...
> ... **what would** [X] **like to do**?
> ... **what would** [Y] **like to have happen**?
> ... **then what happens**?

"No, but ..." — In rejecting your invitation, the client may be prompted to provide what is required instead. They may say "No, X isn't interested in going to Y, but Y wants to go to X," or "No, but Z wants to go to Y." You continue the introduction with, "And [repeat client's words]. And can ...?" This acknowledges the client's idea, discovers whether the symbol can do what it says it wants, and encourages the client to take charge of their own process.

WHEN TO INTRODUCE

There is no formula or recipe for when to introduce because it is entirely dependent on having a sense of the whole organisation of the client's Metaphor Landscape and what is happening in the moment. Sometimes introducing one symbol to another will seem entirely logical, while at other times there may be no obvious rhyme nor reason other than it feels right. There are a number of factors which can inform your decision of when to introduce.

The first requirement for a successful introduction is that a significant enough resource exists. Obviously a resource symbol has to exist (have a name, an address and some useful qualities) before you can ask if it would be interested in going to another symbol. It also has to have sufficient significance for the client so that its application triggers a change in other symbols. However "it is not the intensity or quantity of a resource state, but its particular *qualities* that make it useful in changing a problematic experience."[20] Providing the client is connected to the resource and has an embodied sense of its significance, you will be able to introduce it to another symbol days, weeks or months after it was first discovered.

Second, the needs of the other symbol or context involved in the introducing should correspond, connect, align with the attributes of the resource. In the Jubilee Clip example it seems likely that a young boy who fears a look of disappointment would find a Master's mature heart useful. But in the Lozenge example it is less obvious that shackles on a baby's ankles would benefit from sunlight—unless you know the organisation of the whole Metaphor Landscape and what is happening for the client at the moment of the introduction.

Third, sometimes a client has never considered the benefit that would accrue from using a resource out of context (transferring it from one time and place to another). As a general rule, the more space and time separating two symbols, the less likely that the client will recognise the potential for connection. For example, if after repeatedly moving time back (Approach D) the client discovers "the key to life" they may not think of using it to escape from a prison cell with a rusty old lock explored an hour ago (or even several sessions previously)—but *you* might.

Fourth, the more you work with clients' metaphors the more you will become *au fait* with the illogical logic of an individual's symbolism. The logic of metaphors is closer to that of dreams than it is to the laws of physics. When a client's Metaphor Landscape is well developed and its organisation well modelled you may get an intuition that symbol 'X' could be of use to symbol or situation 'Y', even though this may seem bizarre. As long as you are not trying to solve the client's problem for them, we suggest you follow your intuition and invite symbol 'X' to go to symbol 'Y'. The safeguards built into the introducing process leave the client or the symbols free to reject your invitation. And whatever happens, valuable information about the organisation of the client's Landscape will emerge.

Fifth, sometimes the client gets to a point where their Landscape is perfectly poised, perfectly balanced but nothing new happens. In these cases almost any introduction may be the catalyst that initiates a chain reaction whereby the Landscape reorganises.

As in most delicate operations in life, timing is everything, and knowing when to introduce symbols is an art which you can only learn from experience. Introducing resource symbols is much like match-making. You think two people will be perfect for each other, and yet there is more to a good match than logic. Either the chemistry is there or it is not, and no one can be sure in advance. The 'Interested?' and 'Can?' questions are the symbolic equivalent of the first date.

Concluding Remarks

Metaphor Landscapes change in one of two ways: their form, order or configuration translate without significantly changing a higher level pattern; or the change is such that an organising pattern transforms. Translations often give the client all they want. But sometimes no amount of translating will satisfy, or translating itself becomes impossible. In these cases, only transforming the binding pattern will suffice.

Neither you nor the client can manufacture a transformation, but together you can encourage the conditions in which it can occur. These conditions arise when the client shifts *the way* they perceive, rather than simply changing *what* they perceive.

The Six Approaches use clean questions in a strategic and organisational manner. They reveal hidden resource symbols and create opportunities for the client to transcend and include their habitual ways of perceiving. Whether this happens in five minutes, five sessions or five months is impossible to predict.

When a change occurs it may not be clear whether it is a translation which changes nothing, a productive translation, or a transformation which changes everything. Only after the effects of the change are known does the client (and sometimes the therapist) get to find out—and this is the subject of the next chapter.

9

Stage 5
Maturing the Evolved Landscape

The real voyage of discovery consists
not in seeking new landscapes
but in having new eyes.
Marcel Proust

When a symbol changes it develops a new form. The changed symbol will usually influence other symbols, which go on to affect other symbols, and so on in a cascade, contagion or chain reaction. If enough changes occur, or a change of sufficient significance occurs, the client's symbolic perceptions reorganise and a transformed Metaphor Landscape emerges.

A Metaphor Landscape can change during Stages 2, 3 or 4. The change may be to a single attribute, to a relationship between symbols or to a pattern which includes many metaphors and perceptions. Whenever and however a change occurs, maturing is what happens next.

Your role during Stage 5 is to facilitate the client to nurture, embrace and enhance changes in their Metaphor Landscape. As this happens, the maturing process is either interrupted by a bind—in which case you revert to Stage 2 or 3—or the changes continue until the reorganisation consolidates into a new Landscape. To more fully explain how Landscapes mature, this chapter includes:

The Maturing Process
Facilitating a Changing Landscape to Mature
Client Transcript: Jubilee Clip – Stage 5
The Results of Maturing
Ending a Session when it is 'Work in Progress'

The Maturing Process

Changed symbols can relate in new ways, do things they could not do before, and stimulate changes to symbols and metaphors elsewhere in the Landscape. Therefore change can be seen, not as the end of the road, but as the beginning of a new one. For example:

- When a butterfly emerges from a chrysalis, it can get used to its wings, learn to fly and decide what it would like to do next.

- When Arthur pulls Excalibur out of the stone, he can get to know his new ally and try out his new-found power before they go off to fulfil their mission.

- After a bully's frozen heart thaws, she stops baiting and provoking. Then she can attract friends to play with, come to understand the value of sharing and the difference this makes to others.

- As a wound heals, it can understand why it got sick, rebuild its strength, and consider the effects of long-term self-care on the organism as a whole.

Some changed symbols not only affect their immediate neighbours, they also have an effect on symbols in other times and places. If a fundamental or significant enough change takes place, then novel forms, unexpected events and brand new connections appear and the whole Metaphor Landscape reorganises. Because the new Landscape will include self-preserving processes which automatically inhibit the replication of previous patterns, the emphasis of maturing alters: from evolving, developing and spreading individual changes to consolidating the new Landscape's entire configuration.

Sometimes maturing is a smooth and continuous process with the Metaphor Landscape reorganising incrementally. Sometimes nothing much appears to happen and then the whole Landscape transforms at breakneck speed. The pace, the amount and the degree to which a Landscape changes is determined by a combination of three factors:

TIME   The more changes during a period of time, the faster the *rate* of change (evolving).

SPACE   The more of the Landscape that changes, the greater the *scale* of the change (spreading).

LEVEL   The higher the level of organisation that changes, the greater the *significance* of the change.

But sometimes, as the Landscape changes and the client moves toward what they want, they experience a counterbalancing reaction — a hitherto hidden conflict, dilemma, impasse or paradox. When this happens maturing is interrupted. This allows the binding pattern to be revealed and incorporated into an updated Landscape (using Stage 2 and 3 processes). Maturing is resumed after the next change takes place (see Figure 9.1).

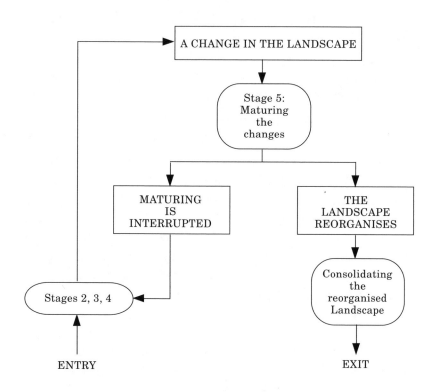

FIGURE 9.1 An overview of the maturing process

Changes to the Metaphor Landscape are not confined to what happens in the consulting room. As much, if not most maturing happens outside of the session as the client adapts to the changes and discovers how these influence their everyday life. In a sense, maturing is not complete until the changes are so familiar that they are perceived as a natural way of being. For some clients this takes minutes, for others, months.

Facilitating a Changing Landscape to Mature

Maturing starts when a client becomes aware of the *effects* of a change. Maturing is not a single process but a number of processes which interact and build upon each other. There are no specialist Stage 5 maturing questions. You use the same Clean Language questions as before, but for a different purpose—to facilitate the maturation of a Metaphor Landscape once it has started to change. This process is summarised in Figure 9.2.

When there is a change in the Metaphor Landscape,
direct the client's attention so that they notice:

- The change   *acknowledging*
- The immediate effect of the change   *evolving*
- The new form of the changed symbol(s)   *developing*
- The effect on other symbols or contexts   *spreading*

Repeat as necessary until:

- Maturing is *interrupted*. Then return to Stage 2 or 3 to uncover the binding pattern

or

- The Metaphor Landscape reorganises. Then support *consolidation* of the new organisation, exit the Landscape and return to everyday dialogue.

FIGURE 9.2 Facilitating a changed Landscape to mature

The following extract from the Jubilee Clip transcript illustrates acknowledging, evolving, developing and spreading. When we left the transcript in Chapter 8, Kung Fu master's red mature heart had just been introduced to young boy with the result that "he feels life again" (C60). This signals the first change and maturing can begin:

T60: **And as** he feels life again, **then what happens**?

C61: The race becomes enjoyable.

T61: **And as** the race becomes enjoyable **and** he feels life again, **then what happens**?

C62: Confidence returns.

T62: **And** confidence returns. **And when** red, mature heart **that's** had lots of experience and deep understanding **goes to that** young boy **and** he feels life again **and** the race becomes enjoyable **and** confidence returns, **what happens to a** mother **who's** just read a letter twice?

C63:   She expresses it's a learning process, not a failure. She's comfortable with him.

T63:   **And** she's comfortable with him. **And** it's a learning process. **And when** mother is comfortable with him, **what happens next**?

C64:   The boy has a different view. A sense of security. Looking forward to life.

T64:   **And** looking forward to life. **And** a sense of security. **And** a different view. **And what kind of** view **is that** different view?

C65:   A wholly confident view. Congruent. Balanced [pause]. In harmony.

T65:   **And when** young boy has a wholly confident view, congruent, balanced, in harmony **what would** he **like to do first**?

C66:   Take the exam again.

T66:   **And can he** take the exam again?

C67:   Yes, and he passes.

T67:   **And** he takes the exam again and passes. **And what happens next when** he passes the exam?

C68:   He begins growing into a Master.

(The transcript completes later in the chapter.)

Acknowledging a change

Directing the client's attention to a change has two purposes: it ensures the client *acknowledges* the change is happening or has happened, and it *prepares* the way for the change to evolve, develop or spread. This is an essential part of maturing because, surprising as it may seem, just because a change takes place does not guarantee the client is fully aware of it. You facilitate the acknowledgement and preparation by starting your questions with either:

> **And as** [description of change] …

or

> **And when** [description of change] …

When a client's language presupposes that change is still happening, begin with 'as'. This recognises its ongoing nature and encourages it to continue (see T60 and T61 above). If the change has already happened, begin with 'when' (see T62 and T63).

Evolving the effects of a change

Every change has consequences and by directing the client's attention to what happens *after* a change, you invite them to consider the effects of that change. As they do they will probably notice further changes which will have their own effects, and so on. Two ways to facilitate this evolution of the Landscape are: *moving time forward* and *enacting a changed symbol's intention.*

MOVING TIME FORWARD

To invite the client to notice the effects of a change, ask one of the two basic moving time forward questions:

> **And ... then what happens?**
>
> or
>
> **And ... what happens next?**

T60: **And as** he feels life again, **then what happens?**

C61: The race becomes enjoyable.

And,

T63: **And** she's comfortable with him. **And** it's a learning process. **And when** mother is comfortable with him, **what happens next?**

C64: The boy has a different view. A sense of security. Looking forward to life.

ENACTING A CHANGED SYMBOL'S INTENTION

When a symbol changes, its intention may be enacted or its function fulfilled when before it could not. Alternatively the change may result in the symbol having a new intention, function or need. In either case, enquiring about the symbol's intention and whether that can be enacted encourages the symbol to continue evolving. To do this ask:

> **And what would** [changed symbol] **like to have happen/do *first*?**

When the client answers with the symbol's intention, you ask:

> **And can** [intention of changed symbol]?

If the intention can be enacted, you invite time to move forward so that the client notices the evolution of the change:

> **And as** [intention of changed symbol], **then what happens?**

For example:

T65:   **And when** young boy has a wholly confident view, congruent, balanced, in harmony **what would** he **like to do first**?

C66:   Take the exam again.

T66:   **And can he** take the exam again?

C67:   Yes, and he passes.

T67:   **And** he takes the exam again and passes. **And what happens next when** he passes the exam?

C68:   He begins growing into a Master.

If the intention cannot be enacted, then maturing may need to be postponed while the client identifies the conditions necessary for the intention to be fulfilled (see the 'Results of Maturing' below and Chapter 8, Approach E).

Developing a changed symbol's new form

While evolving matures a change by moving time forward, *developing* matures by holding time still. Once a symbol, relationship or pattern changes there is value in the client getting to know more about the form of these changes. By asking basic and specialist developing questions you establish a changed symbol's name, address and relationships:

T64:   **And** looking forward to life. **And** a sense of security. **And** a different view. **And what kind of** view **is that** different view?

C65:   A wholly confident view. Congruent. Balanced [pause]. In harmony.

In addition, there are certain types of metaphor which, when developed, automatically evolve to a new form. These are metaphors of *naturally-changing processes,* such as:

- Environmental processes (heating, melting, filling, emptying)
- Biological processes (birth, death, growing, aging, healing)
- Chemical processes (rusting, burning, dissolving, crystallising)
- Cyclical processes (sleeping/awakening, night/day, the seasons)

Asking developing questions of a naturally-changing process invites the client to notice what is changing and to encourage the process to continue (see Jubilee Clip T68 and T69 below for an example which develops 'growing'). Naturally, moving time forward questions also support this process of change.

Developing questions encourage clients to embody the changes taking place so that the new becomes as real and meaningful as was the old.

Spreading the effects to other symbols

As a symbol evolves and develops other symbols and metaphors may spontaneously change. A significant change may be able to influence every part of the Landscape. It is therefore important to keep track of which parts have been touched and influenced by the change process. If the client does not mention that the changes have spread to a particular part of the Landscape, you should check whether or not they have. You can do this in two ways: *enquiring about the spread of change* and *introducing a changed symbol* to another, yet-to-be-changed symbol. When a client has a large symbol inventory, Metaphor Maps can be a valuable aid in keeping track of the spreading process.

ENQUIRING ABOUT THE SPREAD OF CHANGE

You can invite the client to notice whether a change has, or can, spread to symbols and contexts not yet mentioned. You do this by enquiring if a change in one place or time in the Landscape has resulted in a change elsewhere:

And when [change X], **what happens to** [symbol or context Y]?

T62:   **And** confidence returns. **And when** red, mature heart **that's** had lots of experience and deep understanding **goes to that** young boy **and** he feels life again **and** the race becomes enjoyable **and** confidence returns, **what happens to a** mother **who's** just read a letter twice?

C63:   She expresses it's a learning process, not a failure. She's comfortable with him.

INTRODUCING A CHANGED SYMBOL

You can also encourage a change to spread elsewhere in the Landscape by introducing a changed symbol to an as-yet-unchanged symbol or context. A successful introduction will result in one or both symbols maturing their form and function, and in so doing becoming available for further introductions. The format for introducing can be found in Approach F, Chapter 8.

Making your questions congruent with the changes

The way you facilitate the maturing of a Metaphor Landscape should be congruent with the inherent logic of the changes that are taking place. In other words, the construction and delivery of your questions should take into account the rate and scale of changes, and how the client is responding to those changes. This means *the way* the Landscape matures should inform whether you speed up, slow down, shorten or lengthen your questions, and whether you ask evolving and spreading, or developing questions. Imagine a client describes a dam breaking with a surge of rushing water. To match this rapid movement we would keep our questions short. Ask them quickly. Repeat only the last thing said, adding "And then what happens?" On the other hand, if a young child emerges from a cave after years of hiding, it would seem appropriate to allow time for the child to get used to their new freedom by ... pausing ... and asking lots of developing questions ... about the world outside ... and the child's reaction to being outside ... before inviting the change to evolve or spread further.

Your job is to synchronise your questions with the system's inbuilt pace of change, whether this is moving at the speed with which lightning strikes or the rate that continents drift.

Client Transcript: Jubilee Clip – Stage 5

The completion of the Jubilee Clip transcript follows. It demonstrates the way maturing processes work together to support the emergence of a reorganised Metaphor Landscape. The transcript resumes immediately after the client reports the first change, that young boy "feels life again." We ask a moving time forward question to direct attention to the *effects* of the change and the evolution of the young boy:

T60:   **And as** he feels life again, **then what happens**?

C61:   The race becomes enjoyable.

T61:   **And as** the race becomes enjoyable **and** he feels life again, **then what happens**?

C62:   Confidence returns.

The young boy's relationship with the race has changed. It is now enjoyable, whereas before it involved him *having* to prove himself and *having* to overtake his ideal self twice. Furthermore, "confidence returns." This is important since the client originally wanted "total confidence in my own abilities" (C1). Even so, the maturing process is far from finished because most of the Landscape has yet to be affected. Have the changes spread to mother, for example? To find out, we first accumulate the three changes which have taken place so far:

T62:   **And** confidence returns. **And when** red, mature heart **that's** had lots of experience and deep understanding **goes to that** young boy **and** he feels life again **and** the race becomes enjoyable **and** confidence returns, **what happens to a** mother **who's** just read a letter twice?

C63:   She expresses it's a learning process, not a failure. She's comfortable with him.

T63:   **And** she's comfortable with him. **And** it's a learning process. **And when** mother is comfortable with him, **what happens next**?

C64:   The boy has a different view. A sense of security. Looking forward to life.

We discover mother has changed (she expresses that exams are a learning process), her relationship to the boy has changed (she is comfortable with him), and the boy has changed (he has a different view, a sense of security and is looking forward to life). These changes contrast with mother's previous "look of disappointment," her distancing herself, and him feeling "something is wrong with himself." Because of the importance of the 'looking' motif in the original metaphor (C3–C4) we direct his attention to the boy's "different view," before enquiring about the evolved boy's intention:

T64:   **And** looking forward to life. **And** a sense of security. **And** a different view. **And what kind of** view **is that** different view?

C65:   A wholly confident view. Congruent. Balanced [pause]. In harmony.

T65:   **And when** young boy has a wholly confident view, congruent, balanced, in harmony **what would** he **like to do first**?

C66:   Take the exam again.

T66:   **And can he** take the exam again?

C67:   Yes, and he passes.

T67:   **And** he takes the exam again and passes. **And what happens next when** he passes the exam?

C68:   He begins growing into a Master.

T68:   **And as** he begins growing into a Master, **what kind of** growing **is this** growing into a Master?

C69: Aware of the world around him. Understanding his place in life. Enjoying the process.

T69: **And** aware, **and** understanding his place in life, **and** enjoying the process. **And is there anything else as** he begins growing into a Master?

C70: It's also being able to interact with people—for their benefit.

T70: **And when** able to interact with people for their benefit, **what kind of** interact with people **is that**?

C71: I feel comfortable and at ease. Almost part of them.

The paradox of not being able to sit an exam because of an inadequate background is resolved, and a new organising metaphor of "growing into a Master" emerges. Notice how 'as' in T68 and T69 helps to develop the naturally-changing metaphor 'growing' and automatically evolves the attributes of the now not-so-young boy. And, as the boy grows the perceiver shifts from "he" to "I," who now feels comfortable and at ease interacting with people. Whereas the old pattern was about vulnerability, disappointment and fear, the new pattern involves awareness, understanding and enjoyment.

The transcript nicely illustrates how one change can evolve and spread to other parts of the Landscape:

Feeling life again leads to the race becoming enjoyable and confidence returning.	C60—C62
Mother being comfortable with the boy leads him to have a different view.	C63—C65
A congruent, balanced, in harmony view leads to passing the exam.	C65—C67
Passing the exam leads to growing into a Master.	C67—C68
Growing into a Master leads to being able to interact with people—almost part of them.	C68—C70

Because changes are happening thick and fast, and a new metaphor has emerged, and "he" has shifted to "I," our next series of questions hold time still so that the form of the new metaphor can develop:

T71: **And when** you feel comfortable and at ease **and** almost part of them, **where do** you feel that comfortable and ease?

C72: [Smiles and touches chest.] In here again!

T72: **And** in here again. **And what kind of** in here **is that** in here?

C73: Totally relaxed.

T73:   **And when** totally relaxed **and** comfortable **and** at ease **and** almost part of them, **what kind of** part of them **could that** part of them **be**?

C74:   Being an influence on their lives. Up-building of productive relationships [pause]. Maybe even intimate.

T74:   **And** an influence on their lives, **and** up-building productive relationships, maybe even intimate. **And what kind of** intimate **could that** intimate be?

C75:   [Long pause.] Could you ask me that question again?

T75:   **And** an influence on their lives. **And** up-building productive relationships, maybe even intimate. **And what kind of** intimate **could that** intimate **be**?

C76:   There's no comfort zone and no barrier.

T76:   **And when** there's no comfort zone and no barrier, **what is** there, **when** there's no comfort zone and no barrier?

C77:   [Long pause.] Love.

The client's last four responses suggest a significant reorganisation is taking place: the length of his contemplations increase; for the first time he loses awareness of a question; he reports that two previously unmentioned metaphors, comfort zone and barrier have changed; and the resource "love" reappears (from C4). With all this happening there is no need to do anything except develop the attributes of the resource:

T77:   And love. **And what kind of** love **is that** love?

C78:   Sublime love.

T78:   **And** sublime love. **And where does that** sublime love **come from**?

C79:   Here again [touches chest with left hand].

T79:   **And** here. **And when** sublime love **comes from** here, **that's** sublime love **like what**?

C80:   Even consider giving your life for another.

    The client indicates he is experiencing "sublime love" coming from the place in his chest where previously he felt vulnerability and fear. So we ask the "When X what happens to Y?" question to invite him to notice if the changes that have happened have spread to jubilee clip and screwdriver:

T80:   **And** even consider giving your life for another. **And when** sublime love **from** here, **what happens to** jubilee clip **and** screwdriver?

C81:   They disappear.

Hallelujah, jubilee clip and screwdriver, the original binding metaphor have disappeared. However just because they disappear does not mean they cannot reappear. We continue to ask maturing questions so that the client discovers their fate:

T81:   **And when** they disappear, where **do** they disappear **to**?

C82:   They evaporate. They're atomised.

T82:   **And** jubilee clip and screwdriver evaporate, atomised [pause]. **And then what happens**?

C83:   They are part of the universe.

T83:   **And when** jubilee clip and screwdriver are part of the universe, **what happens next**?

C84:   The child becomes the Master. Wholeness pervades [long pause]. He's undoing jubilee clips for other people [pause]. He's a Master at doing it [laughs]. I feel like I've stopped climbing [very long pause]. Thank you.

All the key symbols have changed and the "thank you" indicates a readiness to leave the symbolic domain, so we accumulate his changed perceptions as a way to consolidate the new Landscape:

T84:   **And now** you've stopped climbing ... **and** the child **has** become the Master ... a Master at undoing jubilee clips for other people ... **take all the time you need** ... **to get to know about** sublime love ... **and** intimate relationships ... **and** feeling comfortable and at ease ... being able to interact with people ... part of them ... **and now** you've stopped climbing ... **you can get to know even more about** balance ... **and** harmony ... **and** confidence ... **and** being a Master at undoing jubilee clips for others [pause]. **And take all the time you need over the next few days and weeks** ... **to discover** ... what ... **happens** ... **next**.

After a long silence the client smiled and mumbled something about not really knowing what to say. Then more silence and contemplation. As the minutes quietly passed we assumed the Landscape was continuing to consolidate and that the silence was our co-therapist. Then, as he was preparing to leave, he said:

> For the last few years I've been asking myself, 'Am I doing what I want to do or is it time to look for something new?' But I kept getting blanks. Now I know what my mission is: helping others to undo their jubilee clips.

And we all laughed.

The transcript demonstrates the value of continuing to ask maturing questions until changes come to fruition. At C68 the boy *"begins* growing into a Master" but it is not until C84 that he *"becomes* the Master." In the meantime change reverberates round the whole system and the three binds—jubilee clip, the race and climbing a mountain—are all resolved. As often happens, in the client's vulnerability lay his strength: now he is a Master at undoing jubilee clips for other people.

Summary of changes

One of the hallmarks of transformation is the emergence of novel forms. The transcript shows how these can materialise in a variety of ways and at a number of levels. Although the client's overall pattern of organisation changes—he stops climbing and becomes a Master at undoing jubilee clips for other people—this could not have happened unless many individual symbols and their relationships had changed along the way. These changes are summarised in Figure 9.3.

The Jubilee Clip transcript demonstrates some general points about maturing which are worth noting. First, in Stage 5 the overall number of questions which facilitated evolving and spreading are approximately balanced by the number of questions which developed and consolidated. Second, maturing accounted for a quarter of the entire transcript. And third, spending this much time maturing enabled the client to embody, rehearse and become familiar with his new patterns.

The Results of Maturing

As changes evolve, develop and spread, new symbols, relationships and patterns begin to appear. Then one of two things can happen: the maturing process is blocked, held back, undone or in some other way *interrupted* by a self-preserving binding pattern; or the Landscape as a whole *consolidates* into a new organisation.

Interruptions to maturing

Interruptions to maturing can happen either in the session or in the client's everyday life.

SYMBOL	CHANGE
The boy:	Feels life again (C60).
	Confidence returns (C62).
	Has a sense of security (C64).
	Has a wholly confident, congruent, balanced, in harmony view (C65).
	Begins growing into a Master (C68).
	Becomes a Master (C84).
Jubilee Clip and Screwdriver:	Evaporate and atomise (C82).
	Are part of the universe (C83).
I:	Feels comfortable, at ease, and totally relaxed in chest (C71–C73).
	Sublime love comes from chest (C77–C79).
	Stops climbing (C84).

RELATIONSHIP	CHANGE
Him and the race:	The race becomes enjoyable (C61).
Mother and exam:	It's a learning process, not a failure (C63).
Mother and boy:	She's comfortable with him (C63).
The boy and life:	Looking forward to life (C64).
The boy and exam:	He takes it again and passes (C66–C67).
The boy and the world:	Aware, understanding his place, and enjoying the process (C69).
I and people:	Being able to interact with people for their benefit (C70).
	Almost part of them (C71).
	Being an influence on their lives (C74).
	Up-building of productive intimate relationships (C74).
	Consider giving your life for another (C80).
	Master at undoing jubilee clips for others (C84).
[Unspecified]	The removal of comfort zone and barrier (C76).

FIGURE 9.3 Summary of changes in Stage 5 of Jubilee Clip

During the session, repeatedly asking questions which evolve and spread change may reveal hitherto hidden obstacles or binds. It is important to recognise that these interruptions may manifest behaviourally ("My head has just started aching"), conceptually ("Surely your other clients don't say these sorts of things"), or within the metaphor. In the following example, maturing was proceeding smoothly until several binding patterns "loomed up" and unexpectedly interrupted the maturing process:

T: **And as** button is pushed [stamps floor], **and** cord is retrieved, **and** thin sheet is triggered **and** goes WHAM [replicates hand movement], and pipes are severed [pause], **and** construction drops away from the base of fire bucket, **then what happens**?

C   It's not a bottomless bucket any more.

T: **And when** it's not a bottomless bucket any more, **what happens next**?

C: [Broad smile.] Then I am more at peace with myself and things don't … [long pause]. A sense of the world becoming right and things are as they should be. The old order being restored. Or maybe it's a new order made up of the old!

T: **And when** you are more at peace with yourself, **and** a sense of the world becoming right and things are as they should be, **and** the old order being restored, or maybe it's a new order made up of the old, **then what happens**?

C: [Long pause. Frowns.] There are lots of gaps in me. My universe has not been realised yet. I don't feel I'm living on all pistons firing. I'm only actually a very small part of my universe. There's a whole seven-eighths I haven't been able to realise. Eight-eighths is like dying and going to heaven [pause]. I'd be happy with seven-eighths. If I could get a job I could start realising my life [long pause]. 'What if' just loomed up. But what if, what if this doesn't work? What if I put everything into this and it doesn't work? Then the whole building will come crashing down.

If an interruption like this happens, you facilitate the client to find out how this new information fits into the organisation of the whole Landscape (using Stage 2 or 3 processes as appropriate).

Maturing can also falter outside of the session. Either an in-session transformational experience proves to be short-lived and the client reverts to old behaviours, or an apparently transformational shift proves to be illusory and the client discovers that they are repeating the same old pattern but in a different form. Whether the transformation was a 'peak experience' or a 'translation in disguise' the client will need to resume the modelling process and incorporate the information contained in the relapse, reversal or return. In a despondent moment the client may think nothing of value has happened, whereas the information about *the way* the change process was interrupted will be invaluable in their search for permanent transformation.[1]

Consolidating the reorganised Landscape

Sooner or later, with or without interruptions, sufficient changes occur so that a reorganised Landscape emerges. Then a process of consolidation begins. Consolidating takes place when the changed symbols, relationships and patterns integrate, amalgamate and synthesise enough for the new Landscape to become a coherent whole and take on a life of its own. From then on homeostatic and binding patterns operate to preserve the new organisation; instead of limiting new growth they nurture it.

Just as Stage 3 is about facilitating clients to model how their *existing* symbolic patterns interrelate, consolidating in Stage 5 is about facilitating clients to notice how *new* patterns fit together as a coherent whole. You do this by directing their attention to the inter-connectedness of new resource symbols, relationships and patterns so that the inherent logic of the matured Landscape emerges.

But how do you know when a Landscape has matured enough to be consolidated? How do you know when the process is finished—at least for now? Sometimes the client tells you. After a long contemplative silence the Jubilee Clip client simply says, "Thank you." But mostly it is when the logic of the changes indicate the client has arrived at a new staging post. For example when:

- The process comes to a natural conclusion—the child becomes the Master.

- A binding pattern is both transcended and included—although jubilee clip and screwdriver evaporate, atomise and become part of the universe, the pattern of wanting to undo jubilee clips lives on, but with a different purpose.

- An emerging pattern of organisation exhibits operational closure (it forms a unity which has a measure of autonomy and the means to activate self-preserving changes)—as the client uses his history and knowledge of jubilee clips for the benefit of others, he will further consolidate his new Landscape.

One way to facilitate consolidation of a newly emerged Landscape is to review the *changes* that have occurred and offer the client an opportunity to reflect on these changes by saying something like, "And now [client words for the last change] take all the time you need to get to know about ..." and then slowly weave the new symbols and metaphors into a tapestry which blesses the new Landscape's organisation.[2] For example the Jubilee Clip transcript ends with:

T84:   **And now** you've stopped climbing ... **and** the child **has** become the
Master ... a Master at undoing jubilee clips for other people ... **take
all the time you need** ... **to get to know about** sublime love ...
and intimate relationships ... **and** feeling comfortable and at ease ...
being able to interact with people ... part of them ... **and now** you've
stopped climbing ... **you can get to know even more about**
balance ... **and** harmony ... **and** confidence ... **and** being a Master at
undoing jubilee clips for others [pause] ...

Exiting the new Landscape and returning to dialogue

Once a Landscape has matured and consolidated enough, the client will need to make a transition from metaphor and trialogue to everyday dialogue.

Often clients take the initiative to exit the symbolic domain. One client stopped, looked around and said, "That's amazing. Now I see the choices in my life as either on my path, or not. When they are not 'on purpose' it will be much easier to say 'no' to them, no matter how attractive they seem. It seems so simple now." If the client does not take the initiative you can encourage the return to dialogue by linking the reorganised Landscape to their everyday life:

> And you can take some time over the next few days and weeks to
> discover what happens in your life as a result of all the changes
> you've made here.

Or,

> And you can begin to consider how what you've learned will influence
> your choices and decisions in relation to your family, work colleagues
> and others in your life.

Some clients may need a few minutes on their own to review the session before they are ready to talk with you again. Others will eagerly want to discuss what they have just experienced. During the discussion you can support them to continue consolidating by asking how specific future events in their life will change as a result of what has happened.[3]

Ending a Session when it is 'Work in Progress'

Of course not every session finishes with a completely reorganised Metaphor Landscape. More likely a session will end during Stages 2, 3, 4 or 5 with 'work in progress'. Three indicators of when to stop Symbolic Modelling are:

- Events in the Landscape come to a natural rest or stopping point, "I'm lying next to a river, enjoying the view and wondering how I'm going to get across."

- The client expresses their desire to stop. "Phew, well, that's certainly given me something to think about."

- You run out of time.

The way you end the session will depend on how much time is left, the events happening in the Landscape and the client's emotional state. If the client and their Landscape are at a convenient stopping point you can summarise the current configuration of the Landscape and then invite them back to everyday dialogue. For example in the Castle Door transcript, the client discovers that she can open and close the door, but by the end of the session she has not chosen to do so. Therefore we say:

T57: **And now** you can open and close that door, **take all the time you need, to get to know what it's like, not to** have to spend all that energy keeping that door closed **any more. And what else can happen now** more gold is inside **and** hollow **is** full and cool **and** all the darkness **is gone** [pause]. **And what difference it makes, now that** you can open and close castle door—**when** you choose. [Pause.]

So take some time to get to know what all this means for you and what difference it will make when you leave here [pause]. **Do you have any comments, thoughts or feelings about what you've experienced**?

Her reply makes clear what needs to be addressed in the next session:

C58: [Long pause.] I know what this is about. My husband is ill and my daughter's dying of cancer. I deserted God. Or God deserted me. I'm not sure which. I lost my link to God and have never got it back.

You can support the client to make the transition to everyday dialogue by employing the opposite behaviours to those used in Stage 1 for Entry:

- Change to a more conversational voice tone and speed
- Ask questions which engage conceptual processing
- Initiate a dialogue by referring to the client by their name and talking in the first person.

If you are running out of time and the client is not at an appropriate stopping point, it is usually preferable to invite them to spend some time attending to an aspect of their Landscape that is resourceful, or at least neutral, before you complete. You do this by reviewing the current state of their Landscape and then backtracking to a safe place, a resource or to their original outcome.[4]

Assignments

Just because the client leaves your consulting room does not mean the Symbolic Modelling process stops. Many clients gain insight, get a different perspective and change their behaviour as a result of noticing correlations between how they think, feel and respond in their 'real life', and the organisation of events in their Metaphor Landscape. You can assist this with a well-chosen assignment.

Assignments are tasks which encourage self-modelling by engaging the client in an activity related to their outcome for therapy and to their Landscape.

Depending where in the Five-Stage Process the session ends, an assignment invites the client to continue developing their symbolic perceptions (Stage 2), modelling their patterns (Stage 3), identifying necessary conditions for transformation (Stage 4), or maturing changes that have taken place (Stage 5). Assignments usually involve some type of: *mapping, writing, researching* or *physicalising*.

MAPPING – DRAWING OR SCULPTING THE CURRENT LANDSCAPE

Mapping has numerous functions. Initially it can help the client develop the form of their symbols and metaphors. Then it can aid them to see patterns that have occurred over sessions, and to contemplate or investigate the relationship between the Landscape and their life: "Now that you know there are six links to that chain, it might be useful to consider what each one of those links represents."

As we explained in Chapter 8, maps can also be used to encourage the client to attend to wholes (Approach B) and broaden attention (Approach C).

If the Landscape has already started to change, an assignment can help develop the changes and encourage them to spread to other areas: "Now that X has happened, you might want to find out what difference this will make to the other symbols on your map."

WRITING – IN JOURNAL, STORY OR POETIC FORM

Some clients report that by writing an account of what happened in the session they can continue the process on their own. Other clients dialogue with their metaphors and symbols by asking them Clean Language questions and writing the answers in a journal.[5]

RESEARCHING – WORDS, PHRASES, SYMBOLS, STORIES

Some clients find it illuminating to research the additional meanings, functions, history and etymology of key words and symbols (see Chapter 8, Approach C). For others, a way to identify their patterns is to research the characters, fairy tales, myths, stories, books and films which have appeared in their Landscape.

PHYSICALISING – ENACTING THE METAPHORS

Clients can make all sorts of discoveries by physicalising their metaphors: visiting or revisiting places which have appeared in their Landscape; finding environments which match features in the Landscape; altering things in their home or work place to replicate the symbolic changes that have taken place; embodying their process by engaging in symbolic acts and creating personal rituals.

At the beginning of subsequent sessions we ask clients to report on what they have learned and what has changed as a result of the assignment. Our aim is to raise the client's awareness of their ability to change. We also regularly review how much has changed since they started therapy and how this relates to patterns in their Metaphor Landscape.

Because change often manifests in unpredictable ways, we listen and look for changes which the client may not have fully acknowledged or appreciated. A client came to us with a very specific outcome: to stop compulsively cleaning her house. A month later, at her second session, she reported that her compulsion was only marginally better but that her relationship with her husband had unexpectedly improved. The next session revealed minimal change to the compulsion but a big improvement in her relationship with her children. At subsequent sessions she reported that she had joined a gym, started working part-time, had been accepted for a place at university and was feeling much better about herself generally. It was not until the eighth session that she casually mentioned that while she still reverted to the occasional bout of cleaning, it was a diminishing and not very important part of her life any more—and that there was no need for a ninth session.

Concluding Remarks

Whether a change manifests as the merest alteration to an attribute of one symbol or as a transformation of a pattern of organisation accompanied by a dramatic display of emotion, you respond in the same way—by supporting the changed Metaphor Landscape to mature.

Your role is to direct the client's attention to each change as it occurs, and then to facilitate that change to evolve, develop and spread to other symbols and contexts. In this way novel patterns emerge which can be consolidated into a new Metaphor Landscape.

Much as clients want to change, they usually have little idea of what they will experience when they actually have changed. When some clients experience the first significant shift they think, "that's it, it's all over" when in fact there may be much more for them to learn. Therefore it is generally better to over rather than to under mature. The more time spent maturing, the more the client will embody and integrate the changes. The more the reorganised Landscape consolidates, the more the client will become familiar with their new way of being. Once this happens, a whole world of possibility opens up for them.

Finishing maturing does not complete the change process—far from it. The reorganised Landscape will continue to influence the client and initiate further unexpected changes long after their work with you is a distant memory.

IV

IN CONCLUSION

10

<hr>

Outside and Beyond

Yes, metaphor. That's how this whole fabric of mental interconnections holds together. Metaphor is right at the bottom of being alive.
Gregory Bateson

While this book has been about facilitating individuals in a therapeutic context, Symbolic Modelling can also be applied outside the consulting room. The components of Symbolic Modelling—metaphor, modelling and Clean Language—can be used in three ways: to model successful strategies and states of excellence, to facilitate change, and to facilitate individuals and groups to create new metaphors (Figure 10.1). The components can be applied together or individually; and can be used in conjunction with other methodologies.

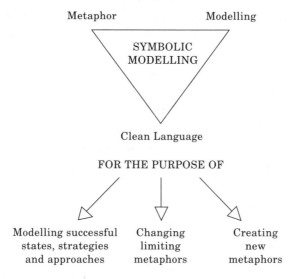

FIGURE 10.1 Three ways of applying the components of Symbolic Modelling

Applications

Below we describe a range of examples where Symbolic Modelling is being applied outside the field of individual psychotherapy: as a modelling methodology, in education, with couples and families, in the spiritual realm, in health, physical therapy, business and organisations.

Modelling success

Symbolic Modelling has been used to identify and codify states of excellence, successful strategies and outstanding approaches. For example, what motivates an author to have their work published? How do people forgive? How do some clinicians have excellent rapport with their patients? To find out, modellers need access to one or more 'exemplars' who demonstrate the successful behaviour. The purpose is for the modeller, or others, to be able to achieve similar results by 'acquiring' a corresponding state, strategy or approach.[1]

One way to model symbolically is to facilitate an exemplar to self-model and to 'take on' or embody their metaphors in the process. Alternatively, you can elicit the organisation of the Metaphor Landscape of one or more exemplars and construct a generic model. Then you, or others, can acquire this synthesised model by adjusting your existing metaphors to correspond to theirs.

The following examples illustrate how metaphors can be a vehicle for the transfer of behaviours, skills and beliefs from one or more individuals to another.

MOTIVATION TO PUBLISH

When we first started writing this book James met an author who had many books and hundreds of articles in print. James wondered what motivated him to publish his work. A little Symbolic Modelling revealed that having his work published was like "leaving footprints in the snow." James asked him to stand up and describe the scene as if it were happening now. The author continued:

> I'm in the open with snow all around. When I look back and see my footprints I get a sense of where I've come from and the value of my life. There are lots of footprints in front of me, but those are not mine and they are not going in my direction. Ahead I see dry-stone walls criss-crossing the landscape. There is a gateway and that's where I'm heading.

I have no idea what's through the gateway until I get there. But each publication means I take a step closer to that gateway. I know the snow will not last forever; I'll die and my footprints will eventually disappear. But that doesn't matter. What matters is that I left my mark, I trod my path.

Later he remarked "I hadn't realised before, but now I understand why I always start my day writing and why I don't consider a piece of work finished until it's published."[2]

James decided to put himself in the author's shoes by physicalising the metaphor. That night he put sheets of white paper on the floor in a line leading from his bed to the door. In the morning when he got out of bed he stepped onto each sheet of paper which sounded like walking through snow. By the time he had crunched his way out of the bedroom his motivation to write had the added element of 'for publication'. James did this every day for two weeks until he no longer needed the paper— and he has been writing first thing in the morning ever since.

FORGIVENESS

The London Clean Language Practice Group symbolically modelled the process of forgiving. Each participant was facilitated to discover their metaphorical representations for what it was like before, during and after a specific act of forgiveness. Here is a selection:

BEFORE	THE PROCESS	AFTER
Tight	Releasing a rubber band	More space and freedom inside
Small minded	Letting go of a helium balloon	Seeing with a wider perspective
Stuck	Being let off the hook	An open heart
Running round in circles	Crossing a bridge	Choice to move toward as well as away from

The group looked for patterns across individual metaphors. They learned that, generally:

Before the process of forgiving could begin, there needed to be an explicit awareness of 'not forgiving' which was experienced as tension, smallness or restriction.

The *process* of forgiving started with a desire to forgive, and this developed into a symbolic movement such as releasing, opening or moving toward.

After forgiving, metaphors of choice, freedom and change in relative proportion were common.

It also became apparent that most people can forgive to a degree, and that the act of forgiving may need to be repeated many times before a completely forgiven state is reached.

CLINICAL RAPPORT

Wendy Sullivan was contracted by the National Health Service to model clinicians with excellent doctor-patient relationships. As part of the project she interviewed each doctor and elicited a metaphor for the way they related to their patients. Examples were 'a good actor', 'a chameleon', 'a detective' and 'attending a Southeast Asian business meeting'. When the clinicians were brought together they were invited to share metaphors and 'to try each other's on for size'. It was surprisingly easy for them to do this, even though some of their metaphors appeared to be very different. In the ensuing discussion they agreed on the common elements of their metaphors. These were: joining another person's world; getting to the heart of the patient's problem; and having the ability to adapt to each patient while remaining true to themselves. They concluded that a 'chameleon detective' was the metaphor that most fitted them all. One senior consulting physician was so pleased with the aptness of the metaphor that he began introducing it into his training of student doctors.

It did not escape Wendy's attention that clinicians who have good relationships with their patients have a natural fluency with metaphor.

Education

Educators are applying Symbolic Modelling in a number of ways. The following five examples from a range of contexts show how, with a little creativity, the use of autogenic metaphor and Clean Language is making a contribution in the field of education.

MATHS PROBLEM

A pupil who had great difficulty doing maths thought he was stupid if he could not give an immediate answer to a maths problem. He said, "I know I know the answers but I just can't find them." Caitlin Walker helped him symbolically model how he found the answers to easy maths problems: "It's like the problem goes upstairs in a lift and when it comes back down I have the answer." He discovered one of the differences between easy and hard problems was the length of time it took for the lift to come back down. He found, to his delight, that if the problem was hard and he waited long enough, the lift would return with an answer or with a clarifying question. He also realised that getting upset with himself prevented the lift returning, and that with some hard problems the lift doors became stuck. When he found ways to oil the doors and to wait, there was improvement in his maths—and also in his self-confidence.

ANGER MANAGEMENT

Caitlin Walker has also used Symbolic Modelling with a group of adolescents whose disruptive behaviour resulted in their exclusion from the mainstream school system. These youngsters had little idea how to manage their anger and would become violent at the slightest provocation. Within the group each was facilitated to identify a metaphorical sequence of events—starting with what happened just before they became angry and how the process of becoming angry resulted in physical violence. Each metaphor gave its owner a language with which to describe their experience, a way of recognising early warning signals, and a means of intervening in their own behaviour to prevent the anger-violence pattern repeating. One youngster had a "radar" that detected when someone was thinking of starting a fight, which led him to attack first. After he modelled his strategy, others in the group said that because they expected him to start fights, they "prepared for war" whenever he was around. He realised that his radar was detecting their fear of him attacking first. Over a number of months he discovered that by "turning down" his radar he could "defuse" many situations before he "started to explode." Although he learned how to control his anger in the classroom, he chose to keep his radar turned up outside, "because it's what keeps me alive on the streets."

CLASSROOM RESPECT

One creative teacher, Susie Greenwood, used Clean Language as a way of responding to a class of 11-year olds when they objected to watching a religious education video. One child shouted, "It's not fair." Susie wrote this exact phrase on the board and said to the class, "And it's not fair.

And when it's not fair, is there anything else about it's not fair?" She was bombarded with replies, including "You're mean," which she wrote on the board. When the class was asked, "And what kind of mean is that mean?" one child ventured, "You're cross," which was also written up. "And what happens just before I'm cross?" received several replies, including "You're not cross, you're upset." As she wrote this on the board, Susie asked, "And what's the difference between cross and upset?" The first answer was, "There's respect." "And when there's respect, what happens next?" So many hands went up that she asked every child to say one sentence about respect. By the time each child had spoken, the class had settled down. Susie then said, "Now I'm going to show you the video, and afterwards I want to know what you thought about it, and what you got out of it."

Susie told us she thought this approach worked well because she asked clean questions of the whole group rather than by singling out any individual. Collectively they could see that she accepted their opinions without trying to change them or defend herself, after which the general discussion and mood of the class could evolve in a mutually respectful way.

LISTENING

As a Speech and Language Therapist, Wendy Sullivan often works with students whose difficulty with their speech is compounded by difficulty in attending to what is being said. Their poor listening skills make it hard for them to understand or remember details, especially during school lessons or lectures. In the past she taught rules for good listening. Now she elicits their metaphors for what poor listening is like, and what good listening is like.

One student "went into a little world" when not listening, and "kept the ear and the eye on the teacher" when concentrating. She helped the student explore the structure of the metaphors—how they got into their little world, how they came out, and what needed to happen for them to keep the eye and the ear more on the teacher.

Wendy says that once the students have identified the way their metaphors for listening work, they can monitor and guide their own behaviour more easily than they could by consciously trying to follow set rules.

MOVING SOUND

Christoffer de Graal runs Moving Sound workshops for people with severe physical or learning disabilities. Some participants are described by their support staff as autistic or as not having developed language comprehension. This does not inhibit Christoffer. "I've been told again and again that they don't understand my questions, yet they still respond, and I utilise their response—whatever it is." He and the participants play a variety of musical instruments "to enable them to get more of a sense of how they can express themselves and to create a conversation between moving and sound, and sound and moving." He begins the workshops by asking each participant "What movement or sound do you have today?" Then he utilises the basic clean questions to enable him to establish a connection with participants' nonverbal behaviour. As a result the participants create new and enjoyable ways of expressing themselves nonverbally.

A sample of the staff's comments from a post-workshop debriefing are "It really got people's personalities coming out"; "I've seen development, people have been more willing to join in and make their own contribution"; and "You can place limitations on people and this blows that out of the water." Christoffer says, "Clean Language creates a container that's respectful and encourages me to have an attitude of curiosity, acceptance and wonder."

Couples and families

Symbolic Modelling is being used successfully with couples and families. A number of therapists such as Clive Bach, Dee Berridge and Frances Prestidge have been utilising client-generated metaphors in couple therapy.

One way to work with couples is to facilitate each partner to develop a metaphor for the relationship, either conversationally or through a symbolic drawing. Each metaphor is then explored using Clean Language so that areas of conflict and compatibility can be identified. Just describing their metaphor to their partner often has a profound effect. In one case:

> A couple were having sexual problems and both felt bitter and resentful—until they gradually evolved the following metaphors.

For him it was like his favourite toy was broken and he was waiting for it to come back from the repair shop but no one could tell him when or if it would ever be ready. He felt helpless and frustrated. He was considering looking for a new toy, but really loved the old one and wanted it back.

For her it was like living in a very small house surrounded by fields. Her favourite companion, a big friendly dog, lived outside. She loved the dog and wanted to go out and play with him but he was always so close to the door that she couldn't get out. She felt angry and trapped. She wanted the dog to move away from the door so she could come out and join him in the fields.

When they shared these metaphors a big shift happened. Each could listen to and understand the others' experience in a way that just hadn't been possible before. They felt compassion for one another instead of blame and were able to identify ways to change their behaviour and solve the problem. They continue to use metaphors to assist them in resolving new issues as they arise.[3]

Another approach facilitates couples to create a *joint* metaphor for how they want their relationship to be, which they draw on one sheet of paper. As events unfold in the combined Metaphor Landscape, frank and eye-opening discussions are stimulated when they are asked:

And what is the relationship between [Y's symbol] and [X's symbol]?

And is [X's symbol] the same or different as [Y's symbol]?

And when [X's event] what happens to [Y's symbol]?

And when [Y's event] what would [X's symbol] like to have happen?

Deirdre Tidy has introduced metaphor into the 'circular questions' of family systems therapy. One member of a family is facilitated to develop a metaphor for the presenting problem. When the metaphor changes and evolves, another member is asked what effect this change will have on a third member of the family. Their response is developed into a metaphor and the process repeated until the question circulates round all the family members.

Couples and families say that by sharing metaphors they have a better understanding of "where the other person is coming from," and that metaphor creates an environment which allows them to say and hear things in a safe and respectful way.

Spirituality

When people speak of God, angels, devils, a life force, healing energy, a power greater than themselves, my mission, a calling or a sacred contract, it is inevitable that they will use metaphor. Because it is so important to honour these experiences and their associated beliefs, Symbolic Modelling is ideal for working in the spiritual domain.

REFOCUSSING

Diane Divett is a Pastor who is undertaking a PhD. She is researching the effectiveness of 'Refocussing', an approach she devised which uses Clean Language and David Grove's metaphor therapy within the context of Christian theology. The aim of Refocussing is to: "Help individuals examine: (1) Where have I come from? (2) Where am I now? (3) Where am I going? (4) How am I going to get there? in light of where God is for them and what He has to offer concerning their life issues, past, present and future."

Central to her approach is the use of Clean Language to help clients "locate, access and develop their own unique God spaces. This enables people to connect to God allowing for divine interaction which facilitates potent healings." She maintains Clean Language is based on "the scriptural mandate to listen." As an example of the effectiveness of her work, Diane describes a client with a decade-long tranquilliser addiction whose "God space was in his stomach, right near the emptiness, tension, anger, guilt and frustration in his life ... God for him was like oil, providing peace, comfort, relaxation and love. As he focused on where God was for him and allowed God, like oil, to pour into the emptiness, he was healed."[4]

AN ETERNAL APPLE

With Clean Language you do not need to be an expert in any particular doctrine to be of value in helping someone identify how they connect with Spirit, find the God-within, clarify their spiritual beliefs or discover their life's purpose—but you do need to be cleaner than clean.

Much of our psychotherapeutic work involves the spiritual content of people's lives. This can manifest as "an emptiness in my life," "God is trying to trick me," "Someone up there's looking after me," or a feeling of 'connection', 'oneness' or 'team spirit'. While metaphors such as 'eternal light', 'infinite ocean', 'endless space', 'universal plan', 'web of life' and 'all powerful energy' are easily recognised as spiritual in nature, the sacred often disguises itself in a mundane pattern or motif.

One client had a metaphor of throwing away a bothersome apple. No matter how often or how far he threw it, sooner or later it would reappear in his hand. He had spent years trying to get rid of it. An exploration of this pattern revealed that he threw the apple away as soon as he had a clear sense of the direction his life should take—only to have it reappear in his hand whenever he felt lost or confused. It was a special moment when he finally realised that rather than trying to get rid of the apple, he could accept it as guiding his decisions and the direction of his life.

Health

Health professionals are using Symbolic Modelling in a variety of ways to facilitate patients and colleagues to increase awareness of illness and wellbeing and to improve communication. Some practitioners are finding it useful to elicit metaphors for a patient's current symptoms, the process of healing and their optimum state of wellness. The practitioners then use Clean Language to facilitate the patient to learn what needs to happen—within the metaphor—to move from illness to health.[5]

SYMPTOM DESCRIPTION

While running a Healthy Language course for a group of nurses who specialised in Multiple Sclerosis, we were told that their patients often had difficulty describing the bizarre nature of their symptoms. We suggested they ask them, 'And that's like what?' and then develop whatever metaphor emerged.

When they did, they got responses such as "It's like ants running all over my body" and "It's like cheese wire wrapped round my legs." Further clean questions encouraged the patients to describe these strange sensations in greater detail. The nurses were surprised at just how relieved the patients felt when they could explain their symptoms in this way. Some patients said it was the first time they felt someone had really understood their illness.

A DOCTOR'S SHORTHAND

Dr. Sheila Stacey uses metaphor to save time and build rapport with patients. "Some patients give lengthy descriptions of their symptoms or problems, so I wait for them to use a metaphor that sums up what the problem is like for them." The metaphor gives both the doctor and the patient a shorthand description for future reference. A patient who was experiencing depression spent a long time talking about her illness and a number of problems in her marriage before she said, "It's like trying to climb out of a black hole." Sheila said that at future appointments "we could both refer to the 'black hole' or the 'climbing out' and know it represented a shorthand description of a very complex problem." This allowed them to make maximum use of the limited consultation time available.

Sheila also says patients classically describe pain with metaphors like knotted, squeezing, stabbing or burning. "I've found patients with cancer use particularly vivid metaphors: 'it's eating away at me' or 'I'm frightened it will spread like wildfire'. There were times when I'd spend hours explaining the technical details of treatment options to patients, but when I'd meet them later it was as if I'd explained nothing. They remember so much more when I use their metaphor to explain the effects that radiation or chemotherapy will have on their cancer."

REACHING AGREEMENT

The parents of a young child who had been born prematurely with major brain damage thought that, given her prematurity, she was developing in a normal way. Paediatrician Dr. Tom Allport's initial diagnosis of cerebral palsy was confirmed, yet the parents continued in the belief that their child would be fine. Because his explanation of the child's illness did not seem to register with the parents, Tom used Clean Language to establish agreement about the child's observable symptoms: her arching back, her strange limb movements and her miserable look. After there was agreement on the symptoms, doctor and parents together could define shared goals aimed at helping to ease the child's discomfort and decide what forms of treatment would be best for her. They could do all of this without the parents having to accept that their child had cerebral palsy.

The child died two years later and Tom clearly remembers a subsequent meeting with the parents where they thanked him for "listening in a different way than everyone else had."

Tom says, "I ask 'What kind of ?' all over the place. Clean Language helps me create a shared language where words and meanings make sense to professionals and patients alike. Thinking in Clean Language, even when I don't speak it, helps me work out what we are understanding, what we are not, and to consider where to take the conversation."

Physical therapy

A growing number of bodywork practitioners are adding Clean Language and the use of client's metaphors to their work. Below we give two examples.

META-AROMATHERAPY

Christine Westwood uses David Grove's metaphor therapy in combination with aromatherapy to address unresolved trauma. "The healing process works through identification of the specific location of associated body symptoms in combination with the aromatherapy massage, which releases ... unconscious childlike components of the personality to emerge [in] metaphor ... Meta-Aromatherapy uses the related metaphors —a succession of mental images and felt sensations unique to each client—as a safe way of resolving these often hidden traumas." She says it is important for the practitioner "not to 'interfere' with this process of release, both [by using] 'clean' language ... and physically through posture and freedom of movement." It is a safe way of working because "Metaphor allows the client to resolve trauma without being engulfed in the actual circumstances" and "neither the client nor the therapist need to know the originating circumstances of the trauma."[6]

PUBLIC SPEAKING

Alastair Greetham, a Chartered State-Registered Physiotherapist, specialises in helping people improve the way they use their bodies in areas such as sports performance and public presenting. He begins working by using Clean Language to elicit a metaphor which represents the client's current sense of their body. He then takes them through a series of developmental physical exercises aimed at freeing the body and creating a balanced, aligned and integrated posture. At the end of the process the client identifies a metaphor for how they experience their body now.

One public speaking client with a tense, compressed and bent spine described his body as like "A bridge that's tipped up and buckling under the stresses and strains." After the exercises this became "A suspension bridge that supports itself. One that spans a beautiful river, with white fluffy clouds in the sky and a setting sun—such a pleasing and relaxing environment." Alastair says that the metaphors enable his clients to measure how much they have progressed. And placing their attention on their new metaphor before a competition or presentation helps them to access and retain their optimum body state.

Business and organisations

There is a growing use of Symbolic Modelling in business and other organisations. We give three examples involving recruitment, computer training and a company whose staff created a corporate metaphor.

RECRUITMENT

Dan Rundle, a recruitment specialist, uses Clean Language to find a fit between employers and potential employees. When a Social Services department calls needing a social worker, Dan responds "So you need a social worker. And if I could get someone for you who was perfect, what would that person be like?" He repeats back their answers, frequently asking 'What kind of?' and 'Anything else?' about the information they have given him. He then calls prospective candidates and asks what the perfect position for them would be like, and this opens up the way for asking more clean questions. Dan uses Clean Language because "repeating back their exact words ensures the information I get is accurate, and asking the questions means I don't make assumptions and I get the specifics right first time. I send fewer CV's, they are closer to what the customer wants (which they really appreciate) and my hit rate is better, so I have an enhanced reputation in the organisation and great performance bonuses." Dan says his job "is like one of those kid's toys with different shapes where you have to find the right hole, except with Clean Language you can fit an odd-shaped piece into an odd-shaped hole perfectly."

COMPUTER TRAINING

Simon Stanton is a consultant who trains National Health Service workers in how to use computer systems. He likes to tailor his training to the particular learning style of his participants, so he helps them identify a metaphor for the type of system they are learning. This sets up a context in which he can illustrate how the computer operates in a way that is already familiar to them. For example, he finds out in detail how a participant organises their office, toolbox or kitchen and uses this as a metaphor to explain how a database works. The system's features and any associated jargon are related to their metaphorical equivalent. If the participant has a problem understanding, it can first be resolved within the metaphor and then the solution applied to the real computer system.

Simon has found a little Clean Language can go a long way. He tells the story of a computer user who, when asked, "What's it like learning about the computer?" replied "It's clear as mud." Simon's next question, "And what kind of mud is that mud, when it's as clear as mud?" gave the user something to think about. She finally replied, "Actually, it's getting clearer." Simon moved on to the next participant, leaving her mud to continue clearing.[7]

CORPORATE METAPHORS

Many companies have created corporate mission and vision statements, but few have created a corporate metaphor. New Information Paradigms (NIP), a niche software development company specialising in knowledge management systems, is one that has. Assisted by consultant Caitlin Walker, each of the 16 staff identified a number of metaphors for 'the company and where it is going', for 'me as a member of NIP', and for 'my relationship to NIP and the way I would like it to become'. As a result, an entire wall next to the coffee machine became adorned with Metaphor Maps. The staff were then taught Clean Language so they could respectfully investigate each other's metaphors. Next, each of the company's four teams was facilitated to incorporate the individual maps into a single group metaphor. With this accomplished, the teams paired up to discuss areas of overlap, disagreement and synergy, finishing with an inter-linked or integrated metaphor. Finally the four teams combined to produce a composite corporate metaphor. The result was a far better understanding of how they could work together and of what they were collectively trying to achieve. NIP found that "meetings are shorter, more constructive and we reach a common understanding quicker," "we are more able to remain objective," and "it allows people to access their emotions without having to be overt about it." Caitlin adds that the process gives them another perspective from which to find agreement and uncover problems: one group metaphor contained a river, and when they saw there was no way for people to cross the river, they realised that *that* was the problem!

Recognising a good thing, the company has devised its own applications for Symbolic Modelling. When NIP customers have difficulty specifying their requirements, the sales team uses Clean Language to help them create metaphors for what they want. When the metaphor is translated into traditional business-speak, the customers feel understood and the sales people have high-quality information. Back at the office, the sales people relay the usual customer information *and* the customer's metaphors to the software designers. NIP say the metaphors provide "a common definition language" with which to discuss the project and to "get to the underlying reasons why something is the way it is." The software developers create their own metaphors to help explain the technical design features to the sales and marketing teams, who in turn use these metaphors in their presentation to customers. In the process, the software developers have found unexpected uses for their systems. NIP has identified three main advantages of using metaphor. In their words:

> Metaphors work because they transmit enormous amounts of information and richness.
>
> Presenting ideas and situations as metaphors gives the receiver the opportunity to understand the message being communicated to them, in their own terms. Perhaps more importantly, any points raised, or criticisms voiced about the metaphor (with its inherent gaps, flaws etc.) isn't personal—the scope for taking offence is greatly reduced ... there is 'room to manoeuvre' without being 'pinned down' ... to get all metaphorical.
>
> Encouraging participants, in a group, to come up with their own metaphors for (apparently) the same thing — a product, a customer situation etc. — often creates a mental or virtual 'shared space'. In this 'shared space', it becomes possible to explore individual metaphors, there is scope to merge or use them as stepping stones towards a metaphor that everyone has contributed to, or at least that can be subscribed to.[8]

The twenty or so examples described are only the metaphorical tip of the iceberg of what can be achieved using Symbolic Modelling. Symbolic Modelling can be applied in so many fields because thought processes are largely metaphorical, because modelling is an innate ability, and because Clean Language, by its very cleanness, adapts to a remarkably wide range of environments.

And Finally ...

Our metaphors are like threads which weave together to create a continually unfolding tapestry—the fabric of our existence. They are so fundamental, pervasive and embedded in thought, word and deed that they tend to remain out of our awareness. As we become aware of the way metaphors define our experience, we open up the possibility for a transformative shift in the way we perceive ourselves and our world.

Facilitating an individual to self-model their Metaphor Landscape requires the integrity of Clean Language. It requires us to accept how little we can know of another person's developmental process. It requires us to think systemically and to trust in the dynamics by which people transcend and include their current state of knowing and being. It requires us to honour, affirm and celebrate every one of their responses as a revelation of their uniqueness. And it requires us to pay due diligence to the evolutionary unfolding of each human spirit.

V

ANNOTATED TRANSCRIPTS

NOTE:

1. Repetitive passages have been deleted from the following transcripts, otherwise they are verbatim.
2. We do not identify which of us asked each question.

Castle Door Transcript

More explanation of this transcript can be found in Chapters 3, 6 and Approach E in Chapter 8.

T0: And what would you like to have happen?

Standard opening question.

C1: I'd like to have more energy because I feel very tired.

T1: And you'd like to have more energy because you feel very tired. And when you'd like to have more energy, that's more energy like what?

Requests entry into metaphor.

C2: It's like I'm behind a castle door.

T2: And it's like you're behind a castle door. And when behind a castle door, what kind of castle door is that castle door?

Asks client to attend to the nature of the perceived symbol, thereby developing its form.

C3: A huge castle door that's very thick, very old, with studs, very heavy.

T3: And a huge castle door that's very thick, very old, with studs, very heavy. And when huge castle door is very thick, very old, with studs, very heavy, is there anything else about that huge castle door?

Further developing—if the door has five attributes, maybe it has more.

C4: I can't open it and I get very very tired trying to open it.

T4: And you can't open it and you get very very tired trying to open it. And as you get very very tired trying to open it, what kind of very very tired trying is that?

Inviting client to notice the nature of the relationship between the perceiver and perceived.

C5: Like I'm struggling on my own and not getting anywhere. It takes a lot of energy. I feel like I'm banging my head on a wall.

T5: And like struggling on your own, not getting anywhere, and banging your head on a wall. And as it takes a lot of energy banging your head on a wall, what kind of wall is that wall?

Developing the form of the new symbol.

C6: A castle wall of thick granite and I get very frustrated and very angry.

Attention shifts to the perceiver.

T6: And a castle wall of thick granite and you get very frustrated and very angry. And when very frustrated and very angry, where is that very frustrated and that very angry?

Locating 'very frustrated and very angry' will determine if this is one or two feelings, and will begin to develop their form.

C7: In here [touches solar plexus region].

T7: And when in here, whereabouts in here?

Locating more specifically.

C8: Exactly in here. Hollow. Full of darkness.

T8: And exactly in here. Hollow. Full of darkness. And when hollow is full of darkness, is there anything else about that darkness?

Developing the form of the new symbol.

C9: It's very dry.

T9: And it's very dry. And when darkness is very dry, it's very dry like what?

Still developing.

C10: It's dry like a desert.

Desert *in* hollow *in* body *in* castle.

T10: And it's dry like a desert. And when dry like a desert, is there anything else about that?

More developing.

C11: It keeps me in one place and it doesn't let me move.

Similar function to C4 and C5.

T11: And it keeps you in one place and doesn't let you move. And dry like a desert, hollow full of darkness in here and struggling on your own and very very tired trying to open huge castle door that's very thick and very heavy and very old. And is there anything else about that door you can't open?

Backtracking to the door and then inviting the client to notice other attributes (now that the relationship with the perceiver has been identified).

C12: Yes. A great big circular handle that's all twisted around.

T12: And is there anything else about that great big circular handle that's all twisted around?

Developing the form of the new symbol.

C13: It looks like twisted pasta. It's big. It's old. It's dull. It's metal, iron, black.

Second reference to 'old' (C3), indicates 'door' and 'handle' have a history.

T13: And when great big circular handle looks like twisted pasta and it's old iron, black, where could that old iron come from?

Inviting time to move *back* to the source of the handle's 'old iron'.

C14: A spear.

T14: And a spear. And what kind of spear could that spear be?

Developing the form of the new symbol.

C15: Like a Roman would use—I've a sense of a centurion standing with it.

T15: And you've a sense of a centurion standing with it. And what kind of centurion could that centurion be?

Developing the form of the new symbol.

C16: [Smiles.] Big and broad with armour on and a spear.

The nonverbal indicates a potential resource.

T16: And when big, broad centurion with armour on is standing with a spear, then what happens?

Invites time to move *forward* to start identifying a sequence of events.

C17: He knocks on the door.

Ah, the 'centurion' is part of the castle context but is on the outside.

T17: And as he knocks on the door, what happens next?

Continues to move time forward.

C18: I can hear him but he can't see me and he goes away. And I can't get out. Then I get very frustrated. It gets almost too much to bear.

Potential solution (No. 1) fails and the pattern repeats.

T18: And it gets almost too much to bear. So when you're behind huge castle door with a twisted iron handle, and you get very very tired trying to open it, and hollow is full of darkness, and a big broad centurion with a spear knocks, and you can hear him but he can't see you, and he goes away, and you can't get out, and it gets almost too much to bear, [pause] then what happens?

Recapitualtes the sequence and then moves time forward to discover the effect of not getting out.

C19: [Pause.] Then I lose all my energy because I don't know what to do.

T19: And then you lose all your energy because you don't know what to do. And when you lose all your energy because you don't know what to do, then what happens?

Continues to move time forward to discover effects.

C20: I sit in the corner and go to sleep.

T20: And you sit in the corner and go to sleep. And as you sleep, and sleep, what happens next?

Moves time forward to after the event 'sleep'.

C21: I have to find a way out. I try to open it again.

'T' is repeating the same pattern.

T21: And you have to find a way out. And you try to open it again. And what happens just before you try to find a way out again? | Directs attention to the moment before the pattern repeats.

C22: [Looks up and squints.] I can see the sky—I never noticed that before—hope is on the outside [long pause]. It's very strong. It gives me determination and the ability to keep trying. | Several potential resources make their appearance.

T22: And you can see the sky. And hope is on the outside. And when it gives you very strong determination to keep trying, whereabouts is it when it's very strong? | Locating the potential resource 'it' invites it into form.

C23: I can feel it right in the middle—at the absolute core of my being. | As 'it' is in the middle and at the absolute core, 'it' is probably not 'hope' which is on the outside (C22). So what is 'it'?

T23: And when you can feel it right in the middle, at the absolute core of your being, it's like what? | Asks for a metaphor for 'it'.

C24: It's gold.

T24: And it's gold. And when it's gold at the absolute core of your being, what kind of gold is that gold? | Continues developing the form of the symbol.

C25: Absolutely pure. It's always been there. | Indicates significance of this resource.

T25: And absolutely pure. And absolutely pure gold's always been there at the core of your being. And is there anything else about that absolutely pure gold? | More developing of the resource 'gold'.

C26: It's incredibly strong but malleable. Powerful. You could shape it but you couldn't break it. An almost silent powerful.

T26: And an almost silent powerful. And is there anything else about that absolutely pure gold that's incredibly strong and malleable and almost silent powerful at the absolute core of your being? | More developing of the qualities of the resource symbol.

C27: It can move. | In contrast to C4, C11, C18.

T27: And gold can move. And where would gold like to move to? | Asks for gold's intention.

C28: To become liquid and fill all the space.

T28: And can it become liquid and fill all the space?

Checking ability to enact intention.

C29: No.

Potential solution (No. 2) fails.

T29: And gold can't become liquid and fill all the space. And gold would like to become liquid and fill all the space. And when gold would like to, and can't, what needs to happen for gold to become liquid?

Acknowledges current reality, and asks for conditions necessary for gold to achieve its intention.

C30: It has to go outside into the sun.

T30: And can gold go out into the sun?

Checks if it can fulfil the condition.

C31: It doesn't want to.

Another conflict emerges.

T31: And it doesn't want to. And for gold to become liquid and fill all the space, it has to go outside into the sun and it doesn't want to. And it has to go outside and it doesn't want to. And when it has to go outside and it doesn't want to, then what happens?

The repetitions acknowledge the conflict of intentions. Moving time forward identifies the effect of the conflict.

C32: Some could go, and some has to stay behind.

Potential solution (No. 3).

T32: And is some that could go the same or different to some that has to stay behind?

Specialist developing question which differentiates each 'some'.

C33: Very very core has to stay behind. I won't let that move. I need that. I won't let it go.

'I' reappears and is now the one that 'won't let it go' outside!

T33: And very very core has to stay behind, and you won't let it move. And when you won't let very very core go outside, where does that won't let it go come from?

Asks for the source of the 'won't let it go'.

C34: If it goes out into the sun I lose it. I lose my strong determination and that's where my power comes from.

But gold 'has to go outside into the sun' (C30) to become liquid so that it can fill all the space (C28).

T34: And when your power comes from your strong determination, where does strong determination come from?

Tracing back the source of 'strong determination'.

C35: Way, way back.

A new context (time-space).

T35: And whereabouts way, way back?

Asks for a more specific address.

C36: A link somewhere but I don't know where.

T36: And a link somewhere, but you don't know where. And what kind of link could that link be?

Developing the form of the new symbol.

C37: It links from something to me. A link I know is there but nobody else can see it.

T37: And what kind of something is that something way, way back that links to you?

Developing the form of the 'something' at the other end of the link.

C38: I don't know [pause].

T38: And when you don't know, is there anything else about a link that's there but nobody else can see?

Directs attention to what client does know.

C39: It's twisted.

Remember 'twisted' handle at C12?

T39: And it's twisted. And when link is twisted, it's twisted like what?

Developing its form.

C40: Very fine thread.

T40: And very fine thread. And what would very fine thread that links like to do?

Identifies fine thread's intention.

C41: To pour some more of the gold into me.

Potential solution (No. 4).

T41: And very fine thread would like to pour some more of the gold into you. And what needs to happen for very fine thread to pour some more of the gold into you?

Asks for the conditions necessary to enact thread's intention.

C42: A tap needs to be turned on.

T42: And can a tap be turned on?

C43: Yes, but it doesn't come out quickly enough.

'Yes, but ...'

T43: And a tap needs to be turned on, but gold doesn't come out quickly enough. So what needs to happen for gold to come out quickly enough?

Asks for the conditions necessary to satisfy the 'but'.

C44: To come out over the top of the vessel.

T44: And to come out over the top of the vessel. And what needs to happen for gold to come out over the top of the vessel?

Asks for the prior necessary conditions.

C45: An unseen hand needs to tip it so it runs round the outside.

A new resource appears.

T45: And can an unseen hand tip vessel so gold runs round the outside?

Can 'unseen' hand enable a link that 'nobody else can see' (C37) to pour some more of the gold into her?

C46: Yes!

T46: And as unseen hand tips vessel and gold runs round the outside, what happens next?

Invites client to enact the intention and notice its effect.

C47: Some of it gets into me [pause]. I get stronger as it goes down.

Gold is fulfilling thread's intention from C41 and (probably) gold's intention from C28.

T47: And when some of it gets into you, and you get stronger as it goes down, then what happens?

Evolving the change.

C48: I feel much more calm and stronger.

T48: And as gold goes down and you feel much more calm and stronger, what kind of calm is that calm?

Developing the effects of the changes.

C49: I don't have to panic behind the door.

T49: And you don't have to panic behind the door. And then what happens when you don't have to panic?

More evolving.

C50: I have to want to choose to open the door.

Note 'I' is three removed from actually opening the door.

T50: And you have to want to choose to open the door. And what needs to happen for you to want to choose to open that door?

C51: I need to take the risk.

Another condition is necessary.

T51: And you need to take the risk. And can you take the risk—to choose to open that door?

C52: Only if I can choose to close it again. I'm worried about the handle on the inside. I need to have control of this door.

'Only if …' is yet another condition. Presumably this 'handle' is the same as that in C12.

T52: And you need to have control of this door. And when more gold goes down and you feel more calm and stronger and you don't have to panic behind the door any more, and you'll take the risk to open that door if you can choose to close it again, what happens to a big, broad centurion with a spear?

Recaps the changes and invites client to notice if the changes have spread to the potential resource.

C53: He can stand outside and protect.

T53: And as centurion stands outside and protects, then what happens?

Enacts centurion's function and directs attention to the effects.

C54: I can open it from the inside and nobody can open it from the outside.

The final condition is fulfilled.

T54: And when you can open it from the inside and nobody can open it from the outside, what happens to hollow full of darkness?

Inviting client to notice if the changes have spread to 'hollow' and 'darkness'.

C55: All the darkness goes.

T55: And when all the darkness goes, what kind of hollow is that hollow when all the darkness goes?

Developing the form of the changed hollow.

C56: Well, gold fills the hollow and cools the desert.

Reappearance of the 'desert' (C10).

T56: And when gold fills the hollow and cools the desert and all the darkness goes, then what happens?

More evolving.

C57: I can open it and close it [pause]. I don't have to spend all that energy keeping that door closed.

Ah, that's where all her energy was going: keeping closed the door that she was trying to open!

T57: And now you can open and close that door, take all the time you need, to get to know what it's like, not to have to spend all that energy keeping that door closed any more. And what else can happen now more gold is inside and hollow is full and cool and all the darkness is gone [pause]. And what difference it makes, now that you can open and close castle door—when you choose. [Long pause.]

It's time for the session to end, and this is a convenient place to finish. So we review all the changes as a way of consolidating the Landscape's new features.

So take some time to get to know what all this means for you and what difference it will make when you leave here [pause]. Do you have any comments, thoughts or feelings about what you've experienced?

C58: [Long pause.]

I know what this is about. My husband is ill with ME and my daughter's dying of cancer. I deserted God. Or God deserted me. I'm not sure which. I lost my link to God and have never got it back.

The client makes some conscious discoveries and connections, so the therapy will proceed with a new outcome. As an assignment we asked her to: draw a Metaphor Map of the current Landscape; to wonder about the relationship between 'I deserted God' and 'desert' (C10, C56); and 'my link to God' and the link 'that nobody else can see' (C37).

Jubilee Clip Transcript

More explanation of this transcript can be found in Chapters 7, 8 and 9.

T0:	And what would you like to have happen?	Standard opening.
C1:	Total confidence in my own abilities. There is a colleague who has incredible self-belief. He believes he is going to succeed no matter what obstacles are put in his way. I became a senior manager by accident and now I feel vulnerable [touches chest with left hand]. It's like I'm waiting to be exposed and then people will say 'We're proved right'. I'm thinking, how can I disguise my weakness?	Defines outcome. This specifies the client's current state and is the fourth time he has used 'vulnerable' since we began the session.
T1:	And you'd like total confidence in your own abilities and now you feel vulnerable. And when you feel vulnerable, how do you know you feel vulnerable?	The entry question asks the client to reflect on his experience of 'feel vulnerable'.
C2:	Failure comes to mind. I failed the 11-plus exam. I realised for the first time I wasn't invincible. I felt different about me.	A memory with indicators of a defining moment.
T2:	And you realised for the first time you weren't invincible and you felt different about you. And when you felt different about you, what kind of felt different is that?	This developing question invites the client to *stop time* and define the attributes of 'felt different'.
C3:	I see me as a young boy looking up at mother. She has a look of disappointment on her face. She's just read the letter saying I failed the 11-plus.	The repetition of 'see', 'looking', 'look' and 'read' indicates a significant visual motif.
T3:	And she's just read the letter saying you failed the 11-plus. And when she has a look of disappointment on her face, what kind of look is that look?	Invites the client to notice the attributes of one of the looks.
C4:	Expressionless, drawn, eyes looking down, jaw set, a serious look of sadness. Almost a look of resignation.	The amount of detail indicates the significance of the look.
T4:	And when mother's read a letter saying you failed and mother has almost a look of resignation, then what happens?	Starting to identify the sequence of events.

C5:   For the first time mother distances herself.

More indication of a defining moment.

T5:   And for the first time mother distances herself. And as mother distances herself, then what happens?

Continues identifying a sequence.

C6:   He feels puzzled as it's never happened before. He knows something wrong has happened. Something has changed in the bond.

T6:   And what kind of change could that change be when something has changed in the bond with mother?

Asks for attributes of the *changed relationship* between the symbols 'mother' and 'son'.

C7:   The child feels it's around love—it's not as strong.

T7:   And it's around love and it's not as strong. And when love is not as strong, then what happens?

Returns to identifying the next step in the sequence.

C8:   A quietness. Mother goes about her housework but doesn't recognise the child in the same way.

This is 'after' the defining moment as mother's location and her relationship with the boy have changed.

T8:   And a quietness, and mother doesn't recognise the child in the same way after she has read a letter. And what happens just before mother's read a letter?

Backtracks to the first step in the sequence so can ask client to attend to the *preceding* step.

C9:   He can sense the affection between them. There is an air of expectancy of success. He's happy.

The perception 'before' is marked by a completely different state.

T9:   And when he can sense the affection between them, and an air of expectancy, and he's happy, then what happens?

Checking if the client goes through the same sequence.

C10: She completely read the letter. In fact I remember the moment—she completed reading the letter twice.

Yes. And note the detail of how many times mother read the letter.

T10: And she completed reading the letter twice. And she completed reading the letter twice. And what kind of moment is that moment when she completed reading the letter twice?

Saying the words twice honours the twice-ness.
Asks him to notice the attributes of the defining *moment* rather than any component of that moment.

C11: Not a pleasant moment. He doesn't want to repeat it.

T11: And he doesn't want to repeat it. And when he doesn't want to repeat it, then what happens?

C12: He feels that something is wrong with himself.

Client's attention has moved from mother's look to his feelings about himself.

T12: And when he feels something is wrong with himself, what kind of feels something is wrong could that be?

Invites client to develop this new source of information.

C13: A bad feeling. He's hurt somebody, caused pain.

T13: And he's hurt somebody, caused pain. And a bad feeling. And where does he feel that bad feeling?

Asking for a location encourages the feeling to develop a form.

C14: Here [touches chest with left hand].

The same hand in the same place as before (C1).

T14: And whereabouts here?

C15: In the chest. In the upper chest.

T15: And in the upper chest. And what's the relationship between a bad feeling in upper chest and vulnerability?

Checking if there is a difference between the two feelings located in his chest.

C16: It's the same as an adult feeling of vulnerability.

T16: And it's the same feeling. And is there anything else about that feeling when it's the same feeling?

Continuing to develop attributes.

C17: Rapid, shallow breathing and a tightness.

T17: And rapid, shallow breathing and tightness. And when tightness, what kind of tightness could that tightness be?

More developing.

C18: [Pause.] It's difficult to explain.

T18: And when rapid, shallow breathing and tightness, and it's difficult to explain, does it have a size or a shape?

This specialist question aims to develop the form of 'it' so the client can 'explain'.

C19: [Client holds left forefinger with right hand.] It's like a finger is grabbed and pressure is applied—I have a picture— it's of a jubilee clip tightening around a hose.

He answers with a metaphor for the binding pattern. The 'ing' indicates the ongoing nature of the symptoms.

T19: And a jubilee clip tightening around a hose. So when jubilee clip is tightening around hose, where does that tightening come from?

Asks for the source of the 'tightening' relationship.

C20: A screwdriver.

T20: And what kind of screwdriver is that screwdriver?

Developing the form of the new symbol.

C21: Flat-bladed with a plastic handle.

T21: And is there anything else about that flat-bladed plastic-handled screwdriver that's tightening jubilee clip?

Honours the detail. Using 'that' rather than 'a' names Screwdriver and Jubilee Clip and gives them an identity.

C22: The handle is yellow.

T22: And handle is yellow. And when flat-bladed screwdriver is tightening jubilee clip around hose, what would yellow plastic handle like to do?

Requests the intention of the *symbol* rather than the client.

C23: Undo it.

T23: And can it undo it?

Checks if intention can be enacted.

C24: There's a conflict.

T24: And there's a conflict. And when screwdriver would like to undo jubilee clip and there's a conflict, what kind of conflict could that conflict be?

Identifies the binding pattern that keeps the metaphor from changing —the conflict between two intentions.

C25: There's a fear about undoing the clip. It's an unknown risk.

As the risk is 'unknown' how can it be calculated?

T25: And when there's a fear about undoing the clip, and it's an unknown risk, what kind of unknown could that unknown be?

Asking client to notice the nature of the other half of the conflict.

C26: Is somebody going to be disappointed at the result?

T26: And is somebody going to be disappointed at the result? And when there's a fear about undoing jubilee clip, where could that fear be?

Locating the symbol named 'fear'.

C27: In the chest again [touches chest with left hand].

The same as C1 and C14. Do we detect a nonverbal pattern?

T27: And in the chest again. And is that the same or different as vulnerable in the chest?

Checks it is the same pattern.

C28: No difference. They're the same.

T28: So fear and vulnerable are the same. And screwdriver is tightening jubilee clip round hose. And screwdriver wants to undo jubilee clip, and there's fear of undoing jubilee clip—is somebody going to be disappointed at the result?

Acknowledging all the components and relationships of the pattern. Hence bringing the *whole* pattern into awareness.

And as screwdriver is tightening jubilee clip, and fear of unknown risk, and vulnerable in chest, and screwdriver is tightening, and screwdriver wants to undo jubilee clip, what happens next?

Invites client to notice how he responds to this kind of conflict.

C29: A feeling of helplessness.

T29: And a feeling of helplessness. And when helplessness, is there anything else about that helplessness?

C30: [Shrugs shoulders.] No.

A helpless response to helplessness?

T30: And no. And helplessness. So when there's a conflict and helplessness, what needs to happen for screwdriver to undo clip?

Enquiring if the client knows what conditions are necessary to resolve the conflict.

C31: A person has to do it [pause]. And that person is me.

He does.

T31: And a person has to do it and that person is you. And what kind of person is that person who has to do it?

Asking for the attributes of 'that person' starts to develop the new symbolic perception.

C32: Not afraid. Confident, comfortable with myself. Congruent. Well-balanced. Focused [pause]. In harmony.

T32: And not afraid, confident, comfortable with yourself. Congruent. Well-balanced. Focused. In harmony. And when in harmony what kind of harmony is that harmony?

Concentrating on developing the attributes of the resource.

C33: With people, with nature, with myself. With the good and bad things in life.

T33: And when harmony with people, with nature, with yourself, and with the good and bad things in life, that's harmony like what?

Invites a conversion to symbolic form.

C34: A truly balanced person. It reminds me of a TV show and the Master from Kung Fu.

T34: And a truly balanced person, the Master from Kung Fu. And what kind of Master is that Master?

More developing of the resource symbol.

C35: He has answers to life. A deep understanding of himself, nature, his place in the world. He can be an example, a guide.

T35: And he can be an example and a guide. And he has answers to life, and a deep understanding of himself, and nature, and his place in the world. And when he has a deep understanding of himself, where could that deep understanding come from?

Invites client to locate the source of the resource.

C36: A large part from himself. And some external. But mostly it comes from within.

T36: And some external but mostly from within. And whereabouts within does deep understanding come from?

Asks for a more specific location of the resource and invites the client to embody it.

C37: The head. The brain. And all the senses.

T37: And when deep understanding comes from the head, the brain and all the senses, is there anything else about where deep understanding comes from?

Which way to go? Don't know. Ask 'is there anything else?' so that the *client* sets the direction.

C38: It includes emotional things — I picture a heart.

T38: And what kind of heart is that heart?

Developing attributes of the symbol within a symbol.

C39: A mature heart.

T39: And a mature heart. And is there anything else about the mature of that heart?

Developing the 'mature' attribute which is complementary to that of 'young boy'.

C40: It's had lots of experience. It's red. It's a picture of a heart, but it doesn't look like a real one.

T40: And when red mature heart has had lots of experience, what happens to a person who has to undo jubilee clip that's tightening?

Specialist question to discover the relationship between the resource and the conflict.

C41: I feel like the pupil. I've not reached the level of maturity required.

An indication that a secondary bind is operating.

T41: And when you feel like the pupil and you've not reached the level of maturity required, is there anything else about the level of maturity required?

Developing the attributes of the new bind.

C42: It's not to do with age. It's to do with upbringing and principles and thought processes. I don't think I've had the upbringing [pause]. I've only started to grow over the last few years.

'Grow' is a naturally-changing process and potential resource.

T42: And you don't think you've had the upbringing and you've only started to grow over the last few years. And what needs to happen to grow to the level of maturity required?

Asks client to identify the conditions necessary for him to become the person who can undo Jubilee Clip.

C43: I wonder if I can ever achieve it. There's an element of doubt. I'm looking for an external experience [laughs]. Like an exam!

A key moment as the pattern has repeated. (Presumably the client realises the situation of the boy and the adult correspond—he still needs to pass an exam!)

T43: And you're looking for an external experience to reach the level of maturity required. And what kind of exam could that exam be?

Invites client to identify attributes of the potentially redeeming exam.

C44: A very difficult exam.

T44: And a very difficult exam. And is there anything else about a very difficult exam?

C45: I haven't got the background to sit it. I'm inadequate to take the exam.

Another part of the organisation of the bind is revealed (see Figure 7.4 for a description of the paradox).

T45: And when you haven't got the background, and you're inadequate to take the exam, what kind of inadequate could that inadequate be?

C46: My childhood upbringing. Not being exposed to intellectual stimuli. I didn't grow as fast as I might. Everything seems to come late.

T46: And everything seems to come late. And when you didn't grow as fast as you might, is there anything else about not growing as fast as you might?

We're not sure who is saying what about whom. So we opt for the all-purpose question, 'And is there anything else?'

C47: I'll have to prove myself more than once.

A further knot in the bind.

T47: And when you'll have to prove yourself more than once, how many times will you have to prove yourself?

C48: Twice, to be his equal.

How many times did mother read the letter?

T48: And twice, to be his equal. And what kind of twice could that twice be?

C49: It's like running round a track and I have to overtake him twice.

T49: And like running round a track and you have to overtake him twice. And running and running. And you'll have to prove yourself more than once. And you have to overtake him twice. And as you're running round that track and you have to overtake him twice, what kind of him could he be?

> The 'ing' indicates the ongoing-ness of the bind as does the recurring motif 'round' (C7 and C19).

> Lots of repetition of running and twice-ness encourages the client to embody the pattern and identify the 'him' he has to overtake twice.

C50: My ideal me.

T50: And your ideal me. And as you're running round that track and you have to overtake your ideal me twice, what happens as you grow?

> Preserves the name 'me' and invites client to explore the relationship between these two symbolic processes. (Can he grow enough to overtake 'me' twice?)

C51: It changes the situation.

T51: And as you grow it changes the situation, and then what happens?

> The first indication of a change is evolved ...

C52: The gap widens. The more I grow the more the gap widens.

T52: And the gap widens. And the more you grow the more the gap widens. And the more you grow the more the gap with your ideal me widens. And the more you're running round a track, the more the gap widens [pause]. And then what happens?

> ... only to reveal a secondary bind. (Note the metaphor is similar to a mother *distancing* herself.)

> Honours the bind and moves time forward to discover the effects of the pattern.

C53: It's a no-win situation.

T53: And it's a no-win situation. And is no-win situation the same or different as helplessness?

> Checks assumption about isomorphic nature of pattern.

C54: It's the same.

T54: And no-win and helplessness are the same. And when no-win is the same as helplessness, that's no-win and helplessness like what?

> Now we've been round the pattern twice!

> Asks for a metaphor for the *whole* pattern of organisation.

C55: It's like I have to keep climbing a mountain that gets higher the more I climb.

> The nature of the double bind is captured in a single metaphor.

T56: And when you have to keep climbing a mountain that gets higher, where did the have to of that have to keep climbing a mountain come from?

> Asks for the source of the 'have to' that keeps the pattern repeating.

C57: Not wanting to see a look of failure. Wondering 'Am I good enough?'. [Touches chest with left hand.]

Nonverbal pattern repeats. He started with 'wanting confidence' but his doubts keep him running round a no-win pattern which means he can't be confident.

T57: And not wanting to see a look of failure. And wondering 'Am I good enough?' [Pause.] And would red, mature heart that's had lots of experience and deep understanding be interested in going to young boy who's not wanting to see a look of failure?

Time to test the interest of the resource in going to 'young boy' with all his vulnerability, fear and not wanting to disappoint.

C58: [Long pause.] Yes.

T58: And yes. And can that red, mature heart go to that young boy?

Testing the ability of the resource symbol to enact its interest.

C59: Yes.

T59: And as red, mature heart that's had lots of experience and deep understanding goes to that young boy [pause], what happens next?

Introduces the two symbols and asks for the effects.

C60: He feels life again.

T60: And as he feels life again, then what happens?

First mention that he had not been feeling life. We ask him to move time forward to evolve the change.

C61: The race becomes enjoyable.

T61: And as the race becomes enjoyable and he feels life again, then what happens?

The result is that the relationship between runner and race changes.

C62: Confidence returns.

T62: And confidence returns. And when red, mature heart that's had lots of experience and deep understanding goes to that young boy and he feels life again and the race becomes enjoyable and confidence returns, what happens to a mother who's just read a letter twice?

Yes. Just what he asked for in C1.

However, the new Landscape has yet to develop a mature form so we accumulate all the changes so far and invite the client to notice if the changes have spread to 'mother'.

C63: She expresses it's a learning process, not a failure. She's comfortable with him.

Two relationships change: mother and exam, and mother and son.

T63: And she's comfortable with him. And it's a learning process. And when mother is comfortable with him, what happens next?

Maturing the effects of the change.

C64: The boy has a different view. A sense of security. Looking forward to life.

Ah ha. A double change. And remember the significance of 'looks' (C3–C4).

T64: And looking forward to life. And a sense of security. And a different view. And what kind of view is that different view?

Maturing by developing the attributes of the changed perceiver.

C65: A wholly confident view. Congruent. Balanced [pause]. In harmony.

Note that the attributes of the Master have transferred to the boy.

T65: And when young boy has a wholly confident view, congruent, balanced, in harmony what would he like to do first?

Maturing by enacting an intention.

C66: Take the exam again.

T66: And can he take the exam again?

C67: Yes, and he passes.

A change to the original sequence.

T67: And he takes the exam again and passes. And what happens next when he passes the exam?

Evolving the change.

C68: He begins growing into a Master.

T68: And as he begins growing into a Master, what kind of growing is this growing into a Master?

A new, naturally-evolving process is matured. 'This' acknowledges the difference with the other growing which could not overtake his ideal self.

C69: Aware of the world around him. Understanding his place in life. Enjoying the process.

The boy's whole relationship with the world and life is changing.

T69: And aware, and understanding his place in life, and enjoying the process. And is there anything else as he begins growing into a Master?

More developing and use of 'as' to evolve.

C70: It's also being able to interact with people—for their benefit.

Yet more relationships change.

T70: And when able to interact with people for their benefit, what kind of interact with people is that?

C71: I feel comfortable and at ease. Almost part of them.

Compare this with the 'waiting to be exposed' (C1).

T71: And when you feel comfortable and at ease and almost part of them, where do you feel that comfortable and ease?

Developing by asking for location.

C72: [Smiles and touches chest.] In here again!

Where before he felt 'vulnerable', now he feels 'comfortable'.

T72: And in here again. And what kind of in here is that in here?

More developing and embodying.

C73: Totally relaxed.

T73: And when totally relaxed and comfortable and at ease and almost part of them, what kind of part of them could that part of them be?

Maturing continues because there are some symbols unaccounted for.

C74: Being an influence on their lives. Upbuilding of productive relationships [pause]. Maybe even intimate.

The up-down motif (C3, C4, C35, C41, C42) now applies to relationships and a new resource 'intimate' spontaneously appears.

T74: And an influence on their lives, and upbuilding productive relationships, maybe even intimate. And what kind of intimate could that intimate be?

Developing the new resource.

C75: [Long pause.] Could you ask me that question again?

Where did the client's attention go?

T75: And an influence on their lives. And upbuilding productive relationships, maybe even intimate. And what kind of intimate could that intimate be?

C76: There's no comfort zone and no barrier.

More changes. This time to previously unmentioned spatial configurations. Not a standard clean question, more an entry into a new Metaphor Landscape.

T76: And when there's no comfort zone and no barrier, what is there, when there's no comfort zone and no barrier?

C77: [Long pause.] Love.

T77: And love. And what kind of love is that love?

Love returns (C7) in a new way and is developed.

C78: Sublime love.

T78: And sublime love. And where does that sublime love come from?

Asks for the source of the resource.

C79: Here again [touches chest with left hand].

Sublime love is now located in the place of vulnerability.

T79: And here. And when sublime love comes from here, that's sublime love like what?

Invitation to convert to metaphor.

C80: Even consider giving your life for another.

Instead of a symbol he describes a symbolic act.

T80: And even consider giving your life for another. And when sublime love from here, what happens to jubilee clip and screwdriver?

Checks if changes have spread to the original symbols.

C81: They disappear.

They have.

T81: And when they disappear, where do they disappear to?

Yes but where to?

C82: They evaporate. They're atomised.

Now the client knows.

T82: And jubilee clip and screwdriver evaporate, atomised [pause]. And then what happens?

More evolving.

C83: They are part of the universe.

T83: And when jubilee clip and screwdriver are part of the universe, what happens next?

Just making sure.

C84: The child becomes the Master. Wholeness pervades [long pause].

He's undoing jubilee clips for other people [pause].

He's a Master at doing it [laughs]. I feel like I've stopped climbing [very long pause].

Thank you.

The child 'becomes' the Master and attention shifts from 'he' to 'I'. His relationship with jubilee clips has transformed and so has the pattern of organisation.

T84: And now you've stopped climbing ... and the child has become the Master ... a Master at undoing jubilee clips for other people ... take all the time you need ... to get to know about sublime love ... and intimate relationships ... and feeling comfortable and at ease ... being able to interact with people ... part of them ... and now you've stopped climbing ... you can get to know even more about balance ... and harmony ... and confidence ... and being a Master at undoing jubilee clips for others [pause].

Time to encourage the new Landscape's organisation to further consolidate.

And take all the time you need over the next few days and weeks ... to discover ... what ... happens ... next.

[When leaving, the client added:]

For the last few years I've been asking myself, 'Am I doing what I want to do or is it time to look for something new?' But I kept getting blanks. Now I know what my mission is: helping others to undo their jubilee clips.

And we all laughed.

Lozenge Transcript

C1: I started a relationship recently but there's insecurity about the relationship. It's "too good to be true." I find it difficult to enjoy the relationship as I get very anxious when I am not with her. I overwhelm her. I have to hold back. I'm waiting for her to say "I can't take it any more." I was last in a relationship three years ago which I managed to sustain for 2 weeks. When I fall in love I get the feeling of anxiety —I feel almost ill—so maybe I engineer the collapse of the relationship so I can manage the anxiety. It gets worse because I'm aware of the effect. I've had to pull back from the brink a couple of times.

How many layers are there to this binding pattern? Two at least. A secondary bind is apparent because *his awareness* that the primary bind—it is difficult for him to enjoy being with her *and* he gets anxious when he is not—causes more anxiety.

T1: And what would you like to have happen?

C2: I've got to give her room to love me back.

An outcome.

T2: And you've got to give her room to love you back. And when you've got to give her room to love you back, is there anything else?

C3: A feeling that I've got to love her as much as I can because she's not going to be around for that long. It's like I've got to eat all the sweets today even though there will be plenty more tomorrow. "It's too good to be true." I don't believe it will be there tomorrow. I'm not meant to be happy, it's not for me. Love brings me happiness but I can't handle happiness and joy. It's as if I have to live my life in the darkness.

Further description of the tangled web of cause-effect relationships reveals the pervasiveness of this binding pattern—it extends to 'my life'.

T3: And when you've got to eat all the sweets today, and you're not meant to be happy and you have to live your life in the darkness, is there anything else about that darkness?

So much complex information so soon that we simply select the *last* metaphor mentioned.

C4: I don't ever remember having been happy. I don't feel I've ever had permanent happiness—sustained happiness. I felt very alone as a child. I don't feel I was ever happy. It's just a feeling within me now.

T4: And you don't feel you were ever happy. And when it's just a feeling within you now, what kind of feeling could that feeling be?

Developing the attributes of the feeling.

C5: A sad feeling.

T5: And a sad feeling. And when a sad feeling, where is that sad feeling?

Asks for the location.

C6: In my stomach.

T6: And in your stomach. And when sad feeling is in your stomach, whereabouts in your stomach?

C7: Here [touches stomach].

T7: And sad feeling is here. And when sad feeling is here, is there anything else about that sad feeling?

More developing of attributes.

C8: A feeling sick and nauseous. I can feel it now. I feel very anxious. I hate this feeling.

T8: And you hate this feeling of sick and nauseous and very anxious. And when you feel sick and nauseous and very anxious, does sick and nauseous and very anxious have a size or a shape?

Inviting feeling into form.

C9: A hand's-span width [makes gesture with right hand].

T9: And a hand's-span width. And when [replicates gesture], that's like what?

Invitation to convert to metaphor.

C10: Like a lozenge.

T10: And like a lozenge. And what kind of lozenge could that lozenge be?

Developing the symbol.

C11: Dark, purple with black and it's oozing negative emotions. I feel if I could get rid of the lozenge I'd be ok.

T11: And if you could get rid of the lozenge you'd be ok. And when lozenge is dark, and purple with black and it's oozing

negative emotions, is there anything
else about that dark, purple, black,
oozing lozenge?

Further developing the symbol.

C12: It's like a black or purple sponge, with
liquid seeping out, acid burning me up.

Classic Stage 2 questions have
enabled the client to identify an
anxious-making, negative-emotion
oozing, acid-burning metaphor.
Now we direct the client's attention to the source of the symbol.

T12: And a black or purple sponge, with
liquid seeping out, and acid burning
you up. And when liquid seeping out,
where does that liquid come from?

C13: A permanent store, a secret store re-
plenishing itself and it never runs out.
When nothing seeps out I feel ok. (I'm
glad you two are not psychiatrists or
you'd be writing out the Section Order
right now!)

T13: [Laugh.] And when nothing seeps out
and you feel ok, what happens to lozenge?

Invites client to attend to the relationship between 'feel ok' and
'lozenge'.

C14: It's always in there, even when I was a
baby. It started off like that [holds up
thumb and forefinger of right hand,
fingers not quite touching]. Now it's
taking up more and more space.

Note all the references to time in
C13 and C14: 'permanent', 'never'
'always', 'started' and 'now'.

T14: And it started off like that [repeat ges-
ture]. And it's always in there, even
when you were a baby. And where could
[repeat gesture] have come from *before*
it was in baby?

As he is reviewing the history of
the metaphor, we continue to move
time back by asking for a prior
source of lozenge.

C15: It travelled down the umbilical cord
into me.

T15: And when it travelled down the umbilical cord into you, where did it come
from?

Tracing back the source of lozenge.

C16: It was given to my mother by my father.

T16: And it was given to your mother by
your father. And what kind of father is
that father?

Develops the new symbol.

C17: He resented her. [Blows a breath out.]
He was angry with her and he didn't
let her know he was giving her the
lozenge.

T17: And when he was angry with her and he didn't let her know he was giving her the lozenge, where did his didn't let her know he was giving her the lozenge come from?

Asks what motivated 'father' to keep 'mother' in the dark about the 'lozenge'.

C18: A feeling of frustration that no matter what he does he can't shake off the shackles of unhappiness. He has to sneak it into her during intercourse. I can't handle this any more.

Is this meta-comment aimed at us?

T18: And you can't handle this any more. And when he can't shake off the shackles of unhappiness, where do those shackles come from?

Don't know, but the metaphor is a repetition of 'I can't handle happiness' (C3). We acknowledge the comment and keep to the process.

C19: Dark distant past which I don't know about. He has been dragging them around on his hands and knees. They are attached to his ankles. Something is being pulled along behind him and it's heavy.

We note that the client will probably need to find out about 'dark distant past' at some time, because he has said 'I have to live my life in the darkness' (C3) ...

T19: And shackles are attached to his ankles. And when shackles are attached to ankles and something heavy is being pulled along behind, how far is that something behind?

... and in the meantime we ask about what he is now attending to—the 'something' being pulled along behind.

C20: Ten feet. Like a huge, massive boulder of unhappiness.

T20: And a huge, massive boulder of unhappiness is being pulled along ten feet behind. And what happened just before those ankles were shackled?

Directs attention to the event which preceded the shackling.

C21: He was free to crawl around as a baby. They were put on by my grandfather, to stop him crawling away, but he forgot to take them off the baby.

T21: And he was free to crawl around. And shackles were put on by a grandfather who forgot to take them off baby. And where did his forgot to take them off baby come from?

(How come 'grandfather' forgot?)

C22: He died and no one else noticed.

T22: And he died and no one else noticed. And what kind of grandfather put shackles on a baby?

Developing the nature of the symbol 'grandfather'.

C23: Mean and vindictive.

T23: And mean and vindictive. And when grandfather is mean and vindictive, and puts shackles on ankles of baby, where does his mean and vindictive come from?

C24: From me.

T24: And what kind of you is a you where grandfather's mean and vindictive comes from?

Given the information has been moving back in time inter-generationally, this answer is unexpected and confusing. But we stay true to the process by developing the attributes of 'me'.

C25: "You're old enough."

T25: And "you're old enough." And when "you're old enough," how old is old enough?

Specialist developing question.

C26: 18 and I can't handle it.

The same metaphor as C3, C18.

T26: And 18 and you can't handle it. And when you can't handle it, then what happens?

A moving time forward question invites him to identify the *effect* of not being able to handle 'it'.

C27: Thank God I got rid of it [pause], but there seems to be another one floating around.

T27: And when there seems to be another one floating around, where is that other one?

Developing the new symbol.

C28: [Laughs.] There is only the one—and that's in me. There's a mirror image of the lozenge. I'm seeing it in my hand and it's big and I'm being shown the future and it's going to kill me—I'm being shown it as a warning. So I passed it back to my grandfather.

The client explains the apparent paradox of receiving lozenge through his genealogy *and* giving it to his grandfather.

T28: And you passed the one and only lozenge back to your grandfather. And where did it come from before grandfather ever had it?

But how did grandfather get the lozenge in the first place? A modified clean question invites the client to find out.

C29: (Long pause.) Been floating around in time for thousands of years.

The motif of a very long time returns (C13, C14).

T29: And it's been floating around in time for thousands of years. And it's been floating around for thousands of years like what?

Invites the 'floating' relationship between 'lozenge' and 'time' into form.

C30: Like a parasite looking for a host.

       Metaphors in Mind

T30: And like a parasite looking for a host. And when a parasite's looking for a host, what kind of parasite is that parasite that's been floating around for thousands of years?

Developing attributes.

C31: Lonely, looking for a home and love and warmth and comfort, saying "I'm really friendly" but when it goes into someone it seeps out the acid. It has to get rid of it and it doesn't mean to hurt.

'Lonely' last appeared in C4 and 'acid' in C12. The client is spontaneously modelling the metaphor's inherent logic.

T31: And it doesn't mean to hurt. And it's lonely, looking for a home and love and warmth and comfort. And it's friendly but it has to get rid of the acid. And where could that acid have come from?

C32: The beginning of time.

Indicates we are approaching the original source.

T32: And the beginning of time. And when the beginning of time, what kind of time is the beginning of time?

C33: A huge black sphere. Huge black spherical sponge that one day exploded and it created billions of lonely lozenges. It became the lozenge.

The defining moment when lozenge came into being.

T33: And a huge black spherical sponge exploded and created billions of lonely lozenges. And what happened just before that huge black spherical sponge exploded?

C34: Behind it was a sun shining from behind and it got so hot it exploded and that let all the light through and suddenly there was light.

(Shining son?) After 12 moving time back questions (since T23) the client is attending to a time before the entire pattern began— when there was 'light'.

T34: And when all the light is let through and suddenly there's light, what kind of light is that light?

Developing the new resource symbol.

C35: The sun is bringing light and love and warmth and happiness and calmness and I want to just sit and bask in the warmth of the sun, so the more sun I get the smaller the lozenge gets. [Eyes closed, face upturned, smiling.]

Presumably 'I' has introduced itself to the 'sun' and is basking. In this context at least, he seems able to 'handle' happiness and love.

T35: And the more sun you get the smaller the lozenge gets. So take all the time you need to just sit, and bask in the warmth of that sun, that's bringing light, and love, and warmth, and happiness, and calmness.

[Long pause until a noticeable movement of the client's body.]

And as you bask in the warmth of that sun, would that sun that brings light, and love, and happiness, and calmness be interested in going to shackles on a baby's ankles?

C36: Certainly.

T36: And can that sun go to those shackles?

C37: Certainly

T37: And as that sun goes to those shackles then what happens?

C38: They melt and disappear.

T38: And as they melt and disappear, then what happens?

C39: The baby can crawl and stand and play.

T39: And the baby can crawl and stand and play. And as baby can crawl and stand and play, then what happens?

C40: All the lozenges disappear.

T40: And all the lozenges disappear. And when all the lozenges disappear, they disappear to where?

C41: The sun. They are absorbed by the sun, gently, without pain, into the light.

T41: And when lozenges are absorbed by the sun, gently, without pain, into the light, are lozenges lonely?

C42: No.

T42: And when lozenges are absorbed by the sun, then what happens?

C43: A baby grows up to be a happy person and he can take his time.

T43: And baby grows up to be a happy person and he can take his time. And then what happens when father has intercourse with mother?

As changes are occurring spontaneously, we utilise the clear cause and effect relationship (the more sun 'I' gets the smaller the lozenge gets), and honour the 'long time' motif by saying "so take all the time you need …" and then just wait.

Then we test the interest of the 'sun' to continue spreading the changes.

Introducing the two symbols …

… results in more changes.

Maturing the latest changes.

Further evolving the change.

Discovering the whereabouts of the lozenges helps bring the new Landscape into form.

Checking if the changes have affected the attribute 'lonely' (C4, C31).

More evolving.

Checking if the changes have spread to 'father' and 'mother' (C18).

C44: There is just happiness.

T44: And there is just happiness. And when there is just happiness, what travels down the umbilical cord into you?

This non-standard clean question spreads the effects of 'just happiness'.

C45: Sunlight.

T45: And sunlight. And then what happens?

Evolving.

C46: Just happiness.

T46: And when just happiness and sunlight, and just happiness, what happens to sad feeling in your stomach?

Checking if changes have spread to stomach (C5–C8).

C47: My lozenge has gone! All I can say is 'just happiness'.

T47: And your lozenge has gone. And does just happiness have a size or a shape?

Developing the form of the symbol called 'just happiness'.

C48: A big warm glow, happiness, peace and calm.

T48: And when there is a big warm glow, happiness, peace and calm, what happens to insecurity about the relationship and overwhelming her?

Checking if the changes have influenced the original conditions (C1).

C49: It just goes. Like sunshine on both of them.

T49: And then what happens?

C50: They go forward together, relaxed, confident, no anxiety, no worries, enjoying being, peace, tranquillity, comfort.

T50: And as they go forward together, relaxed and confident with no anxiety and no worries, what needs to happen for you to handle all the enjoying being and peace and tranquillity and comfort and happiness?

The 'as' continues to evolve the changes and the question checks that the client knows the conditions necessary for him to continue to 'handle' the changes (C3, C18, C26).

C51: I need to get out into the sun.

T51: And where are you when you need to get out into the sun?

Developing the new Landscape by locating the perceiver.

C52: Living in a dungeon where no light comes in.

T52: And when living in a dungeon, what kind of dungeon is that dungeon where no light comes in?

Developing the new context.

C53: It's my basement flat where I've been since 1979.

T53: And when your basement flat is a dungeon where you've been since 1979, what's the first thing that needs to happen for you to get out into the sun?

Evolving by identifying conditions necessary for him to continue to 'handle happiness'.

C54: I need to empty it.

T54: And you need to empty it. And what is the first thing you will empty in your flat?

Checking client knows how he is going to start the process.

C55: The lozenges! [Long pause.] I'm going home and opening the front door and saying "Ok buddy, time to go."

T55: And you're saying "time to go." And do lozenges want to go?

Checking if the intention of lozenges matches the intention of 'I'.

C56: Yes [long pause]. They want to get out.

T56: And lozenges want to get out. And can lozenges get out?

Checks if lozenges are able to enact their intention.

C57: I'll see them float out the door. I'll go around the flat and check they've all gone.

T57: And you'll see them float out the door. And when they've all gone, where have they gone to?

Identifying the location of lozenges in the new Landscape.

The lozenges go home (C34).

C58: To the sun.

T58: And when lozenges have gone to the sun, then what happens?

Evolving.

C59: [Very long pause, then looks up and around room.] There's space here [touches stomach]. Things seem different.

This contrasts with when lozenge was 'taking up more and more space' (C14) in the place indicated by the same nonverbal (C7).

T60: And now there's space and things seem different, can you give her room to love you back and enjoy the relationship?

Checks if changes have spread to the client's original outcome (C2).

C60: [Nods. Tears in eyes.]

T61: And is there anything else you need now that there is space and things seem different?

C61: [Long pause.] No. I'm feeling very weird. It's amazing what I came out with.

Twelve months after this session the client called to say he was getting married—not to the woman referred to in the transcript, but to another woman with whom he had "fallen in love in a different way."

Appendix

Summary of David Grove's Clean Language

The Function of Clean Language

To acknowledge the client's experience exactly as they describe it.
To orientate the client's attention to an aspect of their perception.
To send the client on a quest for self-knowledge.

The Four Components of Clean Language

FULL SYNTAX	**And** [client's words/nonverbals]. **And when/as** [client's words/nonverbals], [**clean question**]?
VOCAL QUALITIES	When using client-generated words, match *the way* they speak those words.
	When using therapist-generated words, s-l-o-w d-o-w-n your speed of delivery and use a consistent, rhythmic, poetic and curious tonality.
NONVERBALS	Reference the client's *nonverbal metaphors,* either by replicating, gesturing to, or looking at a body expression; or by replicating a nonverbal sound.
	Reference the client's *perceptual space,* with hand gestures, head movements and looks that are congruent with the client's perspective of the location of their material and imaginative symbols.

CLEAN QUESTIONS

	BASIC DEVELOPING QUESTIONS
IDENTIFYING	**And is there anything else about** [client's words]? **And what kind of** [client's words] **is that** [client's words]?
CONVERTING	**And that's** [client's words] **like what**?
LOCATING	**And where is** [client's words]? **And whereabouts** [client's words]?

	MOVING TIME QUESTIONS
FORWARD	**And then what happens**? **And what happens next**?
BACK	**And what happens just before** [client's words]? **And where could** [client's words] **come from**?

Specialist Questions

Opening	**And what would you like to have happen**?

Entry via a

CONCEPT	**And how do you know** [abstract concept]?
LINE OF SIGHT	**And where are you going when you go there** [gesture and/or look along line of sight]?
METAPHOR MAP	[Look at map.] **And where are you drawn to**?

Identifying Attributes

SIZE OR SHAPE	**And does** [X] **have a size or a shape**?
NUMBER	**And how many** [X's] **could there be**?
AGE	**And how old could** [symbolic perceiver] **be**?
	And what could [symbolic perceiver] **be wearing**?

Locating Symbols

DISTANCE	**And how far {is}** [symbol's address]?
DIRECTION	**And in which direction is/does** [symbol's movement]?
INSIDE/OUTSIDE	**And is** [symbol's name] **{on the} inside or outside**?
PERCEIVER	**And where is** [perceiver] [perceiving-word] **{that} from**?

Identifying Relationships

GENERAL	**And what's the relationship between** [X] **and** [Y]?
FORM	**And is** [X] **the same or different as/to** [Y]?
TIME	**And when/as** [event X] **what happens as/to** [Y]?
SPACE	**And what's between** [X] **and** [Y]?
INTENTION	**And what would** [X] **like to have happen/to do**?
	And would [Y] **like** [intention of X]?
	And what needs to happen for [X] **to** [intention of X]?
	And can [X] [intention of X]?
INTRODUCING	**And would** [resource X] **be interested in going to** [symbol / context Y]?

Notes

I: Background Knowledge

Chapter 1, Metaphors We Live By

1. We recognise that technically all words represent concepts. However we maintain that in practice there is an experiential distinction between words which are processed sensorially, conceptually or symbolically. For example, whether the word 'mother' refers to the person who is 'my mother', or to the concept of 'a mother', or to the symbolic 'Mother Earth', makes all the difference.

2. See Bibliography for works by Julian Jaynes, Mark Johnson, George Lakoff, David Leary, Andrew Ortony, and Steven Pinker.

3. George Lakoff and Mark Johnson, *Metaphors We Live By*, p. 5.

4. This is close to Gene Combs and Jill Freedman's definition. They "use the word 'symbol' to refer to the smallest units of metaphor—words, objects, mental images, and the like—in which a richness of meaning is crystallized." *Symbol, Story and Ceremony*, p. xiv.

5. Carl Jung, *Man and his Symbols*, p. 3.

6. In *Man and His Symbols*, p. 88, Carl Jung calls this potency a symbol's 'numinosity':
   [A symbol's] relationship to the living individual. Only then do you begin to understand that their names mean very little, whereas the way they are *related* to you is all-important.

7. Gregory Bateson, in Daniel Goleman, *Vital Lies, Simple Truths*, p. 7:
   The pattern which connects is a 'metapattern,' a pattern of patterns. ... the right way to begin to think about the pattern which connects is as a dance of interacting parts, secondarily pegged down by various sorts of physical limits and by habits, and by the naming of states and component entities.

8. George Lakoff, *Women, Fire, and Dangerous Things*, p. 389.

9. 'Educational Uses of Metaphor' in *Metaphor and Thought*, edited by Andrew Ortony, p. 622.

10. George Lakoff and Mark Johnson, *Metaphors We Live By,* p. 158.

11. We were first introduced to this idea by Richard Bandler and John Grinder, *The Structure of Magic I*, p. 14:

    The most pervasive paradox of the human condition which we see is that the processes which allow us to survive, grow, change, and experience joy are the same processes which allow us to maintain an impoverished model of the world ... [and] block our further growth.

12. This is a similar exercise to one presented by John McWhirter in his talk entitled "Modelling Thinking" at the Association for NLP conference, London, 5 July, 1998.

13. Mark Johnson, *The Body in the Mind,* makes it clear that metaphor and embodiment depend on each other:

    Through metaphor, we make use of patterns that obtain in our physical experience to organise our more abstract understanding. Understanding via metaphorical projection from the concrete to the abstract makes use of physical experience in two ways. First, our bodily movements and interactions in various physical domains of experience are structured, and that structure can be projected by metaphor onto abstract domains. Second, metaphorical understanding is not merely a matter of arbitrary fanciful projection from anything to anything with no constraints. Concrete bodily experience not only constrains the "input" to the metaphorical projections, but also the nature of the projections themselves, that is the kinds of mappings that can occur across domains. (p. xv)

    The centrality of human embodiment directly influences what and how things can be meaningful for us, the ways in which these meanings can be developed and articulated, the ways we are able to comprehend and reason about our experience, and the actions we take. Our reality is shaped by the patterns of our bodily movement, the contours of our spatial and temporal orientation, and the forms of our interactions with objects. (p. xix)

14. Steven Pinker, *How The Mind Works,* pp. 354-357.

15. Aniela Jaffe´, 'Symbolism in the Visual Arts' in Carl Jung's *Man and his Symbols,* p. 257.

16. See John Grinder and Richard Bandler, *Structure of Magic II*.

17. Julian Jaynes, *The Origin of Consciousness,* pp. 59-60:

    Moreover, things that in the physical-behavioral world do not have a spatial quality are made to have such in consciousness. Otherwise we cannot be conscious of them. ... You cannot, absolutely cannot think of time except by spatializing it.

18. Daniel Dennett, *Consciousness Explained,* p. 107: "The Cartesian Theatre is a metaphorical picture of how conscious experience must sit in the brain." Dennett shows how the Cartesian Theatre exists as an object of heterophenomenology (in the mind) but not an object of real phenomenology (in the brain) because there is a:

> ... distinction between the spatial location in the brain of the vehicle of experience, and the location 'in experiential space' of the item experienced. In short we distinguish representing from represented, vehicle from content. We have grown sophisticated enough to recognise that the products of visual perception are not, literally, pictures in the head even though *what they represent* is what pictures represent well: the layout in space of various visible properties. (p. 131)

19. See Ian Robertson, *Mind Sculpture.*

20. Carl Jung, *Memories, Dreams, Reflections*, pp. 250-252.

21. Fritjof Capra , *The Web of Life*, p. 170:

> The new concept of cognition, the process of knowing, is thus much broader than that of thinking. It involves perception, emotion, and action—the entire process of life. In the human realm cognition also includes language, conceptual thinking, and all the other attributes of human consciousness. ... The Santiago theory [of Maturana and Varela] provides, in my view, the first coherent scientific framework that really overcomes the Cartesian split. Mind and matter no longer appear to belong to two separate categories but are seen as representing merely different aspects, or dimensions, of the same phenomenon of life.

22. George Lakoff and Mark Johnson, *Metaphors We Live By,* p. 6.

23. Karl Pribram, 'From Metaphors to Models: the Use of Analogy in Neuropsychology', in *Metaphors in the History of Psychology,* edited by David Leary, p. 79.

Chapter 2, Models We Create By

1. In *The Structure of Magic I,* Richard Bandler and John Grinder discuss the idea of "a model of our model of our world, or, simply, a Meta-model" (p. 24) and pay homage, like many before and since, to Alfred Korzybski and his famous dictum "the map is not the territory."

2. We recognise not influencing is an impossible outcome since the observer by simply observing inevitably influences the person being observed. However this does not affect the desire of a modeller to not influence.

3. Steven Pinker, *How the Mind Works,* p. 21.

4.   The field of NLP (Neuro-Linguistic Programming) was established as a result of several modelling projects conducted by Richard Bandler and John Grinder. They, in collaboration with Judith DeLozier, Leslie Cameron-Bandler, David Gordon, Robert Dilts and others, did much of the original work to codify the process of modelling sensory and conceptual domains. See 'Modelling in Organisations' at www.cleanlanguage.co.uk or Robert Dilts' *Modelling with NLP* for further references. The only systematic methodology for modelling metaphors and symbolic perceptions that we know of is our development of David Grove's approach.

5.   We borrow the term "bring forth a world" from Humberto Maturana and Francisco Varela's theory of cognition which Fritjof Capra summarises in *The Web of Life,* p. 260:

> Cognition, then, is not a representation of an independently existing world, but rather a continual *bringing forth a world* through the process of living. The interactions of a living system with its environment are cognitive interactions, and the process of living itself is a process of cognition.

6.   George Lakoff and Mark Johnson in *Metaphors We Live By,* p. 25, say:

> Understanding our experience in terms of objects and substances allows us to pick out parts of our experience and treat them as discrete entities or substances of a uniform kind. Once we can identify our experiences as entities or substances, we can refer to them, categorize them, group them, and quantify them — and, by this means, reason about them.

Also, we appreciate there are 'higher' forms of consciousness which transcend and include views of the universe based on separate things, events and people, and that these sometimes, albeit rarely, occur during psychotherapy. As these experiences are typically described in metaphor, they too are amenable to Symbolic Modelling. For a clear introductory description of these higher states we recommend *The Essential Ken Wilber.*

7.   Fritjof Capra, *The Web of Life,* p. 98.

8.   David Grove, *And Death Shall Have No Dominion,* p. 9. This is one reason why David Grove says "Clean Language is information-centered. It is neither client nor therapist-centered." See 'The Philosophy and Principles of Clean Language' at www.cleanlanguage.co.uk.

9.   There are some overlaps between Symbolic Modelling and Eugene Gendlin's *Focusing* process, p. 10:

> [Focusing] is a process in which you make contact with a special kind of internal bodily awareness. I call this a felt sense. A felt sense is usually not just there, it must form. You have to know how to let it form by attending inside your body. When it comes, it is at first *unclear,* fuzzy. By certain steps it can come into focus and also change. A felt sense is the body's sense of a particular problem or situation.

Symbolic Modelling differs from Focusing in that: (a) it incorporates awareness other than "felt" and "inside" the body; (b) it explicitly makes use of autogenic metaphors; and (c) it uses Clean Language.

10. David Grove, personal communication.

11. Arthur Koestler, *The Act of Creation,* p. 178.

12. Ernest Rossi, *The Psychobiology of Mind-Body Healing,* p. 53 (Rossi's emphasis).

13. Win Wenger and Richard Poe in *The Einstein Factor,* describe how the technique of 'Image Streaming' can "condition your mind ... and improve your performance in virtually all aspects of mental ability, including memory, quickness, IQ, and learning capacity" (back cover).

   There are enough similarities between Image Streaming and Symbolic Modelling to believe that any benefits derived from Image Streaming would also accrue to long-term Symbolic Modelling clients. The primary differences relate to Symbolic Modelling: (a) being designed as a therapeutic process; (b) using Clean Language; (c) facilitating the self-modelling of the *organisation* of the image stream; and (d) making use of non-visual modalities.

14. Fritjof Capra, *The Web of Life,* p. 98.

15. Chapter 2 of Ken Wilber's *Sex, Ecology, Spirituality,* provides a comprehensive summary of "twenty basic tenets (or conclusions) that represent what we might call 'patterns of existence' or 'tendencies of evolution' or 'laws of form' or 'propensities of manifestation'" characteristic of self-organising systems. (p. 32)

16. We recognise that 'level' is a metaphor which helps us conceive of an intangible pattern in nature (or in our perception of nature, if you prefer). And that once there are levels, the metaphor inevitably extends to 'higher' and 'lower' levels. As long as we remember that these are metaphors, and that all metaphors bestow advantages and disadvantages, we can use them as useful distinctions. In *Sex, Ecology, Spirituality,* p. 55, Ken Wilber emphasises that levels may be metaphors but they are not arbitrary:

   A level ... is established by several objective criteria: by qualitative emergence (as explained by Popper); by asymmetry (or "symmetry breaks," as explained by Prigogine and Jantsch); by an inclusionary principle (the higher includes the lower, but not vice versa, as explained by Aristotle); by developmental logic (the higher negates and preserves a lower, but not vice versa, as explained by Hegel); by a chronological indicator (the higher chronologically comes after the lower, but all that is later is not higher, as explained by St. Gregory).

17. Ken Wilber, *Sex, Ecology, Spirituality,* p. 33:
     Reality is not composed of things or processes; it is not composed of
     atoms or quarks; it is not composed of wholes nor does it have any
     parts. Rather, it is composed of whole/parts, or holons. This is true
     of atoms, cells, symbols, ideas ... There is nothing that isn't a holon
     (upwardly and downwardly forever).

18. Ken Wilber, *A Brief History of Everything,* p. 31:
     A molecule transcends and includes atoms. Transcends, in that it
     has certain emergent or novel or creative properties that are not
     merely the sum of its components. This is the whole point of systems
     theory and holism in general, that new levels of organisation come
     into being, and these new levels cannot be reduced in all ways to
     their junior dimensions—they transcend them. But they also
     include them ... So, transcends and includes.

     In Sex, Ecology,Spirituality, p. 530, Ken Wilber also says:
     This does not mean that every transcendence necessarily includes
     every predecessor in every detail, but simply that each transcendence
     builds upon some of the fundamental features of its predecessor(s).

19. For example, "I'm beside myself" indicates two, or possibly three perceivers
     ('I', 'my', 'self') perceiving from different locations. David Grove realised
     the importance of perceiver location after he began exploring the then
     bizarre notion: When people dissociate and fragment, where do they
     dissociate and fragment to? He found that some of the client's 'essence'
     'went to' very specific places which had great symbolic significance for
     them. Thereafter certain perceptions were always perceived from, or
     influenced by, those locations. Thanks also to Steve Briggs for helping
     clarify our ideas about perceivers and their 'point of perception' (his term
     for the location from where a perception is perceived).

20. Fritjof Capra, *The Web of Life,* p. 81.

21. The higher the level, the more significant; the lower the level, the more
     fundamental: "More significant ... because more of the universe is
     reflected or embraced in that particular wholeness ... More fundamental,
     because everything above it depends upon it for its existence." Ken Wilber,
     Sex, Ecology, Spirituality, p. 63. By this definition symbols are more
     fundamental, relationships and patterns are more significant and
     patterns of organisation are more significant still.

22. For a full account of this example see 'A Client's Eye View' at
     www.cleanlanguage.co.uk.

23. Fritjof Capra, *The Web of Life,* p. 154.

24. Gregory Bateson, *Steps to an Ecology of Mind,* p. 452. Bateson adds in
     Mind and Nature, p. 97: "The interaction between parts of mind is
     triggered by difference, and difference is a nonsubstantial phenomenon
     not located in space or time."

25. Fritjof Capra, *The Web of Life,* p. 215:

    A living system is determined in different ways by its pattern of organization and its structure [form]. The pattern of organization determines the system's identity (i.e. its essential characteristics); the structure, formed by a sequence of structural changes, determines the system's behaviour ... However, rather than being determined by outside forces, [change] is determined by the organism's own structure—a structure formed by a succession of autonomous structural changes. Thus the behaviour of the living organism is both determined and free.

26. Brian Goodwin, *How the Leopard Changed its Spots,* p. 165:

    The relevant notion for the analysis of evolving systems is that of dynamic stability. A necessary (though by no means sufficient) condition for the survival of a species is that its life cycle be dynamically stable in a particular environment. This stability refers to the dynamics of the whole cycle, involving the whole organism as an integrated system which is itself integrated into a greater system which is its habitat.

27. David Grove refers to such binding patterns as "replicating mechanisms" because they perpetuate themselves. He says, *In the Presence of the Past,* p. 22, "A set of symptoms from an earlier experience reproduce themselves in the adult over and over again. This replication is the same as mitotic cell division."

28. Ken Wilber, *Sex, Ecology, Spirituality,* p. 61.

29. *The Essential Ken Wilber,* pp. 141-142.

30. The idiosyncratic nature of binding patterns means that no one, least of all the client, can know in advance what will emerge when a bind is transformed. This is why, no matter how painful a binding pattern may be, clients tend to hold on to them for dear life—better the devil they know than to step into the unknown and risk breakdown. Even when a client is willing to trust the unknown, they may have little idea how to take the required leap of faith.

31. Gregory Bateson, *Mind and Nature,* p. 109.

32. Ken Wilber, *Sex, Ecology, Spirituality,* p. 54.

33. Robert Dilts, 'Identity and Evolutionary Change', Workshop Manual, February, 1999.

34. In David Grove's early work he identified seven therapeutic operations: "Separation; Individuation; Maturation; Solution; Recombination; Proclamation; and Splitting" which typically happen in that order, *Healing The Wounded Child Within,* p.38. The first four loosely correspond to our Stages 1 to 4, and the last three are included within Stage 5.

35. David Grove, *Healing The Wounded Child Within,* p. 5.

36. Bart Kosko, *Fuzzy Thinking,* p. 148 quotes Lotfi Zadeh, the originator of the term 'fuzzy':

    As the complexity of a system increases, our ability to make precise and significant statements about its behavior diminishes until a threshold is reached beyond which precision and significance (or relevance) become almost mutually exclusive characteristics ... a corollary principle may be stated succinctly as, "the closer one looks at a real-world problem, the fuzzier becomes its solution."

37. These principles have been influenced by some of the 'Presuppositions of NLP'. These were derived from studying outstanding psychotherapists such as Milton Erickson, Virginia Satir, Fritz Perls and others. They may not have held these presuppositions consciously—they just acted as if they did. See Robert Dilts' *Strategies of Genius, Volume 1,* pp. 305-307.

II: The Heart of Symbolic Modelling

Chapter 3, Less is More – Basic Clean Language

1. David Grove and Basil Panzer, *Resolving Traumatic Memories,* pp. 8-10.

2. One of the ways language influences is by *orientating or directing the attention* of the listener. This is a far from simple process for two reasons. Firstly, much of the attention-directing capacity of language is not in the words, but in the presuppositions, voice qualities and nonverbal aspects. Secondly, language can only trigger a response that is already specified by the listener's mindbody system. From this perspective, communication is a property of the system and not a conduit from speaker to listener. See Michael Reddy, 'The Conduit Metaphor' in *Metaphor and Thought,* edited by Andrew Ortony; and Humberto Maturana and Francisco Varela, *The Tree of Knowledge,* Chapter 9.

3. David Grove and Basil Panzer, *Resolving Traumatic Memories,* p. 21.

4. There are a further 20 or so specialist questions which we list in the Appendix, and describe in Chapters 5–8.

5. An alternative construction of the 'full' syntax is:

    And [client words]. And [clean question], when/as [client words]?

    e.g. And you'd like to have more energy because you feel very tired. And is there anything else about that more energy you'd like to have when you feel very tired?

6. The exception is 'So' which is occasionally used to start Clean Language sentences, especially when 'backtracking' and 'accumulating descriptions'.

7. Audio taped workshop in The Lake District, England, November 1997.

8. George Lakoff and Mark Johnson, *Metaphors We Live By,* p. 136:
   > Almost any change in a sentence—whether a change in word order, vocabulary, intonation, or grammatical construction—will alter the sentence's meaning, though often in a subtle way.

   This is why in Clean Language staying clean takes precedence over the rules of English grammar. If a client says "All my soldiers is lined up neat" a clean response would be "And all your soldiers is lined up neat. And when soldiers is lined up neat, is there anything else about those soldiers lined up neat?"

9. Mark Johnson in *Moral Imagination*, p. 166 says:
   > In order for an account of events to become a story it must pass beyond a mere succession of events in serial order to become a "configuration." What is required is a synthesis of parts into a unified whole with a certain structure, one which, as Aristotle was first to note, "has a beginning, middle, and an end" ... [This] structure is an instance of an even more basic recurring imaginative pattern—the SOURCE-PATH-GOAL schema—that structures much of our bodily movement and perception, and that is present in our understanding of temporal processes (via the metaphor of TIME IS A MOVING OBJECT).

   NLP has a similar, although more tightly defined concept of a sequence called a strategy. Robert Dilts, in *Changing Belief Systems with NLP,* says that a strategy is "A set of explicit mental and behavioural steps used to achieve a specific outcome. In NLP, the most important aspect of a strategy is the representational systems used to carry out the specific steps" (p. 220). Note that in this sense 'outcome' does not necessarily mean desirable result; people have plenty of strategies that consistently get them results which they, and others, do not want.

   Another example of a sequence identification technique is the Game Strategy elicitation from Transactional Analysis (see Stewart and Joines, *TA Today*). This process can be used to identify the client's 'macro' sequences of behaviour within the predetermined metaphor of a psychological game.

10. If the client gets the "more energy" she wants, this will only enable her to repeat the pattern more often or more intensely, rather than to resolve it. Thus, as often happens, the client's proposed solution will perpetuate the problem. (See Paul Watzlawick, *Munchhausen's Pigtail*, p. 204.) Once she came to realise this, she could turn her attention to other, more productive ways of organising her metaphors.

11. David Grove and Basil Panzer, *Resolving Traumatic Memories,* pp. 9-13. Also, Milton Erickson explained the value of trance:
    > The induction and maintenance of a trance serves to provide a *special psychological state in which the patient can reassociate and reorganize his inner psychological complexities* and utilize his own capacities in a manner in accord with his own experiential life. ...

Therapy results from an *inner resynthesis* of the patient's behavior achieved by the patient himself.

Quoted by Ernest Rossi, *The Psychobiology of Mind-Body Healing*, p. 88.

Chapter 4, Clean Language Without Words

1.   Humberto Maturana and Francisco Varela, *The Tree of Knowledge*, p. 166. See also Robert Dilts, *Roots of NLP*, p. 53 of Part II:

Because all behavior, microscopic or macroscopic, is a transform of internal neurological processes, it will carry information about those processes. All behavior then is in some way a communication about the internal neural organisation of an individual.

2.   Quoted in Gregory Bateson, *Steps to an Ecology of Mind*, p. 137.

3.   See our interview, "And What Kind of a Man is David Grove?" in *Rapport 33*, Autumn 1996, p. 21, and at www.cleanlanguage.co.uk.

4.   There is a similarity between this part of David Grove's approach and that of Ernest Rossi described in *The Symptom Path to Enlightenment*.

5.   Edward Hall, *The Silent Language*, p. 158.

6.   David Grove workshop, 'A Sense of Place', London 1997.

7.   David Grove workshop, 'A Sense of Place', London 1997.

8.   Sometimes a client's Metaphor Landscape retains its overall configuration irrespective of the external environment. Other Metaphor Landscapes adjust themselves to the physical surroundings. And some clients are attracted to certain items, shapes or patterns because of the correspondence with symbols in their Landscape—irrespective of their location.

9.   See Ernest Rossi, *The Psychobiology of Mind-Body Healing*, Chapter 3, and Robert Dilts, Tim Hallbom and Suzi Smith, *Beliefs: Pathways to Health and Well-Being*, Chapter 4.

10.   Although lines of sight as described by David Grove, and NLP eye-accessing cues noted by Richard Bandler and John Grinder in *Frogs into Princes*, p. 25 differ, they do not necessarily conflict, but rather they acknowledge different aspects of subjective experience. Bandler and Grinder suggest that eye movements are systematically indexed with the process of creating or remembering images, voices, sounds, emotional responses and body sensations. In a later development Bandler uses the metaphor of a "globe with latitude and longitude lines" surrounding a person for recording the 'sub-modality' of location (*Design Human Engineering™ Manual*, 1993, Section One, p. 3). This is similar to Grove's mapping of lines of sight except for how each of them perceives the information. For Bandler, "Experience is represented, coded and stored at the Sub-Modality level" (Section Four, p. 3). His globe acts as a three-dimensional container for

defining the *content-free* sub-modality of location of any perception. Grove on the other hand, is interested in the *symbolic nature of the content* along a line of sight.

11. Personal communication from psychotherapist Philip Harland.

12. See 'A Client's Eye View' at www.cleanlanguage.co.uk.

III: The Five-Stage Process

Chapter 5, Stage 1: Entering the Symbolic Domain

1. Caroline Myss defines 'symbolic sight' as "the ability to use your intuition to interpret the power symbols in your life." *Anatomy of the Spirit,* p. 57.

2. David Grove has a more spontaneous approach. Sometimes he begins by asking questions of the client's most overt metaphor, while at other times he uses a completely unexpected cue such as the client catching their breath. He may even start the process before the client is ready by asking about a line of sight, as he did with Penny's tissue box example in Chapter 4. And sometimes he just waits until a cue "begs to be asked a question."

3. See Petruska Clarkson on the implications of psychotherapy outcome research 'Beyond Schoolism' in *Dialogue,* Issue 1, no. 1, February 1998.

4. David Grove, *Resolving Traumatic Memories,* p. 15.

5. Philip Harland has developed a useful way of recording clients' first words. See 'The Mirror-model: a guide to reflective questioning', *Rapport* 42, Winter 1998, pp. 8-16, and at www.cleanlanguage.co.uk.

6. Richard Bandler and others have coded some of these distinctions as 'sub-modalities', the finer gradations of the visual, auditory and kinesthetic sensory modalities (see *Using Your Brain for a Change*).

7. These examples are based on Charles Faulkner's ANLP Conference Presentation (London, 1999). See also Cecile Carson's 'The Vestibular (VS) System in NLP' in *Leaves Before The Wind,* edited by Charlotte Bretto.

8. David Grove, *Healing The Wounded Child Within,* p. 19.

9. If waiting does not produce more information, you have the choice of:
   • Directing their attention to a symbol they *do* know about.
   • Asking 'And when you don't know, is there anything else?'
   • Asking 'And what kind of don't know is that don't know?'
   • Asking 'And how do you know you don't know?'

   Knowing there is an absence of information *is* information about an absence. Each 'don't know' response may have a different meaning for the client. And if this means they have entered the land of the unknown, it is a land full of learning and possibility.

10. For some clients, words *themselves* are symbols, either in the form of an image of the word or via an internal voice. If this is the case, you continue as usual by inviting them to develop the form and location of the words.

11. Although clients display lots of nonverbal information related to emotions, feelings and other sensations, many of these (e.g. blushing) are not easy for the therapist to reference *cleanly*. However if a client is obviously having an emotional response and makes no reference to it, you can ask 'And what is happening?'

Chapter 6, Stage 2: Developing Symbolic Perceptions

1. See 'A Client's Eye View' at www.cleanlanguage.co.uk.

2. Gregory Bateson in *Mind and Nature,* p. 15:
    Without context, words and actions have no meaning at all. This is true not only of human communication in words but also of all communication whatsoever, of all mental process, of all mind, including that which tells the sea anemone how to grow and the amoeba what he should do next.

3. In the world of metaphor, rather than thinking in the traditional psychological terms of 'association' or 'dissociation', it is more useful to consider 'where is the perceiver perceiving from', and 'what is their means of perceiving' (as the perceiver will always be 'associated' into a symbolic form, and perceiving from a place in perceptual space).

4. See *Strategies of Genius,* Volumes I-III by Robert Dilts for examples of how creative people like Aristotle, Einstein and Walt Disney made use of multiple perceptual positions.

5. Once the client has an awareness of a perceiver that is engaged in the act of perceiving, its form can be developed. This process will produce a symbolic representation of the perceiver. But who is perceiving the symbol of the perceiver? It is self-reflective consciousness all the way down.

6. David Grove, *Healing the Wounded Child Within,* p. 19.

7. Although it is unusual, an apparently benevolent symbol may turn out to have an unwanted or restrictive function once it, or the context, has been fully developed. It is likely that how and when this shift takes place will itself be symbolic of what happens in the client's life. We have also witnessed examples of a resource in one session ceasing to be one in the next. In these rare cases a 'de-resourcing' higher level pattern was operating (see Chapter 8).

8. See George Lakoff and Mark Johnson, *Philosophy in the Flesh,* p. 31-32.

Chapter 7, Stage 3: Modelling Symbolic Patterns

1. Guy Claxton in *Hare Brain, Tortoise Mind,* details scientific evidence showing that people base decisions on patterns they are unconscious of having detected. We are also grateful to John Grinder for showing that there are signals that let people know they have detected a pattern *before* they are conscious of the content of the pattern. ("Pattern Detection" workshop, London, 1998.)

2. For a technical description of presuppositions in language see Richard Bandler and John Grinder, *The Structure of Magic I,* pp. 211-214.

3. David Grove often uses this example to show how metaphors can have an antibody-like effect. Note that the change from the knot being in the client's stomach to tying a perpetrator's hands may be a very welcome *translation*. It is unlikely to be a *transformation* because the knot is still tying and at this stage little has changed in the *organisation* of the Metaphor Landscape (Chapters 2 and 8 explain these terms).

4. The 'Circles of Excellence' exercise—modified from Charlotte Bretto, *A Framework for Excellence* (Formats 11-12)—is available in 'Change Your Thinking—Change Your Life with NLP' at www.cleanlanguage.co.uk.

5. We first realised the construction and value of this clean question while observing psychotherapist Teresa Sherlock at work.

6. The standard opening question (And what would *you* like to have happen?) is a particular formulation of this question with 'you' being a specific example of 'X'.

7. In those days, the '11-plus' was an examination taken by 11-year olds who, if they passed went to Grammar school and if they failed went to Secondary Modern school. A child's chance of going to university largely depended on which type of school they attended. Thus the 11-plus not only segregated children by academic ability, it also had a major bearing on a child's future and self-image.

8. We would have asked the same question in the same manner even if the intention appeared 'bad, negative or destructive'. If the client had said screwdriver wants to crush hose into pulp, we would have honoured the symbol's desire by asking "And can it?". Our thinking is, if a symbol wants to annihilate another symbol, how come it hasn't? Whatever has prevented the annihilation from happening will likely be a resource whose form can be developed. Also see Chapter 8, Approach E.

Chapter 8, Stage 4: Encouraging Conditions for Transformation

1. Ken Wilber, *Sex, Ecology, Spirituality*, p. 54.

2. Ken Wilber in *Sex, Ecology, Spirituality*, p. 58 makes:
    > ... the distinction between depth and span, or the distinction between vertical richness and horizontal reach. We have two different scales here: a vertical scale of deep versus shallow, and a horizontal scale of wide versus narrow ... evolution is *not* bigger and better, but smaller and better (greater depth, less span).

    In psychotherapeutic terms this means you cannot determine the *effect* of a change by the amount of *affect*.

3. *Sex, Ecology, Spirituality*, pp. 60–61 (his emphasis). Ken Wilber further clarifies the distinction in a footnote, p. 531:
    > Of course, both translation and transformation actually deal with whole/parts (there are only holons); but transformation deals with emergent holons that subsume those of its predecessors, and thus is "more holistic." The wholes of the previous level are now parts of the senior level, so that "whole units" of the previous translation are now "parts" of the new.

4. Ken Wilber, *Sex, Ecology, Spirituality*, p. 63.

5. Ken Wilber, *A Brief History of Everything,* p. 40:
    > Evolution has a broad and general *tendency* to move in the direction of: increasing complexity, increasing differentiation/integration, increasing organisation/structuration, increasing relative autonomy, increasing telos. ... evolution meanders more than it progresses.

6. Ken Wilber, *Sex, Ecology, Spirituality*, p. 63: "Holons do not evolve alone, because there are no alone holons ... this principle is often referred to as *coevolution.*" And p. 66 "The micro is in relational exchange with the macro at all levels of its depth."

7. A resource symbol might not be applied immediately for two reasons: the appropriate symbol in need has yet to be identified; or there is a symbol in need but it is not an appropriate time to introduce the resource (if, for example, the organisation of a pattern is not clear). An example of the latter is Jubilee Clip where the Kung Fu master's red mature heart was discovered at C38 but was not introduced to the young boy until T57.

8. Ken Wilber, *Sex, Ecology, Spirituality*, p. 76, calls binds "stick points" and notes that it is only because evolution has a direction and develops that the process can get stuck or repeatedly diverted:
    > The psyche, for better or for worse, *is* going somewhere, and that is why the process can get stuck, why it is fraught with frustration, arrest, fixation, stick points, logjams. If the mind weren't going somewhere, it could never get stuck, never get "sick". And these "stick points" can only be understood in terms of the mind's omega point, of where it wants to go.

9. By our definition "damned if I do, and damned if I don't" is *not* a double bind. It is a single bind because there is only one level of bind —whatever the client does they are damned. A double bind would require a further bind at a higher level, precluding escape from the primary bind, such as, "and terrible things happen to people who reject damnation." (Also see footnote 13.)

10. R. D. Laing, *Knots,* p. 30.

11. R. D. Laing, *Knots,* p. 32.

12. Paul Watzlawick, *Munchhausen's Pigtail,* p. 203.

13. Gregory Bateson (and others) in *Steps to An Ecology of Mind,* pp. 206–207, defines the "necessary ingredients for a double bind situation" as:
    1. Two or more persons.
    2. Repeated experience.
    3. A primary negative injunction.
    4. A secondary injunction conflicting with the first at *a more abstract level*, and ... which threatens survival.
    5. A (possible) tertiary negative injunction prohibiting the victim escaping from the field.
    6. Finally, the complete set of ingredients is no longer necessary when the victim has learned to perceive his universe in double bind patterns. Almost any part of a double bind sequence may then be sufficient to precipitate [the symptoms].

    (Note that by the time the "victim" reaches No. 6 they are double binding themselves without the need for outside assistance.)

14. "Current reality" comes from Robert Fritz, *The Path of Least Resistance,* p. 139. We have wondered how much of the success of Alcoholics Anonymous and other 12 Step Programs is due to the very first of the 12 Steps: "I admit I am powerless over alcohol and my life has become unmanageable." In our language, the alcoholic is accepting that their binding pattern is unresolvable (given their current pattern of organisation), as a prelude to change.

15. Client-therapist transcripts often seem to have a logic and a flow in retrospect that is rarely evident at the time. At this point in the session we had no idea where the process was heading (which is isomorphic with the nature of helplessness and no-win). But we took comfort from knowing that when clients become aware they are responding within their binding pattern (i.e. that they are experiencing 'it' right now) an opportunity for transformation arises.

16. Although the client will probably respond to developing/concentrating by 'shifting down a level' to a metaphor/symbol's constituent parts, they may 'shift horizontally' to an isomorphic metaphor/symbol or spontaneously 'jump' to a different place in the Landscape. In the latter case, they usually find value in what happens just before their attention jumps.

17. We are grateful to Caitlin Walker for demonstrating the effectiveness of this approach and how it can be enhanced by simultaneously indicating nonverbally where each symbol is located in the client's perceptual space.

18. We borrow the term "operational closure" from Humberto Maturana and Francisco Varela although we use it in a wider sense than their definition: "Metacellular systems ... have *operational closure* in their organisation: their identity is specified by a network of dynamic processes whose effects do not leave that network." *The Tree of Knowledge,* p. 89.

19. David Grove has developed a process he calls 'Inter-Generational Healing' (see his article 'Problem Domains and Non-Traumatic Resolution through Metaphor Therapy' at www.cleanlanguage.co.uk). Having facilitated hundreds of clients he noted a general pattern to the sequence of their journeys back in time:
    Personal history -> Parent's history -> Inter-generational history -> Social history -> History of the land -> New cosmology.

20. Steve and Connirae Andreas, 'Selecting a Resource to Anchor', *Anchor Point,* Volume 14, No. 7, July 2000.

Chapter 9, Stage 5: Maturing the Evolved Landscape

1. How long does a transformation have to last for it to be a transformation? In *One Taste,* Ken Wilber discusses 'peak', 'plateau' and 'permanent' transformations (pp. 314–321). A short-lived peak experience is still a transformation while it lasts. It provides a direct experience of what is possible. This registers in the client's neurology and acts as a beacon during future dark nights of the soul.

2. This format is a favourite of David Grove. It is common for him to improvise a ten minute entrancing 'rap' which recapitulates a multitude of changes that may have taken place over many sessions.

3. See Chapter 18 of *Solutions* by Leslie Cameron-Bandler for a description of the NLP technique 'future pacing', which 'anchors' changes in the session to expected future events in the client's life.

4. David Grove calls this process 'parking'. *In the Presence of the Past,* p. 57.

5. For a description of how a client uses writing, see 'Using Writing to Explore Issues through Metaphor' at www.cleanlanguage.co.uk.

IV: In Conclusion

Chapter 10, Outside and Beyond

1. 'Exemplar' and 'acquisition' are terms used by David Gordon and Graham Dawes who offer excellent training in their own type of modelling. See www.experiential-dynamics.org.

2. Thanks to Tony Buckley for his contribution to this modelling project.

3. See Dee Berridge at www.metaphormorphosis.co.uk.

4. Quotations are from personal communication with Diane Divett and her *Refocussing* training manual, CCC Publications, Auckland, 1998.

5. Some of these approaches have evolved out of a method devised by Arun Hejmadi and Patricia Lyall, 'Autogenic Metaphor Resolution', in Charlotte Bretto and others, *Leaves Before the Wind.*

6. Christine Westwood, 'Healing Unresolved Trauma Through Meta-Aromatherapy' in *Positive Health,* April, 1998. Reproduced at www.cleanlanguage.co.uk.

7. Simon Stanton in 'Using metaphors in IT training', *Rapport 37,* Autumn 1997. Reproduced at www.cleanlanguage.co.uk.

8. Caitlin Walker's work with NIP has been presented in a video entitled "Working with Imagery and Metaphor in Creativity," produced in 1999 by the Open University for their MBA course. See the web sites of NIP, www.nipltd.com and Training Attention, www.trainingattention.co.uk.

Bibliography

Andreas, Connirae, and Steve Andreas, *Change Your Mind—And Keep the Change,* Real People Press, Moab, Utah, 1987.

Andreas, Connirae, with Tamara Andreas, *Core Transformation,* Real People Press, Moab, Utah, 1994.

Bandler, Richard, and John Grinder, *The Structure of Magic I*, Science and Behavior Books, Palo Alto, CA, 1975.

Bandler, Richard, and John Grinder, *Patterns of the Hypnotic Techniques of Milton H. Erickson, M.D. Volume 1,* Meta Publications, Cupertino, CA, 1975.

Bandler, Richard, and John Grinder, *Frogs into Princes,* Real People Press, Moab, UT, 1979.

Bandler, Richard, *Using Your Brain for a Change,* Real People Press, Moab, Utah, 1985.

Bandler, Richard, *Design Human Engineering™ Manual,* NLP Enterprises Ltd., London, 1993.

Bateson, Gregory, *Steps to an Ecology of Mind,* Ballantine, New York, 1972.

Bateson, Gregory, *Mind and Nature,* Bantam, New York, 1979.

Bateson, Gregory, and Bateson, Mary C., *Angels Fear,* Bantam, New York, 1988.

Berne, Eric, *Games People Play,* Penguin, Harmondsworth, 1968.

Bretto, Charlotte C., *A Framework for Excellence,* CPD, Capitola, CA, 1988.

Bretto, Charlotte, Judith DeLozier, John Grinder, Sylvia Topel, (Eds.), *Leaves Before the Wind*, Grinder, DeLozier & Associates, Bonnydoon, CA, 1991.

Calvin, William H., *The Cerebral Code,* MIT Press, Cambridge, MA, 1996.

Cameron-Bandler, Leslie, *Solutions,* Real People Press, Moab, Utah, 1985.

Capra, Fritjof, *The Tao of Physics,* Shambala, Boston, Massachusetts, 1991.

Capra, Fritjof, *The Web of Life,* Harper Collins, London, 1996.

Chalmers, David J., *The Conscious Mind,* Oxford University Press, 1996.

Claxton, Guy, *Hare Brain Tortoise Mind,* Fourth Estate, London, 1997.

Cohen, Jack, and Ian Stewart, *The Collapse of Chaos,* Penguin, London, 1995.

Combs, Gene and Jill Freedman, *Symbol, Story, and Ceremony,* Norton & Co., New York, 1990.

Damasio, Antonio R., *Decartes' Error,* Papermac, London, 1996.

DeLozier, Judith, and John Grinder, *Turtles All the Way Down,* Grinder, Delozier & Associates, Bonnydoon, CA, 1987.

Dennett, Daniel C., *Consciousness Explained,* Penguin Books, London, 1993.

Dilts, Robert, John Grinder, Richard Bandler, Leslie Cameron-Bandler, Judith DeLozier, *Neuro-Linguistic Programming: Volume I,* Meta Publications, Cupertino, CA, 1980.

Dilts, Robert, *Roots of Neuro-Linguistic Programming,* Meta Publications, Cupertino, CA, 1983.

Dilts, Robert, Tim Hallbom, and Suzi Smith, *Beliefs: Pathways to Health and Well-being,* Metamorphous Press, Portland, OR, 1990.

Dilts, Robert, *Changing Belief Systems with NLP,* Meta Publications, Cupertino, CA, 1990.

Dilts, Robert, *Strategies for Genius, Vols. I–III,* Meta Publications, Capitola, CA, 1994–1995.

Dilts, Robert, *Modeling with NLP,* Meta Publications, Capitola, CA, 1998.

Edleman, Gerald M., *Bright Air, Brilliant Fire,* Basic Books, New York, 1992.

Faulkner, Charles, *Metaphors of Identity,* (Audio Tape set), Genesis II, 1991.

Fritz, Robert, *The Path of Least Resistance,* Ballantine, New York, 1989.

Fields, Rick, (Ed.), *The Awakened Warrior,* Putnam's Sons, New York, 1994.

Gell-Mann, Murray, *The Quark and the Jaguar,* Abacus, London, 1995.

Gendlin, Eugene T, *Focusing,* Bantam, New York, 1981.

Gleick, James, *Chaos: Making a New Science,* Viking, New York, 1987.

Goleman, Daniel, *Emotional Intelligence,* Bloomsbury, London, 1996.

Goleman, Daniel, *Vital Lies, Simple Truths,* Bloomsbury, London, 1998.

Goodwin, Brian, *How the Leopard Changed Its Spots,* Phoenix, London, 1997.

Grinder, John, and Richard Bandler, *The Structure of Magic II*, Science and Behavior Books, Palo Alto, CA, 1976.

Grinder, John, Judith DeLozier, and Richard Bandler, *Patterns of the Hypnotic Techniques of Milton H. Erickson, M.D. Volume 2*, Meta Publications, Cupertino, CA, 1977.

Gordon, David, *Therapeutic Metaphors*, Meta Publications, Cupertino, CA, 1978.

Grove, David J., and Basil Panzer, *Resolving Traumatic Memories: Metaphors and Symbols in Psychotherapy*, Irvington, New York, 1989.

Grove, David J., *Healing The Wounded Child Within*, (Audio tape set and workbook), David Grove Seminars, Eldon MO, 1988.

Grove, David J., *Metaphors to Heal By*, (Audio tape set and workbook), David Grove Seminars, Eldon, MO, 1989.

Grove, David J., *Resolving Feelings of Anger, Shame and Fear*, (Video, audio tape set and workbook), David Grove Seminars, Eldon MO, 1989.

Grove, David J., *In the Presence of the Past*, (Audio tape set and workbook), David Grove Seminars, Eldon MO, 1991.

Grove, David J., *Reweaving a Companionable Past*, (Audio tape set and workbook), David Grove Seminars, Eldon MO, 1992.

Grove, David J., *And Death Shall Have No Dominion*, (Audio tape set and workbook), David Grove Seminars, Eldon MO, 1992.

Hall, Edward T., *The Silent Language*, Doubleday, New York, 1981.

Hall, Michael, *Meta-States*, (second edition) Empowerment Technologies, Grand Junction, CO, 1996.

Hillman, James, *The Soul's Code*, Random House, New York, 1996.

Jackendoff, Ray, *Languages of the Mind*, The MIT Press, Cambridge, Massachusetts, 1996.

James, Tad, and Wyatt Woodsmall, *Time Line Therapy*, Meta Publications, Cupertino, CA, 1988.

Jaynes, Julian, *The Origin of Consciousness in the Breakdown of the Bicameral Mind*, Houghton Mifflin, Boston, MA, 1976.

Johnson, Mark, *The Body in the Mind*, University of Chicago Press, Chicago, 1987.

Johnson, Mark, *Moral Imaginations*, The University of Chicago Press, Chicago, 1993.

Jung, Carl, *Man and his Symbols*, Picador, London 1964.

Jung, Carl G., *Memory, Dreams, Reflections*, Fontana, London, 1983.

Koestler, Arthur, *The Act of Creation*, Macmillan, New York, 1994.

Kopp, Richard R., *Metaphor Therapy,* Brunner/Mazell, New York, 1995.

Kosko, Bart, *Fuzzy Thinking,* Flamingo, London, 1994.

Laing, R.D., *Knots,* Penguin, Harmondsworth, 1992.

Lakoff, George, and Mark Johnson, *Metaphors We Live By,* The University of Chicago Press, Chicago, 1980.

Lakoff, George, *Women, Fire, and Dangerous Things,* University of Chicago Press, Chicago, 1987.

Lakoff, George, and Mark Johnson, *Philosophy in The Flesh*, Basic Books, New York, 1999.

Leary, David E., (Ed.), *Metaphors in the History of Psychology*, Cambridge University Press, Cambridge, 1990.

LeDoux, Joseph, *The Emotional Brain,* Orion Books, London 1998.

Margulis, Lynn, *The Symbiotic Planet,* Phoenix, London, 1999.

Maturana, Humberto R., and Francisco J. Varela, *The Tree of Knowledge,* Shambala, Boston, 1992.

Myss, Caroline, *Anatomy of the Spirit,* Harmony Books, New York, 1996.

O'Connor, Joseph, and Ian McDermott, *The Art of Systems Thinking,* Thorsons, London, 1997.

O'Connor, Joseph, and John Seymour, *Introducing Neuro Linguistic Programming,* Mandala, London, 1990.

Ortony, Andrew, (Ed.), *Metaphor and Thought*, (Second edition), Cambridge University Press, 1993.

Pinker, Steven, *How The Mind Works,* The Softback Preview, UK, 1998.

Reber, Arthur S., *The Penguin Dictionary of Psychology,* (Second edition), Penguin, London, 1995.

Robbins, Anthony, *Awaken the Giant Within,* Simon & Schuster, London, 1992.

Robertson, Ian, *Mind Sculpture,* Bantam Press, London, 1999.

Rose, Steven, (Ed.), *From Brains to Consciousness?*, Penguin, London, 1999.

Rossi, Ernest, *The Psychobiology of Mind-Body Healing*, (Second edition), Norton & Co., New York, 1993.

Rossi, Ernest, *The Symptom Path to Enlightenment*, Gateway Publishing, Palisades, CA, 1996.

Searle, John R., *The Mystery of Consciousness,* Granta, London, 1997.

Senge, Peter M., *The Fifth Discipline,* Doubleday, New York, 1990.

Solso, Robert L., and Dominic W. Massaro (Eds.), *The Science of Mind: 2001 and Beyond,* Oxford University Press, New York, 1995.

Stewart, Ian, and Vann Joines, *TA Today: A New Inroduction to Transactional Analysis,* Lifespace Publishing, Nottingham, 1987.

Tompkins, Penny, and James Lawley, A variety of articles on Symbolic Modelling and NLP published in *Rapport*, 1993–2000 and reproduced at www.cleanlanguage.co.uk.

Varela, Francisco J., Evan Thompson, and Eleanor Rosch, *The Embodied Mind.*, MIT Press, Cambridge, Massachusetts, 1993.

Watzlawick, Paul, J. Weakland, and R. Fisch, *Change,* Norton, New York, 1974.

Watzlawick, Paul, *Munchhausen's Pigtail,* W. W. Norton & Co., New York, 1990.

Wenger, Win, and Richard Poe, *The Einstein Factor,* Prima, Rocklin, CA, 1996.

Wilber, Ken, *Sex, Ecology, Spirituality,* Shambhala, Boston, MA, 1995.

Wilber, Ken, *A Brief History of Everything,* Shambhala, Boston, MA, 1996.

Wilber, Ken, *The Essential Ken Wilber,* Shambhala, Boston, MA, 1998.

Wilber, Ken, *One Taste: The Journals of Ken Wilber,* Shambala, Boston, MA, 1999.

Index

Numbers in *italics* refer to Notes

ABOUT THE AUTHORS

Penny Tompkins and James Lawley are co-developers of Symbolic Modelling and leading authorities on the use of client-generated metaphor for personal and professional development. They have had numerous articles published which are available on their web site.

They are both practising psychotherapists registered with the United Kingdom Council for Psychotherapy (UKCP). Together they train and supervise therapists, counsellors, coaches, managers and teachers in the use of Symbolic Modelling.

Penny was co-managing director of a manufacturing company in the oil industry, and James was a senior manager in the telecommunications business. They use this experience when they coach managers and executives to become more self-aware and to develop their ability to think systemically. They also facilitate teams in the use of Clean Language and metaphor so they can model and learn from themselves. They are married, and live in England.

They are available for:
- training in Symbolic Modelling
- private client sessions
- executive coaching
- supervision
- team development
- using metaphor with large groups
- modelling in organisations
- seminars, conferences and workshops

Video available: *A Strange and Strong Sensation* is a training video of a complete Symbolic Modelling client session with on-screen annotation. It comes with a full transcript and unique 3-perspective explanatory booklet.

For more information please email info@cleanlanguage.co.uk

The Developing Company
www.cleanlanguage.co.uk